D0480598

Maria Anderson has been an NHS midwife for over 25 years. She has worked across the UK and is now based in Inverness with her husband and two children.

Tales of a Midwife

MARIA ANDERSON
WITH CHARLOTTE WARD

headline

First published in 2012
by HEADLINE PUBLISHING GROUP

2

Cataloguing in Publication Data is available from the British Library

ISBN 978 0 7553 6274 5

Typeset in Adobe Garamond by Palimpsest Book Production Limited,
Falkirk, Stirlingshire

Printed and bound in Great Britain by
Clays Ltd, Elcograf S.p.A.

HEADLINE PUBLISHING GROUP
An Hachette UK Company
338 Euston Road
London NW1 3BH

www.headline.co.uk
www.hachette.co.uk

I dedicate this book to all of the midwives I have worked with and to all of the women and babies I have cared for throughout the UK.

To Michael, my husband, for his continual support in my life, career and in writing this book, and to Rosie and Molly Kate for the joy they bring to my life.

The names of individual patients and some colleagues have been changed to protect their privacy.

Chapter One

Carefully, the midwife examined my baby brother Christopher.

Holding him slightly propped up on her knee and facing towards her, she stared at him while he blinked back. He looked so floppy and vulnerable.

I watched, enthralled. She seemed to be taking in every inch of detail from his face and movements. 'What a little smasher he is,' she said, as she continued to look him over methodically.

'I'm just checking that your brother is doing OK,' she explained, glancing up at me. 'What's your name?'

'Maria,' I replied shyly.

'That's my name too!' she exclaimed. 'If you come over here I'll show you what I am doing.'

It was February 1982. I was fifteen and big sister to three younger brothers: Michael, eleven, Peter, eight, and now little Christopher, just three days old. I couldn't take my eyes off my new baby brother. I'd been fascinated from the moment I'd run home from school (I'd been let out early to see him again now he was back at home). As I dashed through the door I still couldn't believe this little podgy thing was the same bump I'd watched grow in my mam's tummy over the past nine months.

The day before Christopher was born was a Sunday morning

and I'd noticed something different about Mam. She seemed quieter than usual. She told me that she wasn't going to church that morning but that I could take Michael and Peter instead.

'Are you OK?' I'd asked.

'Yes, I'm fine,' she'd said. 'But I think I might have the baby today.'

Although I took my brothers I wasn't happy about leaving Mam on her own. It seemed like the longest mass ever.

Back home I was relieved to see Mam preparing the Sunday dinner as normal. Michael and Peter went outside to play in the garden, oblivious to what was going on, but I kept a close eye on my mother – watching as every so often she would stop and breathe heavily before carrying on.

When Dad came in from work at 2 p.m. he was very keen to get Mam to hospital but she insisted on serving the food first. Finally, at 4 p.m., Aunty Mary was summoned to take over the childcare and we waved them off.

Aunty Mary passed the time by telling us stories about how the news was broken to her when each of us had been born. I was delighted to hear how in my case Dad had shouted through the letterbox, 'It's a girl! Maria!'

Just as Michael and Peter were starting to get a little tired the phone rang. We all ran towards Aunty Mary as she picked it up.

She held the receiver down so we could all hear Dad whooping, 'It's a boy! He's a beauty!'

Then Mam came on the phone to say she was fine. She said she was holding our new baby brother and all of a sudden she put him next to the phone. Gurgling noises filtered down the line and we could not contain our excitement as we all tried to get as close to the phone as possible. It was a very happy day in our house.

I was a fifth-year pupil at St Wilfrid's R.C. School in South Shields and the next morning I was so desperate to see my baby brother that I couldn't concentrate on my work. I had told my teacher, Mrs Jones, all about our 'new bairn' and seeing my impatience she eventually allowed me to visit the hospital during lunchtime.

I could have kissed her. The hospital, South Shields District, was almost across the road from the school and after running there I followed the signs for the maternity unit.

After being directed to the ward by a receptionist, I opened the door and was met by a woman wearing a uniform.

'My mam is Mrs Joyce,' I said.

'You know it's not visiting time,' she told me sternly.

'Oh,' I said, my eyes pleading.

'OK,' she said, her voice softening. 'Come with me.'

Quickly I followed her to where my mam was sitting.

'Maria!' she said, astonished.

Without even saying hello I just walked up to the cot beside her and stared at this perfect little baby, lying there fast asleep. He had dark hair, a pale complexion, long fingers and tiny nails peeping out from the blanket.

He was all wrapped up like a parcel. I turned to Mam and gave her a big hug.

'He's beautiful,' I told her.

After an hour Mam told me I should go back to school but I could come back later with Dad.

'OK,' I agreed, reluctantly. I decided I wouldn't tell Michael or Peter that I had already seen our new brother.

As promised, after school, Dad took us to the hospital. There was Mam sitting with a mixture of pride, excitement and happiness on her face, with the baby in her arms. This time he was awake and I immediately noticed his pale blue eyes. He looked quite mesmerised to see us as we all stood over him, staring in admiration.

'He's got big feet!' Michael observed with a sigh of relief. 'I think he will be able to play football!'

Mam told us she had decided to call him Stephen.

'But he doesn't look like a Stephen!' I protested. 'Can't we call him Christopher instead?'

I was backed up by my dad and both my brothers. Poor Mam. But she must have had some doubt about the name Stephen, as after being badgered by the family she reluctantly agreed and Christopher it was. (Christopher, now an adult who has played professional football and was recently married to Katharina, is grateful to this day!)

Now Christopher was back at home, and as the midwife examined him I told her how my brother's birth had coincided with a school project for my O level biology course, which was called 'Life'.

Everyone else in the class was choosing to report on animals or plants but I'd had the idea to study the first year of Christopher's life. As a result I was writing a journal every day about my new brother. So far I'd detailed the time he was born, his weight, his blue eyes and even the frown across his forehead that made him look like he was thinking as he stared at you.

I pointed to the yellow plastic thing that looked like it was attached to his tummy.

'What's that?' I asked. 'Why does it smell and look so dirty?'

Maria explained that it was the cord stump and would eventually rot off.

I turned my nose up. How disgusting! But I couldn't tear my

4

eyes away as she proceeded to clean it with swabs that she had pulled from her black bag. She had clearly done this hundreds if not thousands of times before and she never flinched as she cleaned around the blackened stump.

Then out came what looked like a pair of scissors and I watched in amazement as she removed the yellow plastic clamp, placing it on a tissue.

'You can have that for your project,' she informed me. 'But wash it first!'

Every day I continued to scribble notes charting Christopher's development. And at every opportunity I would hold him, talk to him, change his nappy and get him dressed. I would even help Mam by pacing the floor trying to get him to sleep when Dad was on nightshift for his job as a welder. Mam and I would take it in turns to get up to him. Oh, how he used to cry!

But despite the hard work, my fascination with babies and midwifery continued. Whenever Maria came to the house I was really interested to watch what she was doing and I'd ask her all about her job. She told me she was a community midwife visiting mums and babies at home after they'd been born.

'Do you deliver babies as well?' I asked.

'I do sometimes,' she said.

I felt so much admiration: this lady could deliver a baby!

'How do you become a midwife?' I asked.

'You need to do nursing first,' she told me. 'You can do that once you're eighteen. Then after that you can train to be a midwife.'

I decided it was something I was definitely going to think about after I left school, but I knew I needed to get some qualifications first. To that end, a year later, I proudly handed my biology project in. I'd taken photos and recorded every detail of Christopher's development from when he was a tiny newborn to the way he was now – a happy, responsive baby, always cooing and laughing and well on his way to walking.

To my delight I was awarded top marks for it and I even received a note from the examiner saying that they had never read such an interesting biology project and that it would be a treasured possession for Christopher one day! They were right: I did eventually give it to Christopher, aged twelve, and he was amazed to see how much hard work had gone into it.

Meanwhile, I never forgot how much Maria's job had enthralled me. And when I eventually left school with seven O levels and two A levels, I remembered her advice that I should do my nurse's training in order to progress towards a career as a midwife.

So as my seventeenth birthday approached I applied to be a student nurse at Queen Elizabeth Hospital in Gateshead.

When I got an interview it was agreed that my Aunty Ada, who had been a colonel in the army in the nursing corps, would give me a mock grilling to prepare me.

The mock interview took place at our house and Aunty Ada sat very upright at the kitchen table, looking at me sternly through her glasses.

'Why do you want to be a nurse, Miss Joyce?' she asked, eyeballing me.

'I enjoy helping people,' I stuttered.

She rolled her eyes.

'Why?' she snapped.

'I would like to help people deal with their illness and care for them,' I added.

'And how will you do that?'

I felt like I wanted to cry but I laughed instead.

'Aunty Ada, I can't do this,' I said. 'You are really scary!'

She laughed and I saw my Aunty Ada return.

'Well, my girl, you need to think about why you want to be a nurse and prepare for the interview,' she said. 'You wouldn't get a job with me at this moment!'

It was a good lesson and I immediately started finding out exactly what nurses did and what skills I had that could be applied to the job. I never asked for another interview from Aunty Ada though.

My real nursing interview took place at Queen Elizabeth Hospital, Gateshead, a few months later. The hospital was a seven-mile journey from my home in Jarrow and I arrived dressed in a blue navy suit and navy court shoes, clutching my certificates with my stomach churning with nerves.

I was greeted by Joan, a slim dark-haired woman, well dressed but with kind brown eyes. She was a midwifery lecturer.

She took me into a small office. The room was set up with three chairs, three glasses on the table and a jug of water.

A man sitting in one of the chairs was introduced as Gordon, a charge nurse working in Accident and Emergency. He was smartly dressed and when he shook my hand it was with a very firm handshake.

Joan beckoned me over to one chair and took another. They both smiled at me in an encouraging manner, which helped to put me at ease. After Aunty Ada's terrifying inquisition this interview seemed quite informal.

'So, why do you want to become a nurse?' Joan asked.

I told them that I had attended St John Ambulance training courses since I was nine years old and had gained lots of certificates in first aid, as well as winning a few trophies in competitions organised by St John Ambulance. I explained that this had sparked an interest and had given me a little insight into nursing. I added that I'd also spoken to nurses about their jobs and that had confirmed that I wanted to pursue it as a career.

Looking at my CV, Joan asked about my Duke of Edinburgh Gold Award and what it had entailed. I glossed over the four days of pain (and bickering) as myself and six other girls survived out in the wild with no contact from anyone. Instead I explained how all the skills I'd learnt and relied on could be transferred to a career in nursing. I felt that I'd really earned that award. I'd received it from the Duke of Edinburgh earlier that year at Buckingham Palace, which had been very exciting.

The interview only lasted thirty minutes and it flew by, but at the end I couldn't tell whether I'd made a good impression. I knew I'd be very lucky to get a place, as there were always lots of applicants for few positions – so when a letter postmarked 'Gateshead' arrived about a month later I took a deep breath and ripped it open nervously.

'I would like to confirm you have been successful in gaining a place to start your registered general nurse training, to commence in September 1985 at Queen Elizabeth Hospital Gateshead,' it read.

I was ecstatic and quickly began to tell Mam, Dad and the rest of my family. However, even in the midst of my excitement, I took a moment to pause and reflect on my Aunty Ada, wishing I could tell her all about it. We'd all been devastated when she'd passed away just a few months earlier. Part of me could imagine her laughing and saying in her cut-glass accent: 'Well, you must have pulled your socks up in that interview. Well done, girl!'

* * *

So in September 1985, having just turned eighteen that July, I arrived at the Bede School of Nursing to begin my three and a half years of training.

My dad dropped me off outside the building.

'Good luck, pet,' he said, kissing me on the cheek. 'You'll be all right.'

Nervously I joined another twenty-two students in the packed classroom. Looking around the room I saw they were all different ages and I felt a bit intimidated. However, I kept remembering what Aunty Ada had told me: 'Be confident, girl.'

I noticed another girl who looked as scared as me and quickly made a beeline for her.

'I'm Julia,' she smiled. We were to become good friends.

To my horror, everyone had to introduce themselves in front of the whole class and I felt as if everyone else was much more interesting than me with a lot more experience. Of course I later found out everyone felt the same way as me!

Next we were shown around the hospital and then in the afternoon we were taken to get our uniforms. We were given five dresses and two hats and told to look after them. The uniforms were white standard nurses' dresses – but then there were the hats, which were starched white into a hilarious round shape. Each one sported an orange stripe that faced forward, and every year another stripe would be added to mark a completed stage of training. My hat was to become the bane of my life. It was such a chore to get it starched or sitting right.

Over the next six weeks I was given an introduction into what would lie ahead. I met union reps and third-year students who dished out lots of advice and survival tactics. Patients, we learnt, had basic needs that must be attended to first. They required food, and needed to be washed, clothed and made comfortable, and to be treated with dignity before anything else. That was the basic rule of nursing care. It was old-style nursing and we would be working towards our registered general nurse qualification. There was no diploma or degree at the end as there is now.

The first ward I was to work on was a geriatrics medical ward at the nearby Bensham Hospital in Gateshead, which had a really high standard of care.

I felt immensely proud walking onto the ward for the first time in my crisp new uniform. That is until I spied a distressed-looking old lady heading my way.

'Nurse, nurse,' she called. I instinctively looked over my shoulder but there was no one there. Oh my goodness, she was talking to me! The shock that I'd be actually dealing with real people in need suddenly hit me and I felt terrified. I didn't know what to do.

She was disoriented and confused. 'Come on, let's get you back to bed,' I said, in what I hoped was a soothing voice.

With the old lady temporarily pacified and returned to her bed I hurried down the ward to find a more senior nurse to help her. She took over in a very confident and efficient way and pointed me towards the office to sit down for 'the report', in which everyone learnt about the patients and their roles for the day.

From the off it was extremely hard work caring for such dependent patients. The ward was split into two, with men on one side and women on the other. At the start of the day, after the report, staff would generally work in pairs. This could be a junior student nurse with a senior student, or a student with a junior staff nurse. There was a nursing auxiliary allocated to each side too – untrained but nonetheless vital members of staff who help with duties such as washing patients, making beds and running errands to other wards.

Our daily routine began with ensuring the patients had their breakfast and that they ate it, even if this meant spoon-feeding them until they were finished. Meanwhile the staff nurse would do the drugs round, which probably lasted about two hours.

Next, each pair of staff would take an area of the ward and stock bed-bath trolleys with sheets, washbasins, towels and an assortment of creams, sheep fleeces to prevent friction for bed-bound patients, and blue roll. Then all patients in that area were either washed by bed bath or accompanied to the bath or shower. We would also brush their hair and clean their teeth.

With everyone clean, patients would be taken to the dayroom or sat in a chair next to their beds for the morning. The ones who were bed-bound were moved or turned on an hourly or two-hourly basis to prevent bedsores.

There were so many characters on the ward. One old lady, Mary, who was about seventy years old, had been a patient for about two years when I started. She had contracted limbs and weighed only about seven stone, and had very poor eyesight that meant she mostly kept her eyes shut unless prompted. But when her eyes were open they were a lovely, sparkling blue. She had a beautiful complexion, and long grey hair tied back in a bun.

On a daily basis she was moved from her chair to her bed where she had two-hourly turns to help prevent pressure sores. Despite her elegant appearance, she would swear like a trooper when you moved her.

'Oh, you bugger!' she yelled, when it was my turn to carry out the duty.

'That's it now,' I reassured her, after she'd called me every name under the sun.

'Thanks, pet,' she whispered, instantly back to her normal affectionate self. All the staff loved her.

The ward was under the charge of Sister Storey, an old-school nurse, probably in her late forties and very petite with dark, perfectly combed hair. She wore a navy uniform with white cuffs and I noticed instantly that her hat was very well starched. I wondered if I'd ever get my hat that perfect.

At first I was not really sure about her role and I was pretty scared of her. I learnt quickly that under Sister Storey's watch everything had to be perfect. If you didn't do it properly you'd be in trouble. I witnessed a couple of occasions when staff were in tears. If something was not done correctly she would tell the person immediately. Thankfully Sister Storey seemed to take a shine to me and would take time to show me how things should be done.

There was a clear hierarchy at the hospital, with student nurses having breaks together and the permanent staff sitting in the office. Never the twain would meet. And although the staff nurses were lovely they were also wicked, playing tricks on all of us student nurses unmercifully.

'Nurse Joyce, can you go to Ward Three for a long stand?' one staff nurse, Sue, ordered me one day.

Duly I arrived at Ward Three and repeated her request.

'OK, go and stand in that corner,' Janet, the nurse there, told me.

It was only when I realised people were walking past and sniggering that I realised I was being wound up.

But this was nothing compared to the time another nurse, Sandra, volunteered to show me and a couple of other student nurses what to do with a freshly soiled bedpan.

'So this is what you do,' she said, dipping her finger into the brown substance and sticking it in her mouth. 'You have to taste it,' she exclaimed, as we recoiled in horror.

It was only when she started to laugh that she revealed the bedpan actually contained chocolate sauce.

Luckily for me, I worked alongside two third-year student nurses called Dorothy and Jessie who really took me under their wing. Both were excellent role models for me. They really taught me how to communicate appropriately with patients and staff and I admired the way they treated the patients with affection.

I worked hard, asked lots of questions and was very eager to learn and care for patients to the highest standard. But of course it was a steep learning curve. Before my nurse training, for example, I'd never seen anyone who'd died before, but eventually the time came for me to go through the various procedures called 'last offices'.

As I followed Dorothy into the room where a dead woman had been laid out I felt so anxious. All I could think was that I was in a room with a dead body. I was terrified. Although Dorothy was showing me what to do, the couple of times she left the room I just stood there, shaking. I didn't dare take my eyes off the lady lying there.

Then her eyelid popped open. I shot out that room like lightning.

I was met by Dorothy.

'What's going on?'

'Her eye! It's just opened!' I stammered.

'Oh, that sometimes happens,' she reassured me breezily.

Eventually I did become a bit calmer and I was quite moved by the tradition of opening the window to let the spirit out.

*　　*　　*

After each placement we'd return to the school of nursing for a couple of weeks and then we'd go back on a ward again. I made some really good friends in my class and after training for three and a half years we had a very special bond, even though we were constantly moving to different places and directions.

Like an apprentice you learnt your trade on the ward. It was hard and exhausting but I was really lucky to meet some really good role models along the way – such as Sister Walker from my surgical placement.

Sister Walker was a junior sister who was working alongside a senior sister called Sister McKenzie, who was due to retire. Sister Walker was a lot more friendly and approachable compared to previous sisters I had met. However she also made it clear that the highest standards were required while working on her ward.

She introduced me to writing care plans for patients and had the neatest writing I had ever seen. On this ward there was no hierarchical segregation and Sister Walker would have her break with trained staff and students. Really she was ahead of her time and I admired the way she challenged the doctors on their practice if she thought it was wrong.

In fact the surgical ward in general was an eye-opener for me. There was a lot of running around on this ward as it had a much higher turnover of patients and a much faster pace. We had all kinds of people coming in and I soon had to get over my embarrassment at having to shave intimate areas of male patients.

It was also on this ward I was first shouted at by an angry patient. He had had emergency surgery during the night and as I helped him the next morning, removing the dressing from his wound to clean it, he caught sight of a tattoo he had on his abdomen.

Previously it had spelt out 'F*** Off' but after the surgery it hadn't been realigned properly.

'Look what you've done!' he screamed.

It didn't seem to have occurred to him that the surgeon had saved his life.

My next placement was in a psychiatric ward at St Mary's Hospital, a good twenty-five miles from where I lived, in a town called Morpeth.

It was not exactly an easy spot to get to so in the lead up to starting there I'd been frantically cramming in driving lessons whenever I could. I had already sat my driving test once before and failed. Now the pressure was on, as I really didn't know how I would get to the hospital if I couldn't drive.

Unfortunately I was very nervous behind the wheel: even my driving instructor was losing patience. I could drive OK when I had my lessons but as my test loomed I seemed to forget everything.

I had booked in for my test on the Friday before I started my placement so everything was riding on me passing. If I didn't I would have to get a train to Morpeth from Newcastle station, then get a bus from Morpeth to Stannington, and then walk at least two miles to hospital.

On the day of my test I felt like I was going to be sick. I couldn't eat my breakfast I was so worried. I had a lesson beforehand with my instructor, which didn't go particularly well. The fact that my instructor kept looking at me and shaking his head hardly filled me with confidence.

At the test centre I was trembling with nerves but after successfully reading a number plate from a distance I got into the car and somehow managed to get my act together.

When I stopped the car I still didn't know what the examiner would say and all I heard were his first three words: 'I am pleased . . .'

My instructor was waiting for me and clearly delighted – after all, he would never have to teach me again.

When Dad came in from work he was also thrilled for me, giving me a big hug. Then the reality set in. 'Does that mean you are going to ask to borrow my car to go to Morpeth on Monday?' he laughed.

On the Monday I was duly sat in Dad's car, driving to Morpeth. I didn't know what was more nerve-wracking: being in dad's new car or the fact I had to drive through the Tyne tunnel. As I approached the first roundabout toward the dreaded tunnel my heart started to beat faster.

Immediately a car tooted at me as I tried to get into lane. 'Sorry!' I waved at him nervously and then another car tooted at me for not going fast enough. In my panic, I somehow managed to stall the car.

As I struggled to get the car into neutral, the air filled with angry horns. Cringing, I finally set off again, driving out the tunnel and turning left towards the A1 to Morpeth. Now I just had twenty-five miles to go!

After about fifteen miles into the journey I started to think about where I was going. I didn't really know what I would be expected to do at the psychiatric hospital and – coupled with the demanding journey – it was a huge stress. As I approached Morpeth, I could feel my heart racing and I started feeling really quite sick from the fear.

The psychiatric hospital was in the middle of nowhere. After leaving the A1, I drove along a very winding road that was lined by trees hanging over the road. It seemed to have no signposts. All of a sudden the road led to an open area in between two huge buildings. There was no one about so I parked up and headed for the small reception area.

I reported to an older-looking man who pointed me in the direction of a waiting area, where I was relieved to see some of my classmates from the school of nursing.

Soon we were met by a charge nurse who split us into two groups, to work on the acute women's and acute men's wards. I was allocated to acute women's admissions with three other class members. The charge nurse showed us around the ward and introduced some of the patients to us.

Most of the women were in a very large room, sitting in armchairs. There were no conversations going on; it was just a collection of women doing different things. One woman was wringing her hands constantly, another was just staring, a third was asleep and one was laughing and talking to herself. Mostly everyone looked unhappy or worried, or were just blankly staring into space.

It was quite scary for me as a student nurse and I knew it was going to be a challenge for my communication skills. I didn't want to do or say anything that would upset these women.

At approximately 10 a.m. the women would line up in front of a hatch where they would receive their medication. Some of them would take it without saying a word and others became quite agitated and abusive to staff while they waited.

I felt very out of my depth, as I did not understand the psychiatric conditions that these women had. It was a huge learning curve and quite frustrating as I felt I didn't know how to help them.

However, I was immediately set to work on the acute admissions ward and it quickly became clear I had to have my wits about me.

At one point I was chased down a corridor by a woman in a wheelchair, who proceeded to run over my feet. On another an old lady with a psychiatric problem who was permanently made up in bright orange lipstick and blue eyeshadow started to stroke my face.

'I like your skin,' she marvelled. 'Ooh, I like your skin.'

Feeling rather uncomfortable, I didn't really know what to do so I just smiled at her nervously. Then suddenly she belted me across the face!

A year later I was working on a surgical ward when she came in looking all smiley and lovely.

'Oh my goodness, no!' I exclaimed to my colleague when I saw her. I was keeping well out of her way!

The charge nurse was very supportive and when we admitted people she sometimes explained to me a little of the women's history.

'This lady coming in now has delusions of grandeur and thinks she's the Queen,' she explained. 'She's been admitted several times before.'

She advised me never to go along with her delusions but to try to steer her into reality.

When I talked to the lady I really had to work hard as she kept thinking I was her granddaughter, but the charge nurse helped me through, guiding me along the relevant questions I needed to ask to admit her. It made me really appreciate the skill and knowledge required to work with patients who have a psychiatric illness.

I certainly found it a fascinating – if sometimes distressing – field of medicine. One of the treatments I witnessed at St Mary's was ECT, or electroconvulsive therapy, a treatment used to treat patients with severe depression. It is one of the most controversial treatments in psychiatry as it involves passing an electric current through the brain to induce a fit, which is thought to change the balance of chemicals in the brain. Although it sounds barbaric it can be an effective treatment when all other avenues have failed, and it is still used in certain cases today. Patients have to give consent and it is done under strict anaesthetic supervision. The patient is given medication to relax the muscles and avoid pain.

I saw it used a few times on a woman who was severely depressed and, although she did appear to be less agitated afterwards, over the course of a month the agitation returned.

After witnessing it a few times I decided I felt uncomfortable observing it, as I didn't really understand the theory behind it. However some psychiatrists believe it has saved lives as it has prevented people from committing suicide.

Meanwhile, as a new driver I was getting used to being on the road alone and working through daily dilemmas about when it was safe to overtake a tractor crawling up the road or how to ignore boy racers determined to sit on my bumper.

But then one day, two weeks in, I got a flat tyre.

I was cruising along the A1 when suddenly I could hear a noise coming from the front wheel. I wasn't really sure what was going on but it seemed to get louder as I drove so I stopped at the next layby.

As I got out to inspect my wheel I realised I had a flat tyre. Great. It was 7.45 a.m. and I was stuck on a dual carriageway without a clue of how to change it. Of course, this was in the days before mobile phones so there was no way I could call anyone for help.

After I'd been pondering what to do and fighting back tears for a while, a motorbike pulled up behind my car. A man dressed in black leathers and a helmet climbed off and started to walk menacingly towards me.

'Oh God, now I'm going to get murdered,' I thought. Quickly I wracked my brains for the self-defence methods I'd learnt at school.

'You all right, pet?' he asked, pulling off his helmet. He was in his late thirties, tall with dark hair and looked quite scary before he smiled. 'Can I help you change your tyre?'

'Er, no, I'm fine,' I replied, aware that the high-pitched tone of my voice indicated quite the opposite.

'It's OK, I'll help you,' he continued, stepping forward as I eyed him suspiciously. 'This happened to my wife a few weeks ago. You need to learn to change a tyre, pet. But don't worry, I'll do it for you now.'

He clearly wasn't going to take no for an answer and as he knelt down to examine the tyre I suddenly felt a bit guilty for being so suspicious.

Within ten minutes he'd replaced the deflated tyre with a perfect new one procured from the boot. Wow, I hadn't even known it was in there! Then he'd climbed back on his bike and zoomed off into the distance. Amazing!

Pulling out carefully, I carried on with my journey, arriving at the hospital two hours late for my shift. Once I quickly explained what had happened to the charge nurse I was told to go into the sitting area and chat to the patients. Within ten minutes I was ducking as a woman threw a cup at me. It smashed off the arm of my chair.

Seeing the state I was in, the charge nurse took me into the office.

'You're having a bad day, so I'm going to let you go home early,' he said. 'Go and get your tyre replaced.'

I was hugely relieved and thanked him, reassuring him I would be fine the next day.

My journey to work nevertheless continued to be traumatic. One afternoon I was driving home from work along the winding road towards the A1 when I noticed the car behind me was sitting on my bumper, flashing its lights.

Panic-stricken, I locked the doors and concentrated on driving at the same speed. After about a mile it flew past me but then to my horror drove slower and slower, forcing me to stop.

Terrified, I sat in the car, my heart racing, as a lad jumped out of the driver's seat and marched up to me. I recoiled in fear as he banged on the windows. He was about eighteen, the same age as me, skinny with short dark hair, wearing jeans and a T-shirt. But rather than the menacing look I was expecting he had a big grin on his face.

'Hello,' he mouthed.

Cautiously I wound the window down by a fraction.

'Fancy going for a drink?' he asked.

I bit my lip. 'No, sorry,' I replied tentatively.

'OK,' he nodded. Then he legged it back to his car, jumped in and drove off, leaving me still feeling decidedly nervy.

Of course as I went through my training I did go out on the odd date but I wasn't interested in anything serious. I just didn't have time for a proper boyfriend and if I ever got one I knew I'd face the ridicule of my three younger brothers.

I remember another occasion when a lad I knew came to the door and asked me out.

'No, you are my friend; I can't go out with you,' I said, primly. Of course my brothers overheard and teased me for ages about that one!

* * *

The time sped by on my placement at St Mary's and soon it was time to move on. I did learn a lot from being exposed to acute psychiatric illness and really saw first-hand how these illnesses can impact on people's lives and their families. But when the end of my placement came it could not have been soon enough and I was very relieved not to be going back. The fact was that at eighteen I wasn't worldly-wise at all. Facing such gruelling circumstances each day was hard and I found it all quite difficult.

In any case, I was looking forward to my next rotation, which was where my true interest lay: the labour ward.

Chapter Two

Feeling hot and clammy I tried to concentrate on the scene unfolding before me.

A woman on all fours was groaning and crying out, clearly in the full throes of labour. Just five minutes earlier I'd had a canary yellow gown and surgical mask thrown at me and found myself being bundled into a labour suite.

A year into my training and at last I had got to my much longed-for maternity placement – only to feel completely overwhelmed.

To my left the woman's husband was stood helplessly, also resembling a rabbit caught in the headlights. We looked at each other, eyes wide, as his wife continued to scream in pain.

I had no idea what was happening. I had no information and felt completely hopeless. As the panic hit me I began to feel sick and giddy. My head started swimming. Oh God: I was going to faint.

I ran towards the closed door with my legs buckling beneath me. I was out cold by the time I'd reached the corridor.

I came to as I was being hauled up by my arms. The midwife and auxiliary deposited me on a chair in the public waiting area.

'Put your head between your legs and breathe,' one instructed, opening a nearby window and heading off.

Although disappointed and embarrassed I put my reaction down to a combination of nerves and an empty stomach. I hadn't had any breakfast prior to my 7.30 a.m. start, assuming I'd pick something up a bit later. Tentatively I headed off to the staff canteen for a cup of tea and toast.

Back on the labour ward half an hour later I felt much better and made my way to the office to await instructions.

'Come on,' a midwife told me, beckoning me towards another labour room.

This time the scene before me was a lot less intense. The labouring woman seemed much calmer but as she began to work through her contractions, breathing heavily in and out, I could feel my anxiety returning. I didn't know what was happening or if the labour was going well. No one was explaining anything.

The midwife was crouching down, urging the woman to push, and from my position behind her I could see the baby's head starting to emerge.

My own head began to pound and the nauseous feeling immediately reappeared in my stomach. I took a deep breath, putting my hands behind my back and pulling on my finger.

'You can't do this again!' I thought. Less than a minute later I was falling out the door again and out cold once more.

Again I was hauled up and dumped in the waiting area. This time I felt quite upset. I'd now fainted twice before 10 a.m.

'I can't believe this!' I thought. 'This is terrible.' I had watched medical and surgical procedures, seen and helped people having cardiac arrests – and here I was, unable to watch a baby being born without fainting!

But it seemed the midwives on the ward were as determined as me to get me through a birth. After a glass of water I was pushed into yet another labour room.

'If you want to be a midwife you are going to have to see a delivery,' one girl, Fiona, told me firmly.

I was desperate to get through it and this time I did manage to watch the baby being born. Then once more I collapsed in the corridor.

Back in my familiar spot in the waiting room by the window I despaired at myself.

'Why do I feel like this?' I thought. 'This is what I want to do!'

To add to my dismay my fainting episodes were now a standing joke amongst the staff on the labour ward. Everyone appeared to be laughing about it and I was mortified.

Right on cue, as I held my head in my hands, a senior midwife walked past, clearly giving someone a tour of the unit.

'There's a student nurse,' she pointed out. 'She's been fainting all morning.'

I could have died of shame.

A few minutes later she returned to see how I was.

'I'm sorry but I'm really not feeling well,' I admitted.

'Well,' she said. 'It's midday so I think you've seen enough for one day. I think it might be best if you go home.'

On my journey home I seemed to spot nothing but pregnant women. Pressing my head against the window I ran through the events of the day in my mind.

Where was the panic coming from? Was it the lack of information that was freaking me out? I'd definitely make sure I ate breakfast in the future too.

The possibility that it wasn't the career for me wasn't an option. I was going to get used to seeing babies born even if it meant fainting twenty times.

* * *

The following morning I was back on the ward feeling much better after a good night's sleep.

To my relief I wasn't just pushed in to watch another delivery. This time I was sent to the antenatal ward, where I was able to meet an expectant mother and her partner prior to the birth.

Susan was in her late twenties and her husband was the same age. They were a lovely couple and it was their second baby. I observed quietly as their midwife did an antenatal check and monitored Susan's contractions.

Within a couple of hours the contractions became stronger and Susan was transferred to the labour ward to use gas and air. Generously she agreed that I could accompany her to see the baby being born. I felt privileged and really hoped I wouldn't faint this time. I was definitely feeling less panicked, as for the first time I understood a tiny bit of what was happening.

As her labour advanced Susan seemed totally in control and focused, and I knew instinctively that I was about to witness a momentous event. After only an hour she started to make groaning noises and looked like she was pushing. Meanwhile the midwife was very calm and encouraging.

Then all of a sudden things started to speed up. I watched while the midwife put on her gloves and set out her trolley without any fuss. I then saw the top of the baby's head emerging from Susan. It had lots of dark hair. With every contraction the head emerged a bit further – and suddenly the head was delivered. There was a short pause then, with a last push, the rest of the baby followed. It was a boy and immediately let out a very loud cry.

As Susan and her husband cooed over their son, out came the afterbirth: a slippery red object that looked a bit like a jellyfish.

The midwife showed me how to clamp and cut the cord, then we checked the placenta after making Susan comfortable.

'Thank you so much,' I said to Susan. 'That was amazing to watch.'

She would never know what a positive impact she had on me.

After that experience I saw other babies born with the mothers delivering standing up, lying on their side or sitting upright. Each one was so different and I found it endlessly fascinating, especially when I had known the women previously and built a relationship with them.

But it wasn't just the deliveries that I loved. It was everything about the process leading up to the baby's birth. I really enjoyed having an opportunity to talk to women who were not ill, building up a rapport and helping in any way I could.

As a student nurse I had time to be available to women to help with the little things that the midwives were too busy to do. I never pretended to know anything but I could do the basics such as make cups of tea, listen, help them have a wash or just stay with their baby while they went in the shower. No one died and I had no pressure on me apart from working really hard to help the midwife where I could.

During my placement I worked in the postnatal, antenatal and labour wards and also in the clinic. I even got to go out into the community for a couple of days with a midwife and a health visitor.

When women were being taught to breastfeed I watched, feeling a little embarrassed, as often the midwife held the woman's breast while the baby 'latched on'.

I must admit it looked so complicated and I felt uncomfortable as I hadn't really seen a baby being breastfed before – Mam would always go into another room to feed Christopher.

Some women made it look very easy and fed their babies with no problems but others seemed to struggle and got very upset when it didn't happen immediately. I wished I had the knowledge to reassure them.

The whole experience was so full of learning opportunities, and I found it hugely exciting and rewarding. Midwives were constantly challenged but appeared to be very confident and made a lot of decisions without consulting doctors.

At the end of the eight-week placement I had definitely decided that this was what I wanted to do.

Meanwhile, I had a stint in the orthopedic theatre to get through.

On my first day I was handed a green surgical gown, a hat that looked like a hairnet and a facemask. As I put them on, I was told I would be observing a hip operation.

It was weird seeing surgery for the first time but I actually took it in my stride.

That is until my face began to feel irritated and my mask started to feel tight and sore. I found myself fiddling with it continually but I just couldn't get it to sit comfortably. Afterwards when I looked in the mirror I noticed a faint pink rash across my nose, cheeks and chin.

The next day the rash became sorer and redder and it was obvious that I was allergic to the latex in the masks.

By now I realised that as a student nurse you were expected to do as you were told and not make a fuss, but the longer I wore the mask the worse my rash got. After a few weeks I was struggling to cover it up with makeup and people were beginning to comment.

Eventually I spoke to the sister who ordered a different type of mask for me. I'd hoped this would solve the problem but no, there

I was back in theatre, my face burning with irritation. To my dismay, seven or eight different types of masks were ordered in for me but none seemed to help and each day I'd leave the theatre with a big red mark on my face.

I wasn't referred to occupational health, as would be the case these days – just sent back in to ride it out.

After five weeks of this I was starting to feel quite unwell. My face felt blotchy and sore and sometimes I felt quite lightheaded.

'I'm really not feeling well,' I confided in the sister.

Sighing, she got up and rummaged in a drawer.

'We've got this old cloth mask,' she said, handing over a flesh-coloured piece of material.

Thanking her I headed to the bathroom to try out the mask. Looking in the mirror my heart sank. It looked ridiculous. The cloth was shaped like a cone at the front and made me look like I had a massive nose jutting out.

Creeping into theatre I tried to hide at the back so no one could see me. No such luck. As soon as the consultant came in he spotted me.

'Good God, girl, what is that?' he exclaimed. 'You look like a duck-billed platypus!'

Behind the mask I flushed red and could feel tears prickling in my eyes. I couldn't do this anymore.

'I'm feeling really unwell,' I told the sister and headed out the door. She followed behind me.

'I'm going to recovery,' I told her. 'My face is tingling.' Her expression darkened.

'Well, if you think you are spending the rest of the time in recovery you've got another think coming, my girl,' she barked. But that's exactly where I stayed, spending the rest of my placement attending to the patients who'd just come round from surgery.

I was never short of drama during my training. For some reason I'm always in the place where something happens.

During our lectures in the school of nursing we were taught about various emergency situations. But as the case studies were explained to us we were told not to worry. 'You'll never see this,' the tutors would reassure us.

Well, I saw everything. People having cardiac arrests on wards; drains being inserted following collapsed lungs; respiratory arrests; allergic reactions to drugs: you name it.

During my second year I did a stint on paediatrics and on my first day I was sent to collect a discharge prescription. The pharmacy was located in an old building across the car park from paediatrics. It was about 2.20 p.m. as I made my way quickly through the parked cars towards the building.

Ahead of me was a man in his late sixties. All of a sudden, to my horror, I saw him trip and fall forward to the ground.

My stomach lurched and I raced over, noticing he was clutching his chest. His face was grey and contorted with pain. I realised quickly that he was not responding to my voice.

Immediately I opened his airway but as I put my face to his I could not feel any breath. He had no pulse and from my limited experience I thought that he had had a cardiac arrest. I gave him a pre-cordial thump on his chest and then started cardiac compressions as I tried to attract help.

This was the first time I had resuscitated someone on my own and I prayed to God I was following all the drills I'd been taught correctly.

I sent a passer-by to get help from reception in the main hospital and continued mouth-to-mouth and cardiac compressions, doing my best to keep him alive. Meanwhile a gaggle of concerned onlookers began to form.

'Can someone go and get someone from inside?' I managed to gasp. 'I'm on my own here.'

Eventually the full crash team came along and took over, bundling him onto a stretcher and whisking him inside. In my shock I still continued on my errand to the pharmacy before heading back to the ward.

'Where have you been, Maria?' Sarah, the sister, chastised. 'You've been ages.'

I looked at her, wondering how to even begin. My hands were shaking and my knees were bleeding.

'There was this man in the car park . . .' I began.

'Lord, Maria, you were never caught up in that drama with the fella who had a heart attack?' she said, dumbfounded.

I nodded wearily.

She took me into a room and got me a drink. I felt in absolute shock and began to relive the drama in my head. Had I done everything right? Was he alive? Sarah rang the coronary care unit for me and asked if he had made it. I was very grateful to learn that he had survived.

Funnily enough I never got sent to the pharmacy again.

Working on paediatrics there was lots of variety. The staff were very nice and I felt very comfortable working with children. But we still saw some distressing things. Often we'd have babies admitted after having fits, as their temperature had got too high. They were rushed in wrapped in bundles of clothes and blankets, as it was a natural reaction for parents to put blankets over children when they were shaking. However, young babies cannot control their temperature, so shivering is a way of cooling down because they are too hot, not too cold. Immediately we'd strip the outer layers off to cool the baby down quickly.

Then there were the babies being admitted with meningitis who were as limp as rag dolls. Meningitis can cause irreparable damage and is potentially fatal but with the correct treatment and antibiotics it was incredible to see the recovery if it was caught early enough. At this time meningitis was not common and health promotion and vigilance for parents was not as apparent.

I also worked with young teenage girls who had anorexia. They had extraordinarily distorted body images: they were often only five or six stone yet thought they were very fat. It was very difficult to reason with them. Dealing with the families of these teenagers was heartbreaking as all they wanted was for their children to eat.

As if all this wasn't enough, I had another steep learning curve to face when I had a stint on the Accident and Emergency ward.

My first day was on a Sunday where I was mostly tending to patients coming in with various sporting injuries, such as strains and broken bones, thanks to bad tackles, collisions or falls.

I was given the task of bandaging up such charges, which all seemed fairly straightforward until someone pulled away a trolley I was balancing against while bandaging up a hunky striker. I lost my footing and fell into his lap. I don't know who was more embarrassed, him or me.

At first it was quite scary seeing people rushing into the department in an obvious panic. But after a while I realised that while genuine emergencies do happen, sometimes all is not what it seems.

Early into my placement I was very alarmed to see a large man in his forties, wearing a checked shirt and jeans, coming through the door clutching his chest and seemingly in the throes of a heart attack.

'I can't breathe,' he gasped. 'I'm sure it's my heart.'

As he staggered to the desk, the charge nurse wandered over.

'What are you doing, Joe? You back here again?' he asked cheerfully.

It was then I learnt that Joe was one of the 'regulars' who frequently believed his panic attacks were heart failure. Thankfully, after taking him to a room and doing his blood pressure, pulse, respirations and an ECG, the nurse managed to calm Joe down and he was sent on his way.

There were other people who had much more serious psychological problems than Joe as well, and I saw a few young people overdosing time and again. I was introduced to 'ipecacuanha', otherwise known as 'ipecac' to staff, which is used as an emetic to make people sick in cases of poisoning or overdose.

The first time I had to give this to someone I was given the advice to hand her a vomit bowl, wait ten minutes and stand back.

As the woman was violently sick I tried desperately to pass her vomit bowl after vomit bowl while dodging the deluge. But it was inevitable she was going into hit my shoes and she did. I learnt the hard way. In many ways it made A&E quite a sad place to be and I got even more of an insight into the ins and outs of psychology.

Thanks to my short experience at the psychiatric hospital I felt I could identify certain patients who had psychiatric issues, either as a result of their behaviour or from the fact that they had made so many repeated visits to the A&E department. Sadly there wasn't any real support for people with psychiatric problems on a day-to-day basis at this time.

I can remember one man who came into the hospital who seemed quite normal at first. I was jotting down his general info when he started to get agitated.

'Who is that sitting on your shoulder?' he asked.

I did my best to deal with him as calmly as I could, remembering what I'd been taught in the past. I guided him to a room while he kept talking about the 'aliens' around him and arranged for a doctor and the psychiatrist on call to examine him.

Although we often came across people with bad psychiatric problems like this there was little we could do. Uncomfortably it was often a case of trying to work out whether they were going to cause any harm to themselves or anyone else and then sending them on their way. Sometimes I laid awake at night worrying about it.

Even worse were the dramatic accidents.

I will never forget seeing a two-year-old girl brought in with second-degree burns to her body. She had climbed into a scalding-hot bath in the split second her mother had answered the phone. Her skin had been immediately covered in Flamazine cream as an emergency measure by ambulance staff and she had been given some pain relief but she was still screaming. Her mum was hysterical and crying uncontrollably while the girl's dad tried to comfort her. It was just awful.

I was responsible for dealing with the parents with one of the staff nurses so we took them to the relatives' room to get a history of what had happened. But of course all the mam wanted to do was see her daughter.

'Why did I leave her?' she kept sobbing. It was heartbreaking.

Once the girl was stabilised, her parents were shown in to see her. They were distraught. Their little girl was very ill and would be scarred for life.

Seeing victims of road traffic accidents was also horrendous. I will always remember one young woman who was brought to A&E with horrific injuries. She'd been hit by a lorry and her feet had been almost completely severed.

It was all hands on deck as the resuscitation team was summoned and the surgeons battled to save her. Sadly her injuries were just too severe and she died shortly afterwards.

I then watched my colleagues going through the unpleasant motions of calling her family and breaking the bad news. I was to learn that the kindest way to deal with relatives was to be honest and direct without giving information that would cause unnecessary distress. It was a difficult balance to get right.

Knowing when to summon the family seemed to be a hard call generally. As family members rushed to reception with pale, frightened faces, and paced the corridors knowing that the life of a loved one hung in the balance, the trauma was only too clear to see. But then not calling could result in them never seeing that person alive again. Either way situations don't get tougher or more heart-wrenching.

There were just so many things to deal with, not just the injuries – it made A&E both an exciting and a terrifying place to work.

Some days nothing would happen and secretly I'd find myself thinking, 'Gosh, this is really quiet – I hope it's going to be busier tomorrow!' But as Christmas approached it was like a war zone. As the party season got into full swing our workload doubled.

My shift that year fell on Christmas Day and I became aware

for the first time how lonely the festive period can be for a lot of people.

On Christmas morning it was initially quiet then the admissions began to come in: old people who'd fallen trying to get out of bed on their own, children having had accidents with new toys or putting small things up their nose, and the cuts and bruises from alcohol-fuelled violence as dysfunctional families were thrown together to celebrate Christmas.

As lunchtime approached a few people were admitted with suspected heart attacks, which thankfully turned out to be just indigestion from overindulging in their Christmas dinner.

Then, as the day progressed, the overdose rate increased. Sadly, Christmas seemed to trigger a lot of bad memories and cause desperation in those who were vulnerable, depressed and on their own.

I went home to my own family quite exhausted and reflective. It really made me stop and think how lucky I was to have my family and friends around me when so many people have no one.

I drew the short straw for New Year's Eve too that year, starting my shift at 9 p.m. and working through until 8 a.m. When I first arrived I couldn't believe the crush in the waiting room. There were hordes of people either sitting, lying or stumbling around. The smell of alcohol and vomit was overpowering.

Every room and cubicle was full of people with a story. Some had started partying early on in the day, which had resulted in them falling over and injuring themselves; others had ended up fighting, sustaining injuries both minor and major, ranging from black eyes and glass cuts to life-threatening stab wounds.

As I quickly set to work with my mentor we also saw numerous victims of domestic violence, after drunken New Year's Eve arguments had got out of control. Unbelievably my mentor, a nurse called Judy, told me that there would be many more cases the following evening: she said that every year they would see domestic violence fuelled by tensions resulting from big football matches on New Year's Day. Generally at local derby matches the feelings ran high and unfortunately women at home were often victims of pent-up anger from their partners if their football team didn't win.

Drink driving was another devastating issue.

That night I saw the parents of a young girl being told that their daughter had died crossing the road after being hit by a driver under the influence of alcohol. The paramedics and emergency crash team had fought to save the twelve-year-old but her injuries were too extensive.

The family had followed the ambulance to the hospital and were quickly escorted into the resus room where it was evident she wasn't going to make it.

The mum was clinging on to the daughter's legs as the last attempts were made to save her, sobbing uncontrollably. It was heartbreaking. I will never forget the sound of her grief. She said she felt as if someone had just torn her heart out.

It was the first time I had seen a child been brought in with such severe injuries and I felt very emotional working with Judy as we looked after this girl's family.

We also had to deal with the drunk driver, a middle-aged man, who had just had a few drinks with his mates before going home to his own family. He had sustained minor injuries in the accident, which also needed to be treated.

When his wife came in there was an obvious smell of alcohol in the room and he just held his hands in his head and said nothing. He had young children at home himself and it was clear that not only had his decision to drive destroyed the lives of the family of the young girl but also his own.

The police were involved and when he was told the girl had died he was devastated and cried uncontrollably. We had to ring a relative to come and be with his wife, as she was also heartbroken and angry at what he had done. It was a highly emotional situation for everyone, including the staff. Going between the two families was difficult but I watched how Judy, who was very experienced, dealt with everything in an appropriate and professional manner, without judgment.

Meanwhile, in the middle of all of this drama, people were shouting about how long they had been waiting and police appeared on the ward as fights broke out in the waiting area.

As I finally finished my shift I drove home to vague shouts of 'Happy New Year 1987!' All I wanted to do was get some sleep after a thoroughly exhausting night. There was no doubt, working in A&E made me grow up very fast.

It's a strange department to work in. When you're seeing horrific situations on a day-to-day basis you have to be able to offload that somewhere and the staff on A&E had definitely developed a very black sense of humour. It is that banter that gets people through it. Otherwise it would be difficult to survive. It's a coping mechanism.

Overall, though, I really enjoyed working on A&E. Once I got used to the uncertainty and bedlam I liked being in an acute situation, so I was actually sad to leave when it came to the end of the placement. I left knowing that I enjoyed the buzz and the challenge of thinking on my feet and that I greatly admired the staff in the department for their calmness, professionalism and humour.

* * *

The next aspect of my training was a very different proposition, but no less of a challenge. This time I was to go out into the community for my first real introduction into how other people lived. I was assigned to a community nurse called Mary, a woman in her fifties, slightly overweight and quite matronly. She had worked for years in the same area. Everyone knew her and she walked with authority and confidence. She wore a navy blue uniform with a white cuff, navy belt and no hat – so thankfully I could discard mine too. She held her equipment in a black case and always carried her diary.

I soon saw that her uniform gave her quite a status in the community. People just seemed to respect her and even when we visited areas of social deprivation there was no worry of anyone attacking you.

As I accompanied her on her rounds in her blue Ford Fiesta I was quite shocked at how some people were living and how people seemed to be content in those conditions. During the time I spent with her I was to visit cold, clammy homes where the smell of damp was overpowering, with black marks on the wall where the wallpaper was falling off. Other houses were full of rubbish and cigarette ends, stuffy and airless, with closed curtains. Ironically they were often the ones that contained the best TVs, DVD players and sound systems that money could buy. I was actually bitten by fleas in one house.

'If you get offered a cup of tea don't accept it and always wash your hands,' Mary advised me from the off. 'It's not like working in hospital out in the community. You will be shocked how some people live but we are not here to judge.'

She added that I should take people as I found them and treat everyone the same. No one was to be treated any better or any worse.

As she drove to our first appointment she gave me a brief outline of the patients we were visiting. The first port of call was the GP practice where she would pick up prescriptions for patients and take them to the pharmacy.

As we went on from house to house it was clear that patients depended on her visits not just to dress a wound or drop off a prescription but for the social aspect too.

Mary clearly cared about her patients and they looked forward to her visits. Sometimes she would be their only contact with the outside world. She would talk about the weather, anything in the news, football scores and – as sensitively as possible – a bit of health promotion where necessary.

'What are you eating to help your leg get better?' she asked an elderly man called Johnny as she dressed his leg ulcer. Then she would suggest foods to him that didn't cost too much.

'What about the pain, Johnny?' she enquired.

'Oh, it's not bad, flower,' he answered.

When we'd first arrived at Johnny's home I'd been shocked at how he was living in such cold conditions. It was February and freezing but he was unable to afford to heat the whole house, so he lived in one room heated by an electric fire. His wife had died three years earlier and he was very lonely.

It made me see how vulnerable people like the elderly can so easily become isolated and how much they relied on you. Sadly we might be the only people they saw that week apart from a neighbour popping in to do a bit of shopping. That hasn't changed today and there are still a lot of lonely old people out there.

As we toured house to house I learnt to have my wits about me, as we often had to dodge huge dogs that were never put away.

On more than one occasion we were chased by a dog as we

made our way back to the car. I'd find myself hopping from foot to foot anxiously as Mary messed around with the key. Of course she jumped in first before she let me in!

On a daily basis we were dealing with ailments such as leg ulcers, chest problems that required oxygen, diabetes and pressure sores. The smell from pressure sores never got any easier to stomach – it was very distinct and unpleasant.

I learnt a lot from Mary and the people I met. It was clear that many older people, while frail, strived for independence and liked their own routines. It was not hard to see how, when they were admitted to hospital, the change in routine could make them feel disorientated, frightened and vulnerable.

The whole experience of working in the community left me both sadder and wiser. It was an invaluable part of my nursing training and I would draw on it when I was working out in the community as a midwife, later on in my career.

Chapter Three

'Now, Mr Jones, please sit down,' Sister Storey instructed. 'It's about your wife, Dolly.'

The elderly man cleared his throat anxiously. Then suddenly he coughed, causing his teeth to fly out and bounce onto the floor and under a chair.

'My teeth, my teeth!' he cried.

As I sat there I saw Sister Storey glaring at me. Her look said it all. There was no way she was going to pick up his teeth.

Sighing inwardly, I bent down to look but they were nowhere to be seen. Reluctantly I started to scrabble around on the floor until finally I found them. I picked them up and put them into a bowl on the desk.

'I think we should get your son in so we can have a chat about Dolly,' Sister Storey concluded, clearly deciding that right now was not the time to break the news of his wife's cancer. 'Now, if you go with student nurse Joyce, she will help you sort your teeth out.'

'OK, pet,' he said, shuffling out behind me.

I was now in my third year and back on the medical ward where I'd originally begun my training.

Once I'd disinfected Mr Jones' teeth and handed them back I returned to Sister Storey's office.

'Close the door,' she instructed. I wondered if she was going to tell me off.

'Now,' she said, bursting out laughing. 'Well done for finding those teeth!'

In the past three years I'd done stints on medical, orthopedic, gynaecology, geriatrics, surgical and paediatrics wards, in the theatre, A&E and the community.

After each placement I'd had to complete practical assessments on each area and had various exams throughout the course. Now as my finals loomed I began to get nervous again. I hated exams.

The test was in January so all over Christmas and New Year that year I studied hard, trying to cram the last bits of information into my head. In order to pass my nursing qualification I had to sit two exam papers over two days, an exhausting prospect.

On the day of the first exam I was sick with nerves. Christopher, who was just coming up for six years old, had made me a 'good luck' card, which was very sweet and thoughtful.

Before the exam I met up with my group of fellow trainees in the common room and we all wished each other good luck. The tension in the air was palpable. We trooped into the examination room and I turned over the paper, scanning the questions quickly. Thank goodness! It was all stuff I'd studied. I just had to read each question carefully and think about my answers before writing them so as not to make any silly mistakes.

The three-hour time limit passed quickly but as I put my pen down I was relieved. Avoiding the other students who were in the common room going over the questions (it would just make me nervous), I headed home, grabbed a sandwich and started revising again for the next day.

The next day it was another three-hour exam and the same process.

That night I joined a few of the girls in our class going out to Newcastle city centre to celebrate. It was a great night and such a relief that we had finished.

We had to go back to the nursing school the following week to tie up the loose ends of our course and prepare for becoming staff nurses, then we were granted two weeks' holiday. During the second week we could collect our exam results from the school.

That week I could hardly sleep. I had been applying for jobs and there was a job on the paediatric ward there for me if I had passed.

On the day my results arrived, I grappled with the brown envelope, my heart in my mouth.

I had passed! I was now a qualified nurse!

My new job was working the night shift but I loved it. I found looking after the children on the ward really satisfying and there was a time when I wondered if I should carry on with my paediatric training. But I also recalled how much I'd loved the maternity ward so I made it my mission to apply for midwifery jobs.

It was difficult to get into midwifery and I knew I would improve my chances if I applied to hospitals all over the country. Although I loved Newcastle I fancied trying somewhere else so began to apply for jobs in places like London and Cambridge.

Eventually a couple of hospitals in the London area invited me for interview. I travelled down without even telling my parents – I didn't want them to talk me out of it!

My first interview was at Chase Farm Hospital so I took an early train to London and found my way to Enfield, where it is situated.

After my interview I had a look around the hospital and was immediately offered a place on the midwifery course.

I was delighted but I had a niggling feeling about the placement so I told them I'd think about it before I accepted it. I then headed off for my second interview of the day at St Helier Hospital in Surrey. It lasted about forty minutes and I was very nervous but I felt afterwards that it had gone well. When I went on a tour of the hospital everyone seemed really friendly and the area struck me as a bit more welcoming to newcomers. I had a good feeling about the place.

However I would have to wait twenty-four hours to find out if I'd been successful. So the next day, back at home, I waited for a call from a tutor. Finally, the phone rang and, to my delight, I was offered a place. Without hesitation, I accepted immediately.

Then I had to break the news to my parents that I would be moving over 300 miles away from home.

'Why are you going so far away?' Mam asked plaintively, but she didn't try and talk me out of it.

'Well, if that's what you want to do, pet, then do it,' Dad said. 'But we'll miss you.'

Michael and Peter were also understanding, but Christopher was really upset.

'I won't see you very much now,' he whispered to me, his sad eyes looking up at me. I tried to gee him along by telling him about the adventures he could have coming down to see me. Once he realised that the Queen lived in London he was much more excited.

I'm not known for packing light and when Dad and Mam took me down to Surrey we literally had our heads squashed against the windows to make space for my belongings. I had duvets and everything.

Mam cried all the way and seeing my new accommodation hardly helped to ease her fears.

'It looks like a biscuit factory!' Dad said. To be fair the imposing old building didn't look particularly welcoming. It was a large, white, featureless block, dating from before the war.

As my dad parked up we all got out. Laying out a picnic in a large field opposite the hospital, we tucked into refreshments after our long journey.

'You can change your mind,' Mam said. 'It's not too late.'

'Give over,' I said, feigning a confidence that I really wasn't feeling.

As we went inside the entrance of the nursing home I noticed how old everything looked. It all seemed quite dismal and dark. The walls and floors were completely bare and there seemed to be no colour anywhere.

I introduced myself to the woman behind the reception desk, who pushed a few forms at me and handed me a key.

'Well, she was a bundle of laughs,' Mam said.

Eventually we found the room and I turned the key. The room was totally bare and gloomy with dirty walls, a bed in the corner, a wardrobe and a chest of drawers that had seen better days. The floor was grey hessian and I thought Mam was going to cry again.

'Oh, Maria, you cannae stay here, it's horrible,' she said.

I decided to be upbeat and make light of the situation.

'Oh, it will be fine once I've given it a lick of paint, got some new curtains and put some pictures up.'

As I unloaded the car with Dad, Mam was off trying to find

someone that she could introduce me to. I was just coming up the stairs with another load from the car when she appeared with a small, flame-haired girl.

'This is Mairead,' she gushed. 'She is on the same course as you.'

'Your mammy has been telling me all about you,' Mairead said in an Irish accent.

Mairead said she was from Tipperary and told me she'd just met another girl called Sharon who was from Waterford in Ireland and had just moved in too. With the car unpacked we found a lovely old English pub in Carshalton and went for a meal before my parents headed back north.

Mam looked visibly happier now.

'They seemed very nice girls,' she reflected. I smiled. As long as she was happy then that was OK. But saying goodbye to my parents, I did feel very choked and fought back tears.

'I'll call you all the time, I promise,' I said.

As the car left I felt quite emotional. This was a big step but it was important for me to have more independence. Imagine how much I was going to learn! I was up for the challenge. I took a deep breath and headed back inside to my new home.

I soon got to know my fellow students in the nursing accommodation. As well as bubbly Mairead, who was always up for the craic, there was Sharon, who was more reserved but with a very dry sense of humour.

Then there was Catherine from Llandudno in Wales with her soft voice and Joanne from Swansea with her much stronger accent.

Jim was a novelty for the hospital; he was the first male midwife they had ever had. He was Chinese and had a very soft, well-spoken voice. He also had a good sense of humour. He would keep saying to me, 'Oh, Maria, you are so funny.' I hadn't a clue why he found me funny at all.

Another girl, Ann, was from Trinidad. She was married but her husband was back in Trinidad and would probably not be coming over for about a year. She was very laid back and had numerous braids in her hair.

When I started my course I met Susan, a girl from Eastbourne with long brown hair and dark eyes. She was very pretty and had an infectious laugh.

'I love your accent,' she said, 'when I can understand what you're saying! Why do you keep calling everyone "man"?'

I had never thought about it before.

'It's just the way I speak,' I said.

Later it was to became a standing joke in the nurses' home that whenever Mam rang me I came back with a stronger accent. It was the same after I'd headed north for the weekend.

'Been home, Maria?' my colleagues would smirk.

'How do you know that?' I'd ask.

'You're speaking really fast again!'

On my first morning I joined the other student midwives in the midwifery classroom, which was located through a set of doors from the nurses' home. After the midwifery tutors welcomed us to the course we had lots of paperwork to complete.

Then we got measured for our cornflower-blue uniforms. To my relief midwives didn't wear a hat! We also had to check our immunisation records and visit occupational health, before being given a tour of the hospital and presented with an overview of the course.

The tutors were very serious. Miss Betterman was tall, with long, neatly tied hair and glasses. She was very ladylike and smartly dressed. She was from Switzerland and spoke with a cut-glass accent.

The other tutor was Miss Wood, who was a little less reserved and a bit more direct when speaking to you. She had curly brown hair and, while still very smart, she wore slightly more flamboyant clothes.

We were informed how the course was very difficult and there was no room for anyone falling behind.

'Be prepared for a lot of hard work,' Miss Betterman said.

She wasn't wrong! The theory started on the second day and I felt like I was learning a new language. There was a lot of anatomy and physiology to master and my mind was soon overloaded with information.

After each day in the school I would go back to my room feeling exhausted, but after something to eat I would start trying to recap what we had learnt that day. I would nip in and out of Mairead and Sharon's rooms for a cup of tea to change environment.

Whereas there had been a lot of camaraderie with my nursing training it wasn't like that at St Helier at all. There was a definite rule of 'you will sit and you will listen' during lectures. We had shorter allocated spaces in the classroom, only a week at a time, but they were very intense. In eighteen months we would cover the female reproductive system, signs and symptoms of pregnancy, physiological changes that take place in a normal pregnancy, normal physiology of childbirth, fetal circulation, complications of pregnancy and the effects of hormones in pregnancy.

I had to understand the theory before I could apply it to practice so often I'd come back from a busy day at work on the wards to find notes from the tutor under the door of my room either returning my marked work or giving me further work to do.

As well as the theory the student midwives were ferried out to different departments to get their essential hands-on experience.

This was my first exposure to patients in the South East. I found St Helier very different to the Queen Elizabeth. Whereas the majority of patients in the North East had been Caucasian with English as their first language, now I was meeting patients from all over the world who spoke all different languages and came from places like Sri Lanka, the Caribbean, Africa and Nigeria.

And it seemed I was quite a novelty to the patients as well!

Not long after I started working in the hospital I was looking after an English couple on the labour ward and was given the responsibility of explaining a procedure to them.

As I chatted away they looked puzzled.

'Do you understand the procedure now?' I questioned.

'What country are you from?' the husband asked, very slowly.

Before I had time to reply he said in a slow, drawn-out voice, 'Are you from Norway or Sweden?'

My face must have been a picture.

'Actually, I am from Newcastle,' I said, laughing. 'Maybe I just need to slow my accent down a bit, eh?'

The man's look of disbelief was hilarious.

'I'm so sorry,' he apologised.

Despite the issues with my accent I very much enjoyed gaining practical experience on the ward. After quickly witnessing five deliveries carried out by more senior midwives the time came for me to carry out one for myself. This was to be the first baby I had delivered on my own so it was a big occasion for me.

To my relief, Julie, the lady I was looking after, seemed very relaxed. She was having her second baby and as she sat in a sitting position preparing to deliver I carefully remembered everything I'd been taught as I guided her through the process.

As she focused and pushed in her own time I could slowly see the top of the baby's head emerging. It had dark hair and was moving closer towards me every time she pushed.

'Well done, Julie,' I encouraged, as I'd heard more experienced midwives do before. I was nervous and really wanted to make sure I did everything correctly.

My supervisor, Sister Mills, who did most of the coaching, was watching closely. Previously I'd made sure I had all of my instruments – bowls, cotton wool and cord clamp – in the correct position on my trolley.

Over the next thirty minutes the head continued to advance slowly. Julie was coping very well and her husband was supporting her. With each contraction I checked the baby's heart rate. It was all fine and I felt excited. I couldn't believe I was going to deliver a baby!

Seeing Sister Mills starting to put on a pair of gloves I figured that the birth would be soon. A seasoned professional, she knew exactly when this baby would deliver.

Then suddenly Julie said she felt uncomfortable.

'I want to turn over on to all fours,' she said.

'You do what you want, lovey,' Sister Mills reassured her. 'You're nearly there.' I shot a look at Sister Mills. I thought I was going to faint, as I'd never seen a baby delivered in that position. The look of fear on my face must have been obvious as Sister Mills immediately sidled up to me.

'It's OK, lovey,' she whispered. 'Whatever you've seen happen before you just do the opposite.'

I had previously delivered a doll through a demonstration pelvis in an all-fours position in the school of midwifery but this was very different!

Trying to stay calm, I observed as the baby's head was advancing well. Then I placed my hand lightly on top of the baby's head to stop it from being born too quickly. I remembered that it is always important to watch the perineum and deliver a baby's head slowly to help prevent tears. This is a really difficult stage for women as all they want to do is push as hard as possible to deliver the baby.

Sister Mills placed her hands over mine.

'Now breathe slowly, Julie,' Sister Mills reassured her. 'Your baby's head is nearly delivered.'

As the head came out I placed my hands either side of it and the baby's body was delivered upwards, 'following the curve' as Sister Mills instructed.

He cried immediately.

'16:11, baby born,' I heard Sister Mills say.

Then she helped me to whisk the baby through Julie's legs so she could see him immediately. Sister Mills dried the baby as I placed my clamps on either side of the cord, showing the dad how to cut it.

'It's a boy,' he said, his voice wobbling.

They already had a little girl so were both thrilled and emotional. As I helped Julie around on the bed to sit more upright she never took her eyes off her baby. 'Thank you,' I said to Julie.

'No, thank *you*,' she replied.

'Now, Julie, we just need to deliver the afterbirth,' Sister Mills smiled.

As the baby was being delivered Julie had been given an injection of Syntometrine to aid the separation of the afterbirth from the wall of the womb.

Sister Mills checked to see that the womb was contracted and then instructed me to use controlled cord traction to deliver the afterbirth.

I pulled the cord in a downwards direction with my right hand as I guarded the uterus with my left hand. It was difficult to know how much traction to put on, so Sister Mills gently put her hand over mine to ensure I had the right amount of pull.

Julie was busy looking at her baby but said she could feel something coming out.

'That's your afterbirth, lovey,' Sister Mills reassured her. Then as the placenta was delivered I scooped it up with both my hands to place it in the bowl, being very careful to make sure the membranes were delivered intact.

'16:20,' Sister Mills said out loud. 'Placenta and membranes delivered.'

After checking Julie didn't need stitches, we got her out of the delivery sheets and placed clean pads below her. The couple were now sat cuddling their baby, counting toes, with the pair of them unable to decide whose nose he had.

As part of the routine check after delivering a baby I covered my trolley over with a sheet, washed my hands and then checked Julie's blood pressure, pulse and temperature. Then I checked to make sure her womb was contracted by placing my left hand at the level of her umbilicus to ensure it felt hard.

She was not bleeding so after giving her a call button in case of any problems, I could leave the room. The couple hardly noticed; they were so engrossed in their baby.

'I can't wait until Grace meets her new brother,' I heard the new dad say.

I was just so relieved and happy that I had delivered my first baby. As I wheeled the trolley to the sluice I had a definite bounce in my step. I couldn't stop smiling.

However my tasks as a midwife were far from over. Sister Mills was waiting for me in the sluice.

'Clean your trolley,' she ordered. 'Then I will come and check the placenta with you.' I quickly did what she said, laying it out on a plastic covering on the sink unit.

'What are you checking for?' she demanded. I felt under pressure again.

'Er . . .' I began. 'The shape of the placenta and the insertion of the cord?'

She said nothing.

As I held up the placenta with my hand I told her I was checking to see if the membranes were complete by noting the small hole where the membranes had ruptured. I put the placenta down again and showed her that there were two membranes as I separated them with my hands, peeling them back to the cord.

'Names?' she asked.

'Um,' I stuttered. 'Amnion and chorion.'

The questions continued until Sister Mills was satisfied that I had done all my checks effectively.

'Never give a woman tea and toast until you have checked the placenta and she has been sutured if necessary,' she instructed. Those words I have never forgotten to this day.

'You did OK with the delivery,' she said, walking off. That was almost a compliment from Sister Mills.

At the end of my shift I gave Julie a cuddle and thanked her again. I almost skipped back to the ward but with Sister Mills walking behind me it stopped me in my tracks – although I happily told my colleagues later that I had delivered my first baby. It felt great!

'What a day,' I thought. 'That is why I wanted to become a midwife!'

* * *

Meanwhile I was enjoying life in the nurses' home. My room was very basic and although I wasn't really supposed to change it I rebelliously decided to paint it blue and add the finishing touch of a border, which was fashionable at the time. I also got a good deal on a baby-blue carpet, which I spread over the grey atrocity on the floor. Finally I put up some curtains and added photos of family and friends and drawings that Christopher had sent me.

My £300 monthly rent took a fair chunk out of my take-home pay of £500 a month, but with accommodation in the area extremely expensive I knew my no-frills home was the cheapest I could get. Rather unfairly, we also had to pay £50 a month for the recently introduced poll tax for our measly little rooms – exactly the same as someone with a huge home in Surrey. There were no discounts because you were a student midwife.

Gradually the place started to feel like home. Outside in the corridor there was a telephone that was always occupied and a board with names on it to indicate whose turn it was next. I shared the communal kitchen and bathroom with the whole floor, around fifteen people. We'd often hang out in each other's rooms eating meals, as there was no communal area to eat.

Sometimes boyfriends or girlfriends (male nurses lived there too) stayed over in the nurses' home. It wasn't allowed as a rule, as we were meant to declare visitors, but there was open access so it was easy to slip a guest through.

There was a clear demarcation of status depending on what floor your room was housed on. It was an unwritten rule that newcomers started on the first floor and over time progressed up to bigger and better rooms on the floors above. The fifth floor was the best, with rooms up there even having their own sinks.

After about a year I got a promotion to another floor as building works were starting on the first floor and my room was to be demolished. I eventually made it to the fifth floor when I qualified as a midwife.

The lift in the nurses' home was practically prehistoric. It was one of those types where you had to pull open a wire shutter first to get into the lift. It was also temperamental. One afternoon I was working in the postnatal ward when I nipped over to the nurses' home during my break to pick up my student folder to work on.

As I jumped in the lift it shuddered to a halt. Panic raced through me. I was now stuck between floors. I was quite frightened as the nurses' home could be quite a deserted place at times. Immediately I started to feel claustrophobic.

There was an emergency telephone but it didn't work so all I could do was shout for help. After what seemed like an age the lift eventually moved. But my relief was short-lived as it stopped a foot shorter than the floor I wanted. Managing to pull the wire shutter open slightly I crawled out and rolled onto the floor.

Dashing back to the postnatal ward I was faced by a fuming staff midwife.

'Where have you been, Maria?' she said. 'Your break is twenty minutes and you've been gone for more than an hour!'

Living on the outskirts of London I was keen to check out the capital. I hadn't been there since I'd picked up my gold Duke of Edinburgh award with Mam all those years earlier. So one day, after painstakingly planning my route, I got a bus from outside the nurses' home to Morden, then jumped on the Northern Line with the plan to change at King's Cross for the Piccadilly line to Covent Garden.

Well, when I saw everyone on the tube I nearly burst out laughing. It was just weird. Everyone was so serious and no one held any eye contact!

As I defied etiquette by grinning and looking around the carriage I soon learnt there was a very good reason for most people's reluctance to hold each other's gaze.

Opposite me was a young lad aged about twenty-three with dark hair who was wearing a slim, smart jacket. He kept looking over at me and smiling. It was fine until I got off at King's Cross and headed for my next tube. Suddenly I realised he was behind me. I assumed he must be going in a similar direction but then on the next platform he stood quite near, just watching me. As I squeezed into a carriage he followed behind, and I started to feel really quite unnerved.

Lo and behold when I got off at Covent Garden I glanced around to see him still shadowing me as I snaked quickly through the crowd.

Trying to look like I wasn't frightened, I kept walking, with the horrible realisation rapidly dawning on me that I hadn't told a single soul where I was going that day. I was terrified in case he tried to grab me and I definitely wasn't going to confront him as I was too scared.

Eventually I went into a busy department store and got amongst a crowd of people. Rushing through, I made my way to a different exit, finally losing him in the throng.

Stopping for breath, I gave myself a little pep talk. 'Maria, you're not in Newcastle!' I told myself. 'You can't go into London and not tell anyone! You need to be careful!'

The rest of the day I wandered around Covent Garden and Leicester Square watching the street performers and gazing into shop windows. I also went to visit Harrods and couldn't believe the prices of the clothes, shoes and bags!

After that I had a coffee and just people-watched. I found it fascinating observing everyone going about their business. It was a whole different world to mine.

On the underground journey home I fell into line, keeping my eyes down. This wasn't exactly easy as this time another young hippish-looking lad was busy swinging on the poles people use to grip on to. Forward and backward he went. In between his acrobatics he paced up and down the carriage asking for money. When he approached me I gave him some because I was frightened. I was amazed by everyone else's reactions though. I couldn't help but look at everything he was doing but everyone else seemed to be able to ignore him. They just had their heads in their books and were not paying attention.

That journey to and from London really was an eye-opener and it was definitely the first time I realised that I needed to be more aware of what was happening around me.

Most of my social life at St Helier, however, was closer to home and revolved around the other student midwives. But even then I inadvertently revealed my northern roots. We had our first night out in Sutton in Surrey after about a couple of months. Feeling very excited I spent ages getting ready. I put on my tailored trousers, a dressy top and heels, did my hair, and finally applied lashings of red lipstick.

When I stepped out I found my friends Sharon, Catherine, Mairead and Susan dressed in jeans and T-shirts.

'Where are you going?' Sharon said, eyeing me in a bemused fashion.

'Out with you!' I replied, puzzled.

'Oh, I thought you were going to a wedding or something!' Susan said. 'You're so dressed up!'

It was at that moment it dawned on me that I was a far cry from Newcastle where everyone gets really dressed up when they go out in the evening. After that it was a standing joke that like all hardy Geordie lasses I would go out in a little light jacket while everyone else put on their big coats. I continued to get dressed up to the nines for several weeks until eventually Catherine wore me down and persuaded me to go jeans shopping with her.

Later I did take a few of the girls up to Newcastle to show them what it's all about. Their faces were a picture as we walked through the Big Market spotting girls in leopardskin shorts and tiny tops in the middle of winter.

Being so far away from home I missed my family so I would try to get back home to Newcastle at least every eight weeks. I'd either travel home by train from King's Cross or Dad would come down to get me. Whenever I'd go away for a few days it would cause much mirth amongst the other staff.

'How did you get back?' they'd ask with mock wide eyes. 'They don't have roads up there, do they?'

They seemed to think that the world stopped at Watford Gap. I'd retaliate as best I could with humour. 'Actually I got the train to Watford, bus to Sheffield and the rest of way I took my horse and trap,' I'd quip.

Despite the good humour it was clear that some people really did think that 'oop north' was another world.

'When you stand at the platform in London you can always spot the northerners,' one tutor told me with conviction. 'They are always very short in stature.' Well, what do you say to a comment like that!

*　　*　　*

St Helier maternity unit had recently introduced a policy known as 'Team Midwifery'. This was a newish concept that hadn't been implemented anywhere but London at that time. It evolved from recent publications that promoted 'continuity of care' as an important aspect of enhancing a woman's journey both during pregnancy and after the birth. Every hospital interpreted team midwifery in a different way. Some hospitals tried to integrate the hospital into the community it served; others had separate teams for hospital-based and community-based care. Other teams had only six to eight midwives in them. It was new and it was trial and error at the beginning. Some midwives liked it and others didn't, finding it unsettling to be required to move to a labour ward mid-shift if one of their women had become established in labour. This meant leaving the other women they'd been caring for behind.

The basic concept was that from the start of their pregnancy women would be allocated to a consultant and certain midwives were allocated to that consultant's team. The idea was to try and cut down on the number of midwives that a woman saw during her pregnancy. I could see benefits for both the women and midwives. Women with high-risk pregnancies that required numerous hospital admissions would get to know staff more easily and staff in turn would get to know women better.

Now on a day-to-day basis I was allocated two mentors who were working in a team under two male consultants called Mr Jones and Mr Day.

My mentors were very different but I learnt so much from them. The first one was Tracey, an Irish lady with a soft accent, who was quiet and thorough. She was excellent with the women, confident but unassuming. Her priority was always the women and ensuring they were OK, whether it was before or after the birth. She had a knack of making each mother feel like they were the centre of her attention even though in reality she was juggling lots of situations. It was a skill I very much admired.

My second mentor was Evelyn. She was younger, very confident and knowledgeable on current practice. She would challenge me on a daily basis about what I thought of different situations and was more confrontational with the doctors. It was extremely useful for me to watch her in action.

In theory the women should always have seen the same members of the team for each check-up and for the birth itself, but with the unit facilitating about 4,000 deliveries a year, in practice it was not so easy. Often you might not have met the woman before and the continuity of care would fall down on the labour ward.

My training required me to deliver forty normal births in eighteen months. A lot of students these days are fighting for deliveries. However it certainly wasn't a problem in our busy maternity unit. I notched up about fifty-five in the end. I was lucky as I always seemed to be there when things were happening. It was just so busy!

I also had to get 100 antenatal checks under my belt, either by attending clinics in hospital or by accompanying Angela, a community midwife, on home visits.

Angela was a petite Brazilian lady with dark curly hair, dark eyes that could look at you and tell a story, a big smile and beautiful teeth. I loved that she always wore lipstick.

'My dear,' she said, when I remarked on it, 'I'm the first person the baby is going to see so I need to be looking good.'

Maybe that's where I got my affinity for lipstick. Everyone knows me for my red lippy and like Angela I always put it on before I go in for a delivery. It is my trademark to this day.

Angela was a great teacher and first taught me how to use a pinard stethoscope, a funnel-shaped instrument that is placed on a mother's abdomen to enable you to hear the baby's heart.

The first time I listened all I could hear was my own breathing. It took me dozens of attempts but eventually I made out the heartbeat. I was ecstatic!

Counting the heart rate for a minute is also a skill and as time passed I eventually improved due to sheer perseverance. Thankfully the women under Angela's care were very patient while I was learning.

Once again, though, I was shocked by some of the deprived areas I saw on my home visits. I didn't imagine Surrey would be like that! At one house I went into I actually had to stand my feet in a puddle to help get the dog dirt off my shoes when I came out.

'You will be more careful next time,' Angela instructed.

Another house was littered with cigarette butts and squashed beer cans and there was nowhere to sit as the settee was covered in rubbish. The bathroom sink was full of dirty clothes and the baby was in a Moses basket on the floor in amongst all the squalor.

As Angela asked me to check the baby over a huge Alsatian dog kept circling me, probably smelling the fear. I wasn't frightened of dogs normally but this one was scary.

It was Angela who warned me I should never clean my hands on anyone else's towels. She carried hand wipes instead! She was a great person for me to go out with and she taught me a huge amount.

When we finished work she'd often take me to her house and cook Brazilian food for us. It was beautiful and with me being away from home it was so good to go into a family home and be made to feel welcome while eating fantastic spicy food.

But there was never much chance to relax. Working in the community you would be on call for home births when pregnant women were between thirty-seven and forty-two weeks. I had to help with a home birth as part of my training so it was with some excitement that I learnt that I would be going on call for a lady named Sarah, one of Angela's women who was fast approaching her due date.

The reality of this was that I would be on call all day, every day, for five weeks if need be. I was given a pager to bleep me whenever I was needed, making me very conscious that I shouldn't go out drinking or make firm arrangements to go anywhere.

I must admit on reflection I didn't know how midwives did it full time when they had a family of their own. Expectations from the women were high and it was the community midwives who juggled their own lives to give the women what they wanted. I saw a few midwives completely burn out as they gave women this gold standard of one-to-one care, sometimes to the detriment of their own health and own lives.

With this particular home birth, the plan was that if the labour started during the night then Angela would pick me up, but otherwise I would get the bus.

As it happened I had just got back from work at 6 p.m. when I heard the phone ring. I had now been on call for four weeks. A girl came to the kitchen to get me.

'Hi, Maria,' said Angela when I picked up the phone. 'I'm at Sarah's house now. She is four centimetres dilated if you want to make your way over.'

'I'm on my way,' I replied quickly. I knew that there was still some time – the cervix gradually opens during labour until it is ready for birth when it is ten centimetres dilated.

I immediately ran to Mairead's room.

'I'm off to a home birth, woohoo!' I announced. 'I've made some food in the kitchen if you haven't made your tea yet.'

Then I quickly put my uniform on and grabbed my bag, running out of the nurses' home to the bus stop across the road. Unfortunately I had just missed a bus but the next one would be in fifteen minutes. The journey would probably take about thirty minutes on top of that.

I hope she won't deliver before then, I thought.

The bus arrived and I sat at the back, impatiently tapping my fingers on the seat. When I reached the right stop I remembered the instructions. Right, get off, turn right and then it was about six doors down . . . Finally I found the house and knocked on the door, and Sarah's husband let me in.

The atmosphere was calm inside. Sarah and her husband were in the sitting room while she laboured. The lighting was subdued and I could hear calm music playing in the background. It was very different to a hospital birth.

After each contraction Angela listened to the fetal heart and then reassured Sarah. In between contractions Sarah moved from room to room, clearly in her zone of concentration, while Angela took a back seat, following Sarah's instructions that she didn't want her midwife to be too hands on.

Being nervous I was quite chatty so when Angela told me to calm down I followed her example of only speaking when it was necessary.

'As long as everything is OK with baby and the mother is coping well you stay well back,' she instructed.

Sarah's husband Paul was the birth partner and was busy massaging her back during contractions. Meanwhile Angela brought me a cup of tea and a biscuit. It felt very strange to be taking a back seat, as I was always used to doing something.

After about two hours of being at the house, Sarah had adapted a position standing up in the sitting room and we had just laid out plastic sheeting to protect the carpet. Angela had also prepared an area near the back of the room with oxygen and warm towels on the radiator.

All of a sudden there was a popping sound and then a gush of fluid hit the plastic sheeting. Sarah's breathing changed and she sounded like she was pushing with the contraction. I put some pads down and Angela called the second midwife who only lived around the corner.

She arrived within fifteen minutes, at which point Sarah was involuntarily pushing – and then all of a sudden I could see the top of the baby's head advancing towards us. Sarah remained standing, leaning over a chair.

Angela knelt down so she could control the baby's head as it delivered. I was mesmerised. I had never seen a baby born with a woman standing up before.

As the baby's head delivered, Angela guided Sarah with very quiet instructions. Paul was facing Sarah, supporting her, and the second midwife listened to the heart rate.

Then with the next contraction Sarah pushed gently and a baby girl was born screaming. Angela passed the baby through Sarah's legs and she scooped her up. 'Happy birthday, little girl,' she said.

I could have cried. Wow, what an experience.

Within about forty-five minutes Sarah was lying in her bed after delivering the afterbirth and having a bath, cuddled up to her baby girl, who they had named Lucy. Meanwhile her other daughter, Ruby, had just arrived with Grandma.

I will never forget Ruby's face when she saw Lucy for the first time. Her eyes lit up.

'Ruby's baby!' she said. It was just amazing for me as a student to be part of something so special. This was what midwifery was all about, I thought.

As well as racking up my normal births, antenatal checks and home births I also had to witness forty complicated births such as instrumental, forceps or ventouse deliveries, breeches or C-sections.

I saw my first forceps delivery as a student midwife and soon learnt that it was yet another one of those large learning curves I was just going to have to get used to.

The woman in question had been in labour for fourteen hours and was clearly exhausted. It was her first baby and after pushing for over an hour and a half the top of the baby's head was just visible but there was no advancement. The fetal heart rate was fine.

I was told by my mentor that the head was in the correct position but the woman was just so tired that she would need intervention. After summoning the doctor on call for the labour ward there was a discussion between the woman, the midwife and the doctor about what would happen.

'Just get it out,' the woman pleaded. So with a full assessment of the situation, it was decided to 'give her some help'.

The bottom of the bed was removed and a forceps trolley was wheeled in from outside the room. A paediatrician appeared and everything was prepared. Meanwhile the woman's legs were placed into the lithotomy position in stirrups. It all looked very clinical and her partner looked terrified.

My job was to stand next to the woman and place my hand on

her abdomen to feel her contractions and tell the midwife and doctor when one came.

The doctor got ready, taking care not to show the instruments to the woman.

Meanwhile, feeling a movement across her abdomen, I broke the silence.

'There's a contraction building,' I said in a shaky voice.

The midwife encouraged the woman to push down at that point, chin on her chest, and at the same time the doctor pulled as the woman pushed to prevent the baby's head slipping backwards.

I remember thinking that doctors need good arm muscles to do forceps deliveries! After the contraction the head had moved a little. After three more, the woman was told to pant as the baby's head was delivered and the instruments were removed.

With the baby's head delivered I waited to feel the next contraction. There it was.

'Push again,' we encouraged her. In a rush, the baby was delivered and handed immediately to the paediatrician.

'Is everything OK?' the mother cried, but within a minute the baby let out a huge scream.

'It's a boy,' the midwife confirmed. Both parents immediately burst into tears and I felt very relieved. The midwife explained that the baby had small marks on his face from the forceps but that they would fade.

Still shaking, I stepped outside. There had been a lot more people in the room compared to a normal birth and it seemed much more clinical but at least everything had been fine in the end.

My first Caesarean came courtesy of a lady called Kerry, who was having an elective section with her first baby. I'd previously met her on the antenatal ward and accompanied Tracey, my mentor, to collect her.

Kerry was having a Caesarean as her placenta was slightly covering the cervix, ruling out a natural birth. She had been in and out of hospital throughout her pregnancy after suffering some bleeding.

As we walked along the corridor to the theatre, Kerry was looking very nervous in her hospital gown, slippers, dressing gown and theatre hat. When we reached the anaesthetic room Kerry was given a spinal anaesthetic so she could remain awake and pain-free during the operation to deliver her baby.

With the anaesthetic now working, Kerry was carefully moved on to her back and a screen was put up for the consultant who was performing the operation to work behind.

Once Kerry was in theatre, I put my theatre hat and mask on, feeling a little nervous about this given my prior allergic reactions. Luckily this time it seemed fine. Kerry's partner was brought in just prior to the operation and sat on a stool next to her. There seemed a lot of people there but everyone had a job to do. I tried my best to observe everything.

The room filled with relaxing music and as the surgery began, Tracey, my mentor, kept whispering information to me in between her jobs – which seemed to be never-ending! She was supporting Kerry, recording all the events in copious notes and seemingly doing a dozen other things at the same time.

The operation was over very quickly. I heard a gush of fluid as the amniotic liquid was suctioned just before the delivery. Then with a quick manoeuvre, the baby was lifted out and was being held over the screen for the mother and father to see.

'It's a girl! Congratulations!'

The baby let out a huge scream and was then bundled into a cot with a sterile drape over it.

'A good set of lungs there!' one of the theatre staff commented.

I went over to Kerry and quickly congratulated her without getting in the way. She was crying with relief, joy and excitement: she had hoped for a girl and both she and her husband were very emotional. When Tracey brought the baby over they were just transfixed by her.

What a privilege to be part of new life with people who were so excited about having a baby, I thought. The placenta was delivered safely and Kerry did not have a larger blood loss than normal.

Once Kerry had seen her baby Tracey took her into another room to be weighed and for first baby check to be done. Nowadays, the baby always stays with the mother and is weighed and checked in the operating theatre.

Then, with proud mother and baby reunited, they were wheeled off to the postnatal ward.

Getting to deliver a breech for the first time was just as much of an eye-opener. A breech birth is when the baby is positioned so that its bottom or feet emerge first, rather than the head as is more common. I'd previously seen about three breech deliveries but on this occasion, as I observed from the back of the room, the doctor suddenly put me on the spot.

'Do you want to do this delivery?' he asked.

'Yes please,' I said. I knew that he was very good at teaching and this was an opportunity not to be missed.

The rule generally is 'hands off the breech', as you let nature do its thing. So moving forward I watched as the bottom came into sight in the vagina. Then with every contraction and push from the woman the sacrum rotated slightly, causing one leg to pop out and then the other. The weight of the baby then brought the baby's head to the perineum area.

Ensuring the cord was not pulled as the body was delivered, the doctor then instructed me to place a warm towel over the baby's back.

'With the next contraction you wait for the left shoulder to rotate to deliver the left arm and then the right,' he explained.

Doing as I was told, I waited for the arms to pop out and then finally the head.

I passed the baby to the overjoyed mother and felt absolutely thrilled.

These days normal delivery for breeches is far less common as medical guidelines recommend a Caesarean section. I was very privileged to have that experience.

Chapter Four

Sitting slumped by her baby's incubator, her shoulders shaking and tears rolling down her cheeks, the mother was visibly very upset.

'Lucy,' I said, going over and placing my hand gently on her shoulder. 'Are you all right?'

'I feel so guilty,' she said. 'I should be with all my babies, not just one.'

My heart went out to her. Lucy was mother to triplets born by Caesarean section the week before at thirty weeks' gestation. Weak and tiny, they'd all needed special care, but because of a shortage of neonatal cots the brothers of the tiny girl sleeping next to us were now being cared for in London and Cambridge respectively.

Now Lucy was clearly wracked with guilt that she could only be with one of her triplets as they all fought for their lives. All I could do was listen and tell her that it was beyond her control.

'You need to rest as much as you can,' I told her. 'You need to give yourself time to recover from your Caesarean.'

It was definitely a very different atmosphere on the special care baby unit where I was now in the midst of an eight-week placement.

A far cry from the elated mothers in postnatal, here new mums performed long vigils by incubators, looking drawn and pale, desperately willing their premature babies to survive.

The first time I walked onto neonatal for my placement I found it quite overwhelming. The unit was split into three separate areas: intensive care, high dependency and then the special care cots.

As a sister showed me around she explained that a couple of the tiny babies in the intensive care area had been born at twenty-four to twenty-five weeks' gestation. It just seemed unfathomable.

When you are not used to working with babies this small it is pretty daunting even as a midwife, so goodness only knows how the parents must have been feeling. I had worked on a paediatric ward but this was a completely different type of nursing. The babies that were in intensive care were generally there because they were very premature. The length of stay varied but a baby born at twenty-five weeks could potentially be in the neonatal unit for fifteen weeks until it reached the date that it was due to be born. Some of these babies weighed as little as 500g, which is the equivalent of half a bag of sugar.

To see a baby this premature was shocking and I have every admiration for the specialist nurses who care for them and have advanced qualifications and skills to look after them properly. But although advances in technology and improved outcomes have meant that more and more premature babies are surviving against the odds it is inevitable that some don't make it or end up with long-term problems. I soon learnt that it can be a very difficult, exhausting and turbulent time for parents. One day their baby may be stable and within twenty-four hours the baby is critically ill again.

Working in the special care unit I spent a lot longer with babies and I did become very attached to some of them as I watched them grow. The most heartbreaking thing was seeing the babies who had no one to come and visit them. This may have been because of the social circumstances of the mother or the distance, but just like me the other staff seemed to really take these babies to their hearts, showering them with attention whenever we could.

Over the course of my placement I got to know Lucy, the mother of the triplets, very well. Thankfully at four weeks, once her other two babies were stable, they were transferred back to the same hospital for special care and she could once again dote on them all.

Now the battle was on to get the triplets to gain weight and to establish breastfeeding. From the off Lucy had been advised to try and express some breast milk for her babies, as the benefits were immense. Breast milk has antibodies, enzymes, hormones and growth factors and is easily digestible. It can prevent lots of complications in premature babies. Even if a baby is not able to breastfeed from its mother the baby can have breast milk via a tube or a special cup.

The hospital even had a milk bank system where women who were producing a lot of milk could donate breast milk for ill babies.

Lucy was also encouraged to have as much skin-to-skin contact as possible with her baby, or 'kangaroo care' as it is known. This is when the baby is placed next to the mother's chest, skin-to-skin, to encourage closeness and the rooting reflex of the baby at the breast. Women love this intimacy with their child and it also regulates the baby's heartbeat and breathing, and gives easy access to the breasts for feeding.

Even if the mother chooses not to breastfeed there are so many other benefits from skin-to-skin contact. I have even seen dads take their shirts off in the theatre after a baby is born by C-section to do it. When this practice was first introduced there were a few comments from staff but it is pretty much standard now.

Lucy's babies all stayed in for a further four weeks while they established breastfeeding and were rotated on to the breast in turn. This involved a lot of time and patience but Lucy eventually managed to feed them all from the breast.

'Try and rest while you can,' the sister warned her. 'When you leave the hospital that's when the hard work really starts!'

'I will,' she smiled, 'although I really can't wait to take them home!'

It was an amazing moment when I saw Lucy and her husband Ben carrying three car seats containing their now-thriving babies out of the hospital.

'Take care,' I said, giving her a hug. 'I will miss you!'

Being a student midwife I'd quickly understood the responsibility of my new career. It was clear that giving birth was a life-changing, emotional and sometimes frightening experience. I vowed that I would never take caring for women and babies for granted.

For me as a student I wanted it to be the best experience possible for them but I also learnt that sometimes such idealistic views went out the window.

My training involved working alongside more experienced midwives to learn the ropes. But in reality having a student was also helpful for the midwives, as limited resources and staffing levels meant that they also relied on you to help care for women in labour when they were stretched to the limit.

I soon learnt that it was a luxury if you looked after only one woman in labour. The norm was for you to be looking after at least two women, with the midwife also running between the two. As a student I had to learn to think on my feet and report immediately if there were any problems with the mother or baby's heartbeat.

On one occasion I was looking after two women with Tracey. They had both had epidurals and were at roughly the same stage.

With an epidural there are additional observations to do so when Tracey had to admit a third lady I was running back and forth between the two women. There was no time to have an in-depth conversation or observe fully the changes in either of them as their labours progressed, and it seemed very mechanical and task-orientated as opposed to the birth experiences I had seen lots of times before. I felt like I was just ticking off the tasks: blood pressure, temperature, pulse and frequency of contractions. I was working my way down the partogram – the progress chart in labour – without really thinking about the whole picture. As soon as I got my observations recorded I had to run out to the next woman to do the same.

The problem arose when it became clear that both women were going to deliver their babies at a similar time. I had no choice but to call the midwife in charge in with me as my mentor was in the other room.

As soon as the baby and afterbirth were delivered by the first lady, the senior midwife left and I continued to make her comfortable, check the baby and then give the mother a bed bath. I then had to dash into the other room and help Tracey with the second baby.

Blimey, I thought, there's no messing about with this job!

In fact the largest number of deliveries I experienced was

probably five in one day. To be honest it wasn't a day I enjoyed, as I was just too exhausted.

As a student midwife you are always focused on getting your forty deliveries. But running in and out of rooms catching babies is not really a good experience for the women or the student.

By far the most enjoyable experience is when you deliver a baby where you have cared for and built up some relationship with the mum and her partner. It makes it more personal as opposed to feeling you're on a conveyor belt.

Sometimes, however, with the best will in the world there simply wasn't time to get to know a woman before she gave birth. The maternity unit at St Helier was spread over three floors, with two postnatal wards on the ground level, special care housed on the second floor and the labour ward, containing about twelve rooms, on the third.

One day I was walking along the corridor on the ground floor when I heard a noise coming from outside the lift. When I went to investigate there was a woman on all fours with her husband looking on helplessly.

'Are you OK?' I asked.

She immediately shot me a look as if to say, 'Do I look OK?'

Immediately I shouted for someone to bring me a pair of gloves and did my best to help the woman as she crawled into the lift.

'I'll call the labour ward and tell them you're on your way up,' a colleague said, dashing over.

In the short journey in the lift the woman was pushing and quickly I established it was her second baby. When the lift reached the third floor I pressed the emergency stop button and she started crawling out, towards where a midwife was waiting at the lift doors.

But immediately she started to deliver her baby on the floor outside the lift. Luckily someone had the presence of mind to run and get a screen to block the area off.

Her baby girl came out screaming, minutes later. What an entrance to the world!

Eventually we managed to help the woman into a wheelchair as she cuddled up to her baby. Thankfully she was laughing at the situation. We took her to a room to deliver the afterbirth and then made sure she was comfortable with tea and toast. Her husband was just as shell-shocked but relieved they had made it to hospital.

After finishing a well-earned slice of toast she turned to him and said, 'See, I told you I was in labour!'

As a student midwife you have to accept that as well as births being unpredictable, sometimes emergency situations do occur. There is special training for midwives and doctors in these situations, so when faced with problems a drill procedure is activated and everyone knows their role in dealing with the unfolding emergency.

Generally when things were fraught I was very much an observer. I didn't ask questions, I just ran for things when I was asked. But I was always fascinated to observe the well-oiled machine set into motion when a complication developed.

One woman had a normal delivery and delivered the afterbirth with no problem only to start to bleed quite heavily ten minutes later, because her womb had relaxed. The blood started gushing out and the atmosphere in the room suddenly became heavily charged as everyone became aware that there was a problem.

Immediately a call for help was put out to a doctor and the midwife in charge. I watched, riveted, as the midwife placed her hand over the top of the womb and started rubbing up a contraction to stimulate the womb to contract and thus stop the bleeding.

As someone else quickly explained to the woman what was happening, I was asked to check the placenta to ensure it was complete. If it wasn't complete then this could have been the cause of the bleeding.

When I hurriedly checked the placenta I could see there was a piece missing and so she was immediately transferred to the theatre to remove the retained placenta.

The whole drama had unfolded very quickly but everyone had played their parts calmly, with no signs of panic.

After the woman had been wheeled out, I sat there with the dad who was holding the baby and looking completely distraught.

'Your wife is in very good hands,' I said, crouching down beside him. Then I explained about how she was having a piece of placenta removed, which had caused the bleeding.

'I'm sure she'll be back soon,' I reassured him. I made him a cup of tea and called his mother to come and be with him. Then as soon as his wife was stable and in recovery I went with the midwife as she told him how the operation had gone. He was so relieved he promptly burst into tears. When you see men cry it really does demonstrate how emotional childbirth is.

Along with the drama there were also some very weird and wonderful sights.

One day I was called over by Tracey to feel a Jamaican lady's abdomen. Gently resting my fingers on her stomach I was amazed to feel very uneven structures under her skin.

I wasn't sure what I was feeling until Tracey guided me to a little bump.

'That feels like a nose!' I said.

Then as she guided my hands I realised that I was actually able to feel the baby's face through the tummy.

Tracey explained that the woman had a 'pendulous abdomen', which meant you could feel the baby through the walls of the abdomen. This lady had previously had five children and because she hadn't done her postnatal exercises between pregnancies her abdominal muscles had completely relaxed.

Poor muscle tone would allow the baby to move into lots of different positions so it was more significant towards the end of pregnancy and in labour. Tracey added that it was very important to determine that the baby was head first and to ensure that it did not end up lying transverse or obliquely across the mother's abdomen, which would make it much harder to deliver. I made a mental note not to forget my postnatal exercises if I were to ever have children!

A year into my training we all had to sit an exam consisting of a practical session where you had to be able to describe what you would need to do in certain emergency situations.

It only had a fifty per cent pass rate but I really wanted to prove to myself that I could pass it first time. It was just a case of linking everything back to my practice and thinking logically.

I studied a lot and would work through emergency procedures in my head over and over again. Generally if I can understand something theoretically and apply it in practice I can learn very quickly. But when it was just theory I really had to work hard. The other problem, of course, was that on a weekly basis you were so busy on the wards or in the community that there was actually limited time left for studying. Whenever we could, the girls who lived in the nurses' home would often meet up and study together, helping each other by talking through the different situations that might arise in the test.

We had a mock exam eight weeks before the real thing, which I passed, but I was keen to score higher in the real thing so I knew I had to increase my revision. The tutors we had were strict markers. I'm sure every student midwife feels the whole world is against them at the end of their training because there really is so much to juggle with theory and practice. Everyone is conscious that they are up against each other too, which adds to the pressure. It's almost as if the exam is a final judgment of how you will rate as a midwife.

Now I appreciate that there are plenty of trainees who failed their exams at first but went on to become excellent midwives. But sometimes I would be in tears, convincing myself that I wouldn't pass. It meant so much to me. It wouldn't be the first thing that I had failed at, either: I hadn't passed all of my A-level exams or my driving test first time round and this added to my nerves.

Whether you passed really affected whether you could get a job or not and I had applied for a staff midwife post within the maternity unit. I'd already had my interview with a senior midwife and one of her colleagues, who'd played 'good cop/bad cop' as they grilled me with questions about my midwifery practice.

'How can you apply what you've learnt into midwifery practice now?' they asked.

'I've been lucky to have good mentors who have given me the skills to move on with my practice,' I said, trying to sound composed. 'I'm not afraid to take on challenges to keep myself on my toes.'

To my delight, I'd been offered a job on the provisory that I passed my exams. But when the dreaded day arrived, the three-hour exam paper was extremely gruelling. I left the examination room utterly convinced that I had failed.

It took eight weeks for the results to come through and every day we would troop down to the post room to check if they had arrived.

Finally, one morning we saw a pile of fat brown envelopes on the counter. They were doled out to us in silence. Slowly I peeled mine open and peeped into the envelope.

My heart was in my mouth as I pulled out the piece of paper. The thought of having to get back from work and study all night again for another six months if I needed to retake was too much to think about. But there it was in black and white. I'd passed!

I laughed and screamed. Mairead had passed too and we hugged each other.

Now, as a staff midwife, my cornflower-blue dress was replaced with a navy-blue frock that I could wear with a band clipped in place by a lovely silver buckle that had been a present from my mam and dad when I'd qualified as a nurse. Sadly no one wears buckles these days as part of their uniform but I still have mine!

I was very proud and delighted to be a staff midwife. I felt I'd really worked hard to get it. At twenty-two, I was one of the youngest midwives to qualify, which added to my sense of achievement.

However, this was of course just the start of my journey. Suddenly I was being thrust out into the unknown, caring for women with no supervision. It was nerve-wracking but brilliant.

On my first day I'd joined the other staff midwives sitting on a little bench in the office waiting for the sister in charge, Sister Murphy, to begin the report.

Sister Murphy was Irish and very tall with short hair. She had a look of authority and wore a navy dress with slingback sandals that made her look even taller.

She took no prisoners and when she walked in she gave the

bench a withering glance. As I was to discover, Sister Murphy was very professional and kind to the women but extremely strict with the midwives. If you said something and she didn't agree with it, all it took was for her to raise her eyebrows and your words would instantly wither on your lips.

After telling each midwife who would be looking after who we were dispatched in different directions to start our shifts.

Walking into Room Five to meet my labouring charge I introduced myself with a mix of pride and anxiety and a huge sense of responsibility. The woman was in mid-labour, standing by the side of her bed, about five or six centimetres dilated and using gas and air.

I knew I had about five to ten minutes to get a full history of where she was at before Sister Murphy would come in to see how you were getting on and start firing questions at you. If she asked a question and you didn't know the answer you'd be in trouble.

I knew I had to make all the right decisions and keep her informed. When she came in I answered every question nervously. She didn't acknowledge I'd got anything right but she didn't tell me off either, so I took that as a good sign.

Eventually the woman reached eight and then ten centimetres and decided to get onto the bed.

'Eek, when do I put my gown on?' I wondered, eventually deciding to do it as I set up the delivery pack and lined the instruments up.

'I feel like pushing,' the woman said, so I began to guide her through.

The couple didn't know it was my first solo delivery and at that stage I wasn't about to let on. Thankfully, it was a textbook delivery and there were no problems. I wasn't used to working without anyone else so I was ecstatic. I hadn't had to call the sister in! My first baby delivered all by myself!

Afterwards I did tell the parents.

'Oh, well *done*!' the mother said, like I'd done all the work!

Now, as a qualified staff midwife, I was seeing all walks of life. One of the saddest things I witnessed was a girl aged twelve delivering her baby. From the off it was a challenge as you can't rationalise with a twelve-year-old. In reality you are speaking to a very frightened child.

As her contractions began it was clear she was terrified and it felt very wrong for her to be in that situation. She was almost cowering behind her mother and kept her head down when you were speaking to her.

She looked very young with her hair in a ponytail, scraped back off her thin face. She was extremely skinny apart from the bump and was cuddling a little rabbit. Her mother was only twenty-eight and, having given birth herself at the age of sixteen, she was very protective and reassuring towards her daughter.

I never found out the circumstances of her pregnancy and there was never any mention of who the father was.

When it came to trying to examine her she was very emotional and started crying. So I just relied on the outward signs of progression as well as fetal heart recordings. It was challenging but I really wanted to help this girl to get through it without causing her any additional stress.

The birth was really quite traumatic: she literally screamed the baby out. There was just no consoling her. She was terrified and although I did my best to comfort her and explain what was happening I just could not alleviate her fear. Afterwards she looked visibly shocked by the whole experience.

She struck me as a very naïve twelve-year-old. When I handed her the baby it was heartbreaking. She seemed happy but there was something so sad about handing a baby to a child.

She had support from her mum but I'll never forget her face and the look of disbelief etched on it. She just didn't know what to do and I got the impression she didn't particularly want to hold the baby.

'Can you take the baby, Mum?' she said, almost immediately. And from then on she kept referring to her son as 'the baby', almost as if she was distancing herself. It was her mum who took over and it was clearly she who was going to look after the baby. I just hoped that the girl would get over the trauma of the experience and that some of her childhood would be preserved.

But there was never much time to stop and reflect on these things; it was always so busy. And so it was on to the next birth . . .

Dashing to the lift I smiled as a woman shuffled out, clutching her bump and huffing and puffing. A tall, gangly husband was by her side, supporting her arm, his forehead wet with nervous perspiration.

'Hi,' I said, stepping forward to help. 'I'm called Maria. Are you Mel?'

She nodded, visibly struggling.

'Just stop and breathe through the contractions if you need to,' I soothed, guiding Mel into the admission room.

Although I gave the impression that everything was calm, in reality Mel was the third patient I had to look after at that moment. I had so many things on my mind I hardly knew where to start.

It didn't help that at the time our admissions process covered women with a whole spectrum of issues. There was no triage system in those days and anyone who had any kind of issue came in. You might find yourself dealing with suspected labours, women who were worried their baby wasn't moving or mums-to-be concerned about bleeding. You could be in the middle of looking after someone in labour and halfway through you'd be given someone else who had just been admitted. It was relentless.

When women in labour arrived at the front reception they'd be told to come immediately up to the third floor where a midwife would meet them and take them into the labour room.

Mel was thirty-two, with blonde hair and a slim build, and despite the contractions she now managed to smile.

Guiding her into a free room, I sat her in a chair and began to ask her about her pregnancy. Were there any problems? Was there anything I should know that may affect her labour?

Mel confirmed it was her second pregnancy and that it had been uneventful. Her contractions were every five minutes, her waters hadn't gone and the baby was moving.

I showed her where the toilet was so I could test her urine as part of the admission process. Then as she went to the loo and changed into her nightdress I quickly read her notes and popped my head in to see Tracy, another lady I was looking after, who was in for her second pregnancy and who was six centimetres dilated.

When Mel returned, I was ready with the pinard stethoscope.

'I'm just going to listen to your baby's heart,' I told her.

With the heartbeat safely identified, I excused myself for a moment and dashed down the ward to check on Sonya, a Polish girl who was forty weeks pregnant, five centimetres dilated, and coping really well.

Assuring her that she still had some way to go I popped into the room across the corridor to see Tracy once more. She was mobilising well and using the birthing ball. Her husband was supporting her. I listened to the fetal heart and ensured that she was OK. After completing my observations I said that I needed to go and see another lady and would be back in about ten minutes. I gave Tracy the buzzer in case she needed me while I was gone.

As I left the room I was now en route back to Mel. My next task was to find a free CTG monitor, which at this time was part of the admission procedure (nowadays this is not standard procedure for women who are low risk if all is well with the fetal heart).

Unfortunately there wasn't a monitor in every room so often you'd have to chase around the labour ward to find one. Knowing that a woman had just delivered in Room Three, I waited outside, hopping from foot to foot before attracting the midwife's attention, grabbing the monitor, wheeling it off for a quick clean and then taking it into Mel's room.

'How are you feeling with your contractions, Mel?' I asked, chatting away.

She said she was having two every ten minutes and they were becoming stronger.

'How did your labour go last time?' I asked. 'Were there any problems?'

She confirmed that everything had gone well and her labour was relatively quick at twelve hours.

'Hopefully it will be even quicker second time around,' she smiled.

'Can I put you on to the monitor for twenty minutes?' I asked.

I had already done an abdominal palpation to determine where the baby was lying.

I told Mel she could remain standing as I wrapped the two belts around her abdomen and attached the fetal monitoring transducers to hear the beat of the baby's heart.

'It sounds like a train!' commented Mel's husband. I reassured them that at 120 to 140 bpm it was perfectly normal.

All sorted, I headed back to check on Sonya and Tracy before going back to see Mel once more. Now, with close observation, I was trying to determine who was going to deliver first. It was a constant juggling act. Predictably my two former charges appeared to be progressing fast and were in real danger of delivering around the same time.

Even the most speedy of midwifes can't perform that sort of miracle and by now I'd learnt that when you are struggling like that you need to tell whoever is in charge. Usually you could get a student or if you were lucky another midwife to help you out. They'd look after your other patients allowing you to deliver a baby then dash back to your other charges.

As Tracy was beginning to feel urges to push I was unable to leave her room. So I informed the sister in charge and it was arranged that one of the other midwives would care for my other two women until I was free again.

As Tracy started to push involuntarily I began to get everything organised for the birth, opening the delivery pack as I knew it wouldn't be long. The baby's heartbeat was within normal limits and would decelerate to 90 bpm with a contraction and then quickly return up to 110 bpm.

Tracy was in all-fours position and I could see the baby's head advancing quickly. All of a sudden she gave a big push and the head was delivered. Within thirty seconds another contraction came and a baby girl was born with a hearty scream.

With Tracy safely cradling her baby with a look of unrivalled joy on her face, my thoughts returned to Mel. Dealing with more than one patient was never ideal, as you'd want to give each of your patients as much time and care as you possibly could.

In reality you could spend anything from twelve to eighteen hours from the onset of regular contractions to the baby being born. When women talk about being in labour for five days they are including the latent phase of labour, which is generally the early stages. This is where contractions are on and off and it is basically the body preparing to go into labour. This stage is frustrating for women as they get very tired and fed up of waiting and may come into the maternity unit thinking they are in labour only to be sent home again disappointed.

I always tried to be positive, explaining that if all the observations are within normal limits then they are better off at home where they can be in their own surroundings and relax more. Women are always given instruction to phone back for any advice if their waters break, the contractions get too painful or they have any concerns.

From the first moment the woman walks onto the labour ward, the midwife is observing how the woman is coping and the length, strength and frequency of contractions. Over time you continue to watch and observe, which is why it is difficult to pick up on all of the observational cues of labour establishing when you are looking after more than one woman.

Some women are fine and don't even breathe heavily while other women start screaming the minute they have a contraction. Everyone has different pain thresholds but sometimes a woman's reaction is down to fear and not understanding what is going on.

As Mel progressed she was clearly finding the whole process difficult. As each contraction hit, her face was contorted.

I hurried over to the bed and she looked at me with panic. 'I can't breathe,' she gasped.

'It's OK,' I told her, placing my hand gently on her arm. 'Mel, you're not breathing out. What I want you to do now is take a breath in through your nose and out through your mouth. Just imagine the contraction is coming like a wave. Sometimes you get small waves then big ones. I'll talk you through it.'

For the next ten minutes I coached her through her contractions, keeping good eye contact.

'When you don't breathe out you start to hyperventilate,' I explained. 'You can do this. You breathe every day of your life. Keep it controlled and always remember the contraction will end.'

When someone is losing control you need to keep a firm and steady tone of voice, as it reassures women and takes away the feeling of panic.

With her latest wave of contractions over, now was the time to broach the subject of vaginal examination. In order to assess Mel properly I now needed to see if there were any changes in the cervix at all.

'You are having strong contractions and it would be useful if I could examine you,' I told her gently. 'Is that OK?'

You always have to take into consideration that sometimes women have never had an examination before and may be embarrassed or anxious. It was also important to ask for permission and to write that I had done so in the notes. Luckily Mel agreed and her husband opted to stay in the room.

Whether the birthing partner stays in the room or not really depends on the woman in question. If it is her sister or mother then she usually wants them to leave but if it is her husband or boyfriend then she might like him in the room.

An onlooker might wonder how some mums get pregnant at all as I noticed many women really didn't like their partner to see them naked. But I suppose pregnancy makes a lot of women feel vulnerable, self-conscious and exposed. Some women have had to deal with difficult experiences including sexual abuse or rape so sensitivity is always important in this situation.

To be honest there is little point in a man sitting watching me doing an examination if he is not supporting his partner. Occasionally I would take the decision to ask the partner to leave the room myself, particularly if you got the feeling that him being there is making the situation feel uncomfortable.

Some midwives don't agree with partners being in the room for the birth either, as when the man is out the room women's inhibitions often disappear. Some women push much better when they are on their own. And as you watch men standing around looking stressed and helpless you do sometimes wonder, 'What is the benefit of you being here?'

But it is on the woman's terms and if she does not consent to an examination it will not be done.

After performing an abdominal examination on Mel to determine the position and how many 'fifths palpable' the baby's head was (in other words, how far down the pelvis it had travelled), I instructed her to sit on her hands to raise the pelvis up, put her ankles together and let her legs flop outwards. I made sure she was covered up to maintain her dignity.

As a student I'd found the process of learning how to do an

examination was difficult, as you can't tell what you're supposed to be feeling. I was told that the cervix feels like the tip of your nose, though to be honest all I could feel was intense pressure on me, as I was aware I was in the middle of a very intimate examination. But you have to do it and you have to learn.

It's actually quite interesting to see how much the cervix changes during labour. It is quite long and tubular normally but as soon as someone starts to have contractions a hormone helps it to relax.

As the cervix starts to shorten, the two openings become one opening, which is termed 'effacement'. How the cervix is effaced and also how many centimetres the cervix is dilated are important in determining the onset and progress of labour.

I also needed to determine whether the baby's head was high or low in the pelvis as the positioning can influence labour. If the baby is in the correct position where the head is looking downwards then the diameter of the baby's head is approximately 9.5 cms at delivery. If the baby is looking to the side the head needs to rotate further into the correct position either through the strength of the contractions or during the second stage when pushing. If it doesn't rotate this is one reason for an instrumental delivery by forceps. That is why, as midwives, we encourage women to do exercises antenatally to promote optimal fetal positioning – which is the baby's head looking downwards.

Lastly I listened to the fetal heart again.

With my checks over I told Mel that she was in early labour, two to three centimetres dilated and that her waters had broken.

I then encouraged her to use the TENS (Transcutaneous Electrical Nerve Stimulator) she had hired to alleviate the pain. The TENS machine is attached to the woman's back with pads and works by transmitting tiny electrical nerve impulses out through the skin. These help to build up the body's own natural endorphins which act as a pain relief.

Like most women Mel had a birth plan – a written instruction of her preferences for pain control during labour and birth that is given to the midwife beforehand.

'Can we go through your plan?' I asked. 'I'll just read it and you can tell me if you're still happy.'

Mel had opted to use TENS, Entonox and Diamorphine for pain relief.

We agreed that she should walk around the ward for a little while and that if she had any problems she could inform a midwife on the ward.

This was good timing for me as I could probably deliver Sonya in the meantime and then would be in a better position to look after her without running from one woman to another.

As the day flew by nothing else occupied my thoughts. Working as a midwife you rarely have time to daydream and a full thirty-minute break is a luxury. Not that I minded that much. For me it was and still is more than just a job.

The rewards are there every day. There was nothing better than seeing someone who was terrified getting their breathing right and watching their fear subside. It is amazing what women can cope with if given the confidence.

As I suspected, Sonya soon delivered a bouncing baby boy and after a couple of hours Mel came back up to the delivery suite with very strong contractions. She had been examined on the ward and was now eight centimetres.

With another midwife taking over Sonya's postnatal care I bid her goodbye and headed back to see Mel. This time there was no time for idle chit-chat as she was focusing very hard. It was important for me to be quiet and not intervene during contractions so as not to distract her.

In this situation midwives 'walk and talk', as things could progress very quickly. Reassuring Mel I checked all of her observations and monitored her contractions which were now five every ten minutes and strong. She was almost at the stage of having involuntary urges to push.

Mel was keen to remain standing so I placed mats on the floor and checked that the resuscitaire (a machine for resuscitating newborn babies) was working properly. Over the next twenty minutes I kept a close eye on Mel, as I was well aware she could give a quick push and the baby would just appear immediately. It was her second baby after all!

Sure enough, not long after I'd put my gloves on she gave one big push and I saw lots of dark hair. The head was advancing quickly and I had to kneel so I could control it. The baby's body followed thirty seconds later.

I passed the baby through Mel's legs and he gave a good cry.

Taking hold of her baby, Mel looked delighted. I sat her down and gave her the injection in the top of her leg to help deliver the placenta. With that all done I got her into a more comfortable position as she was keen to breastfeed immediately.

It was now thirty minutes past the end of my shift and she thanked me for staying late to deliver her baby. I was glad I had delivered him too. Giving her and her husband a big hug I left, promising I would catch up with them in the morning, as I would be on the ward again then.

Job done, I went back to the nurses' home, my feet pounding after all the running about. Now I was just happy to have a cup of tea and a biscuit, and aimlessly watch a bit of TV. Something that didn't involve me thinking too much so I could wind down and relax.

Then it was off to bed to get some rest before my 7.15 a.m. start the next morning!

Chapter Five

As the doorbell went on the postnatal ward, Kate, the auxiliary nurse, ran to see who it was. From a distance I could see her talking to a young blonde lady, dressed down in a jacket, jeans and baseball cap.

Kate then came down the ward to where I was checking in on my patient Lydia and her newborn son, Oscar.

'There's a friend of yours arrived,' Kate said to Lydia. 'She says she's travelled quite a way to see you and she's asked if she can come in for a few minutes.'

Visiting hours had ended half an hour before and Lydia immediately looked to me for permission.

'You're OK for a few minutes,' I agreed. 'The baby is feeding well.'

The woman stayed five to ten minutes before leaving again.

When I went back to check on her later Kate was refilling her water jug.

'Gosh, I'm sure I recognised that lady,' she said.

Lydia smiled. 'Um, well actually that was Princess Diana,' she revealed.

'What?!' both Kate and I exclaimed in unison.

As word got round the ward everyone found it very amusing

– particularly as the story filtered back that security had moved Diana's chauffer on from the area where he'd parked in the hospital grounds.

Funnily enough Diana had opened the maternity unit a few years earlier with all of the pomp and ceremony that went with it. Now here she was sneaking into the unit to visit her friend. It did make me laugh. She was definitely the most famous visitor the ward had ever had.

Generally, amongst midwives, visiting time is viewed as a nightmare as it brings with it a whole host of problems. Firstly you can't access the women and make sure the baby is feeding. Then we find ourselves wincing as a baby barely a few hours old is juggled about between relatives.

People walk in, not bothering to wash or sanitise their hands, to pluck a sleeping baby from its cot, with no regard for whether the mother has just managed to settle it or not.

You'd be amazed at the people who roll up to visit a newborn baby. Some of these people aren't even that close to the mother. I once saw a woman looking less than impressed when suddenly her neighbour arrived to see her baby.

'Unbelievable,' the woman exclaimed after she left. 'She hardly talks to me normally. She only came to have a nose.'

Sometimes the new mums themselves feel a bit awkward about asking their family or friends not to pick up the baby. For the sake of politeness they would sit there looking very uncomfortable as their baby, wriggling agitatedly and clearly looking for food, is passed from person to person. In those cases I was only too happy to play 'bad cop', announcing: 'The baby had a terrible night, please can you put her back.'

With visiting hours over, off the wellwishers go to wet the baby's head down the pub, leaving the mother close to tears with a crying, unsettled baby.

Visitors aside, I loved my job at St Helier. Since my student days I'd grown in confidence, found my feet and done my best to do everything by the book.

However you'd have to be practically perfect to win the approval of Sister Murphy. All the midwives on my ward were terrified of her and we'd all been on the receiving end of her acid tongue at some point or other.

One day I was busy doing an admission and looking after two further women in labour. The new admission needed a speculum examination to confirm that her waters had broken.

At the time I had a junior doctor called Felicity with me, to whom I was teaching the procedure. After observing, Felicity offered to take the trolley away for me while I continued to chat with the patient.

Suddenly Sister Murphy came banging on my door.

'Come out of the room please, Maria,' she said gravely.

Then she walked me to the sluice area (an area where we kept dirty bed pans and measuring jugs ready to be sanitised) and pointed to the sink. As I stood there feeling confused she told me to follow her to the staff office, which was full of doctors and midwives.

'If you think everyone else is here to clean up after you, you've got a lot to learn, girl,' she barked.

I was completely dumbstruck. I didn't have a clue what she was talking about.

'Sorry?' I replied. 'I don't know what you mean.'

'The speculum!' she snapped. 'It was in the sink in the sluice area!'

I've always believed that you should own up if you've done something wrong but I really had no idea how it had got there. Being accused of something I hadn't done in front of all my colleagues was humiliating.

I could feel tears prickling in my eyes but I was determined not to cry.

'I'm sorry, Sister Murphy,' I stammered blushing redder by the minute. 'I really don't know what to do, I didn't put it there!'

I walked out in a daze where I met a flustered-looking Felicity.

'Maria, I've left the speculum in the sluice,' she said. 'What shall I do with it?'

'It was you?' I said incredulously. 'I've just been shouted at!'

Felicity immediately turned pale. 'Oh, I'm really sorry,' she replied.

'Can you go and tell Sister Murphy it was nothing to do with me?' I asked, and together we headed back into the staff room.

'Can I have a word, Sister Murphy?' she asked. 'It's about the speculum.'

Sister Murphy immediately folded her arms indignantly. 'I'm not interested!' she exclaimed. 'I know what happened. I've spoken to the midwife. Go away.'

Perhaps I should have just licked my wounds and carried on but the injustice of the situation really riled me. Hardly a shift seemed to go past without Sister Murphy reducing someone to tears and everyone seemed terrified to stand up to her.

I got on with the rest of my shift but back at the nursing home that night I was very upset. All I wanted was for her to listen to what I said and acknowledge that I'd done nothing wrong.

I talked to my mentor Tracey, who agreed I should try to speak to Sister Murphy again. So the next day, shaking in my shoes, I asked to speak to her in a private office. She followed me in, rolling her eyes in her usual fashion.

'Can I have a word with you about the incident yesterday?' I began.

'It's been dealt with,' she snapped.

'But I want to explain what happened . . .' I continued.

There was clearly no reasoning with her. 'Go away and get on with your work!' she ordered.

Later that day I went back to talk to Tracey.

'I really tried to put my point across but she just won't listen,' I said. 'I'm not a person that lets other people pick up after me. I want her to know that.'

I had a real bee in my bonnet and all the other midwives thought I had lost the plot. No one ever tried to confront Sister Murphy or even had conversations with her but this time I was determined.

It was agreed that my mentor would go to see her and organise a meeting for the next day in which she would be a mediator. I didn't sleep a wink that night. I was petrified. 'What is she going to do to me?' I wondered, but I also had the conviction that I must see it through.

As I walked through the door the next morning Sister Murphy was facing a window and as she turned around she gave me such a glare.

'What's all this tittle-tattle for?' she said, once more rolling her eyes.

'All I want is an opportunity to explain what happened with that situation the other day,' I said. 'The doctor was trying to help me. It was she who left the speculum in the sluice. I am a junior midwife and I respect you are in charge but I've tried to speak to you on numerous occasions and you won't listen.

'What I'm working towards is care for the women at the highest standard. I am a member of the team and so are the other midwives. I want you to understand that I'm a human being trying to work as part of a team. I didn't appreciate you speaking to me like that in front of everyone. All I want is to be treated the same as I would treat other people.'

To my utter astonishment Sister Murphy didn't say a word. It was almost like her jaw had hit the ground. She didn't interrupt.

'OK,' she said, finally. 'If it wasn't you, that's it.'

As I stood there, awestruck, it was like I had all these cheers going off in my head. Call me melodramatic but it felt like a real victory. I felt like I was speaking for every midwife in the unit who'd been reduced to tears.

Amazingly from that day onwards I never saw Sister Murphy speak badly to anyone again and she certainly never spoke to me in a derogatory fashion. I do think it made a slight bit of difference. It was almost like she had had to reflect a little on how she was coming across to other people.

And as it turned out she wasn't immune to mistakes herself. One of the rules at the maternity unit was that you always have two name bands on a baby. When you transfer a baby to the postnatal ward the receiving midwife does the postnatal checks and confirms the baby's identification, checking that the cord is clamped and that the baby is the correct sex.

A few days after our breakthrough meeting I was on the postnatal ward when Sister Murphy brought down a baby with no name band on. I think we were both cringing. She couldn't believe it was me who had witnessed her mistake and neither could I!

To be fair, aside from her attitude to staff she was actually a great midwife and teacher and to my relief she didn't appear to hold a grudge against me.

In 1990 the World Cup was in full swing and the excitement spilt out onto the maternity ward. The first match was against the Republic of Ireland, which England drew 1-1, and then after a 0-0 draw with the Netherlands they beat Egypt and Belgium and then faced Cameroon for the quarter-finals.

I was supporting England and my friend Mairead from Tipperary was supporting her national team, Ireland, so the first match in particular was a rowdy affair. There was always camaraderie and banter and frequently Mairead and the other Irish girls would try and swing my allegiance by pointing out that my fellow Geordie Jackie Charlton was managing Ireland. It was the first time Ireland had qualified to play in the World Cup since the 1930s. Sadly Ireland got knocked out at the quarter-final stage and England – famously – in the semi-final penalty shoot-out against Germany.

Shortly after the World Cup had ended, Mairead invited me home to Ireland for the weekend to meet her mammy and family. I'd accrued a few days off so just beforehand I'd been visiting my own parents in Newcastle. I'd booked on a flight to Dublin from Newcastle airport and duly checked in.

But after heading through to departures and joining the queue for my boarding gate I was horrified to catch a glimpse of the plane I would shortly be travelling on. It was the smallest plane I'd ever seen! A twenty-seater propeller plane that people used to nickname 'vomit comets'.

'Oh my goodness!' I exclaimed out loud.

The man in front turned round and grinned.

'Aye, pet, it's not that big, is it?!'

His face was instantly recognisable to me. It was Jackie Charlton!

'You'll be allreet,' he added, as I stared, speechless, at him.

I got on the plane and sat at the rear with the back of Jackie's head visible a few rows in front. I tried very hard not to think about what a horrible windy, cloudy day it was.

As the plane took off and began to climb to the right altitude I have never been so scared in my life. We were thrown around like it was a funfair ride and the plane was seemingly hitting every bit of turbulence. Gripping my nails into the armrests I literally felt nauseous with fear and had to ask the attendant for regular glasses of water.

All I could think was, 'Well, girl, if you're going down, you're going down with Jackie Charlton!'

When we finally made our bouncy descent and landed in Dublin I staggered off the plane with wobbly legs to find Dublin airport besieged with Ireland fans, out in force to mob Jackie.

As the roars and shouts echoed around the arrivals hall, Mairead came hurtling over to me.

'I cannot believe you came in on a flight with Jackie Charlton!' she shrieked.

For the rest of the weekend Mairead was telling everyone: friends, family, the woman in the corner shop . . . 'She was on the plane with Jackie Charlton!' It must have gone around the whole of Tipperary!

I arrived at Mairead's mammy's just in time for tea, which started off with homemade bread and a cup of tea. But that was just the beginning. I'd heard about the hospitality of the Irish but this was something else. I was nibbling away at everything but it kept on coming in such huge amounts: home-made soda bread and soup, a full roast dinner and all the trimmings, cake and custard to finish and then an encore of cheese and biscuits. It just seemed to go on forever. When I finally retired for the evening I lay down on my bed and groaned. My stomach was so full.

I was up at 8 a.m. the next morning to be greeted by a huge Irish cooked breakfast.

As Kate, Mairead's mammy, attempted to pile yet more sausages onto my plate I politely declined.

'Oh, you've got to have another bit,' she protested. 'You're a grown girl, so!'

'Yes,' I thought. 'I'm growing by the second.'

At half past ten, Mairead suggested we go into town but en route we got collared by one of her neighbours.

'Hi, Mairead!' she welcomed. 'You're looking well! Come in for a cup of tea and a slice of tart!'

As I tried my hardest to bypass the tart, the neighbour, clearly a very friendly woman, frowned. 'Come on, what's wrong with you?' she chided.

As I staggered out the house rubbing my swollen belly I hoped the walk to the bus stop would help work off the gluttony. No such luck.

'Oh, hello, Mairead,' came the call across the street two more times. 'I've never seen you for ages, come in for a slice of cake!'

By the time we arrived at a café to meet Mairead's friend it was coming up to twelve o'clock.

'Oh, we should have lunch!' Mairead quipped.

'No, I'll just have a coffee,' I replied firmly. 'Mairead, I can't believe how much food we've had!'

'Welcome to Ireland, my girl,' she laughed.

We'd been there for an hour when Mairead's little sister arrived to get us.

'Mammy has dinner ready – you've got to come home now!'

'Mairead,' I said, 'I can't eat any more.'

'Maria, you have to,' she replied. 'Otherwise she'll get offended.'

We walked in the door to the smell of fish cooking.

'Hello, girls, you must be starving!' Kate trilled.

'Starving?' I thought. 'I'm going to die of gluttony.'

If I thought I'd got away with the tiny portions I deliberately piled on my plate I had another think coming.

'Dear me, you've hardly eaten anything at all!' Kate exclaimed.

Eventually I excused myself and fell asleep in a chair.

Of course this went on for the whole three days and by the time it came for me to head back to England I felt like I'd put on a stone.

Mairead took me to the airport and after bidding her goodbye I headed to the check-in desk, dreading the 'vomit comet' I would once again be travelling in. But as I handed over my passport at the desk the attendant looked at me apologetically.

'I'm afraid your flight is overbooked,' she said. 'I can offer you a flight to London where you can transfer to Newcastle. And because of the inconvenience I can give you an £85 voucher for Air Lingus and upgrade you to first class on both flights.'

Well, she didn't have to ask me twice!

When I arrived at Newcastle airport four hours later than originally planned, I was met by my concerned-looking mother.

'Oh Maria, you must be starving!' she cried.

'Mam,' I exclaimed, 'you have no idea. If I didn't eat for another four days I'd be fine!'

* * *

By now I was ten months into my midwife career and feeling slightly out on a limb. I definitely had a case of itchy feet.

My friend Catherine had confided that she was looking at opportunities to be a midwife in Saudi Arabia. She wanted me to go with her. I wasn't convinced. The fact that the culture was so different worried me. I didn't think I'd settle in there.

But Catherine's thoughts of leaving only cemented my own reservations about my job. As much as I'd met nice people and it was a good experience I felt I needed to go somewhere else.

Despite qualifying as a midwife I knew that everyone at the hospital would always remember me as a student. I was grateful for everything I'd learnt and all the support but I wanted to stand on my own two feet. In my heart of hearts I wanted to try somewhere else.

My living situation wasn't exactly helping either. The nurses' home was being renovated at a time when I was coming off the night shift and it was horrendous. I'd stumble in exhausted, my whole body aching for sleep, only to be constantly disturbed by the sound of hammering and drilling. It was so bad that as I finished one night shift with four days off, I immediately headed to King's Cross to get the train to Newcastle where I could collapse in peace.

With or without the disturbance I wasn't sure that I wanted to live in the nurses' home indefinitely anyway. Yet I couldn't envisage ever being able to afford a house in Carshalton with my paltry budget.

I had just started going out with an Irish guy who lived in north London but I decided I couldn't let him influence my decision. Equally, I didn't tell my mam that I was coming back until I had handed in my notice. I didn't want anyone to talk me out of it.

I'd been overwhelmed by my first ten months as a midwife and I needed time to digest what I'd learnt back at home.

I handed my resignation letter in to a senior midwife called Mrs Orku, who seemed surprised but accepted it graciously. I think they knew I wouldn't stay forever. It was generally encouraged for newly qualified midwives to move on once they'd found their feet. We agreed it was time for me to get out there and get more experience.

I gave four weeks' notice but I had holiday owing so in the end I worked around ten days and then I was gone.

On my last day I reflected on my time at St Helier. I felt that I had come such a long way from when I had arrived and was starting to become more confident in my work. There was still so much for me to learn but I knew I could gain that experience elsewhere.

I was sad to leave, having made so many new friends, but not being one for big goodbyes I just organised a small meal with some of my closest colleagues and friends.

Dad came down for me and once more the car was crammed with my belongings. As I took a last glimpse at the scaffolding-clad nurses' home I didn't regret it. In fact I was quite relieved.

Now I just had to work out what to do next . . .

Back in the 'toon' I quickly arranged to see friends like Lesley, Hazel and Julia, who I had trained as a nurse with. It was great to go out again in the North East where everyone understood my accent!

Keen to get another job I trawled midwife magazines for adverts and began to ponder over the different parts of the country that I'd like to live. But in my heart I knew I was going back down south to London. Nipping into the capital at weekends and on my days off I had been intrigued by it. I felt I had a lot more of London to explore. So within two months I found myself back there again . . .

I'd decided it was a toss-up between the Royal Free Hospital in Hampstead and Whittington Hospital in Archway, both of which I had interviews for. When I'd investigated further, former colleagues confided that the Royal Free was extremely busy. The general consensus about the Whittington was that it was less hectic and the staff were really friendly.

From a learning point of view I wanted to go into a hospital that was smaller and less busy. So I got a train down to King's Cross and boarded the Northern Line to Archway, finding my way to the hospital there.

The interview lasted about an hour and I felt that it had gone well. Afterwards I asked if I could be shown around. I was eager to see how everything worked. It seemed more compact than St Helier hospital and everything seemed to be in one place. It was completely different but I had a good feeling about it and I could imagine working there. As I thanked them for the tour, I was met by the senior midwife.

'We'd like to offer you the job,' she told me.

I accepted without hesitation and her secretary immediately sorted out my start date. I was thrilled and couldn't stop grinning to myself on the train back up to Newcastle.

But oh my goodness! I'd have to move everything down again! I wasn't sure my parents would be that chuffed.

'What are you going back there for?' Mam exclaimed. 'What about a local hospital?'

'No, Mam, I'm not ready for that,' I said.

Then, as I tentatively broached the subject of Dad ferrying my stuff back down, he sighed in a long-suffering fashion. So after two months Dad and I set off once more on the now-familiar journey south, this time to north London.

I didn't want to live in the nurses' home and I knew a couple of people who lived in Dollis Hill so I replied to an advert for a room in a house which I'd seen in the paper. Three Irish girls from Donegal lived there and we hit it off straight away. As soon as Susie, a petite brunette, opened the door I knew that I'd love it there. She was so friendly and welcoming.

Susie lived in a rambling four-bedroomed detached house that was nicely decorated with a decent garden, along with two Irish girls called Mary and Morven. I knew immediately it was an environment I could relax in and I quickly moved in, enjoying nights in with the girls chilling, cooking and watching telly.

It was great to be living in a house again and my new housemates were so good to me. Two of the girls were sisters and they had four brothers living in London too who I had good banter with as they supported Man U and I supported Newcastle United. I quickly settled into the shared house and made myself at home.

However, on my first morning at the Whittington I felt completely out of my depth. Everyone around me seemed to know what they were doing while I was like a rabbit in the headlights. Oh my goodness, what had I done?

But by lunchtime I was beginning to get excited about working there. It was very different to the Surrey hospital, not least because there were so many multicultural midwives – a mix of Caribbean, Irish, Chinese and English.

'I'll learn so much here!' I thought.

The sister in charge was Sister Giles from Barbados. She was in her late fifties and looked cross until she spoke, at which point her eyes would light up mischievously. I could not believe how laid back she was.

We were working on a nightingale ward, one of those old-fashioned wards where there were no bays. Everyone's beds were positioned on either side of a central nurses' station and you could stand at the desk and see everything going on.

People were constantly bringing women up of all different nationalities with all sorts of different problems, yet this sister was so calm. She seemed unfazed by anything and during our meetings I was intrigued to see she didn't write a thing down even though we were all frantically scribbling away.

I soon discovered that all the senior sisters were from the Caribbean and shared the same relaxed attitude to life combined with big, warm characters. One of the sisters even had bright red hair and pink lipstick that was only overshadowed by her booming laugh.

These midwives didn't take turns to go for their breaks but would all go together, setting out a three-course meal of the Caribbean food they'd cooked in the staffroom. The laughter that came from their table reverberated around the room. They were so loud! Nothing would interrupt them.

On the ward they looked after the women so well, their calmness and experience making the women much more relaxed in turn.

'Hello! How are you doing?' they'd ask when I came on my break too.

They never treated me as being English but had a good laugh about my accent. They thought it was hilarious.

'You are from Newcastle!' they'd mock. 'Where's that, my girl? Scotland?'

'I'm English!' I'd sigh.

As the weeks went by it was apparent that my name was causing a few problems too.

One curly-haired Caribbean woman named Sister Poppleworth didn't suffer fools gladly so when she called me the wrong name I bit my tongue at first.

'Joyceee,' she'd say, sucking her teeth.

'It's Maria,' I would explain. 'Joyce is my surname.'

'Oh yes, oh yes,' she'd reply.

Then one day as she yelled, 'Joyce! Joyce!' for the millionth time I couldn't help myself.

'Yes, Poppleworth!' I replied cheekily. Well, everyone nearly hit the deck.

Sister Poppleworth stopped in her tracks and turned round, a slow smile appearing on her face.

'Why you callin' me Poppleworth?' she asked.

'You keep calling me Joyce and that's my surname!' I replied, now wondering if I was about to get the mother of all telling offs.

'Ah, riiigght,' she said and off she went, sucking her teeth.

She never called me Joyce again and I always referred to her in full as Sister Poppleworth from then on. I didn't want to push my luck!

Although I quickly settled into the job, I found the daily commute was a nightmare. Despite living just ten miles from the hospital it could take me up to two hours to get to work by public transport as I didn't have a car.

If I was on a late shift I would get the 226 bus to Golders Green and then take another bus to Archway, which wasn't so bad. But if I started on the 7.20 a.m. shift I'd have to juggle my travel arrangements. First of all I'd catch a bus to Cricklewood then a train to King's Cross before finally getting the Northern Line to Archway. It meant setting my alarm very early and on a cold November morning I would struggle out of bed in what seemed to be the middle of the night.

One such morning I stood at the bus stop for what seemed like an age but there was no sign of the bus. I didn't have a watch and finally, feeling stressed, cold and exasperated, I headed home again.

When I looked at the clock I couldn't believe it. It was actually 3 a.m! I had to go back to bed and get up again at 5 a.m.

I think that episode was the last straw. Dollis Hill was lovely and I didn't want to move but it was ridiculous that I was getting up so early. So finally, after saving up for several months, I bought myself a red Vauxhall Astra.

It was a revelation. Now I needn't get up until 6.15 a.m. and it also meant I could get straight on the M1 and head north for Newcastle whenever I liked.

However, just as I was getting settled, my landlord revealed there was going to be some building work going on in the house. After my experience at the nurses' home previously there was no way I was staying while the builders were in. I had to get out. I answered an ad for a room in another house in Dollis Hill.

Then two months after I moved in, the owner announced he wanted to sell. Great!

Immediately we all started looking around together in the same area. To our dismay we quickly realised there were slim pickings, as we visited dark, dirty house after dark, dirty house.

In one house our eyes were immediately assaulted by the bright orange wallpaper.

'Oh my goodness, that wallpaper!' I said. 'How could anyone live with it that bright?'

Suddenly a voice filtered out from behind the door to the lounge. 'Yes, it is pretty bright, isn't it?' Mary and I just looked at each other wide-eyed and covered our mouths with our hands to try and stifle our giggles. Suffice to say we didn't take that place.

In the end we decided we'd have to up sticks and pay a little bit more but, just as we started looking around other areas, a house became available on the same street! It belonged to an Indian family who lived practically next door and it was freshly decorated with brand-new carpets. We had a huge area with a big garden, gym equipment, a pool table and an outdoor barbecue that meant we could have fun summer parties. We were very lucky to get it and very happy.

At work I continued to settle in, finding my feet and getting to grips with it all.

The maternity unit had a Team Midwifery system where midwives rotated on a day-to-day basis, doing one day on the postnatal ward, one day on the labour ward or one day in the community. There were two different maternity wards with women allocated to a team depending on which ward they were on. Over the year the hospital staff and the community staff eventually became more integrated so people worked between all areas if necessary. This was useful to maintain skills in both types of midwifery care.

This was not the only difference I would have to get used to at the Whittington. A shocking revelation for me was the fact that we had women prisoners from Holloway Prison on the ward at the hospital.

The first time I was handed a report and told I would be looking after a prisoner I felt a little bit intimidated. What would she be like?

Heading over to the bed I was unnerved to see a woman in her twenties with wild hair and cold eyes. She looked skinny and unkempt and had an icy glare that went through you. She was being watched by an accompanying prison officer. Despite her appearance, I felt sorry for her. It seemed like an invasion of privacy when the prison officer insisted on being behind the curtain with her while I examined her. The ward windows only opened two inches; was there really any need to cuff her and watch her so intently? Where would she be able to go?

I was to learn afterwards that this was an extreme case as the woman was a high-profile prisoner and deemed to be potentially dangerous. And it was only later that I realised that the officer was present to stop people trying to break *in*, either to free her or attack her. Her presence at the Whittington was putting us all in a vulnerable situation but like any woman she had a right to have her baby in hospital.

As soon as I started to assist her I felt very scared. As she progressed through labour she was really quite violent and verbally aggressive. When I checked her blood pressure she hissed, 'Get off us,' pulling her arm away.

Listening to the baby's heartbeat proved equally taxing. Her strength was unbelievable. If she grabbed you she would really get a hold of you. In labour women often gain immense strength and sometimes they'll grab you by your top and you feel like you're being strangled, or they'll grab you by the arm, digging in their nails. But this woman was something else.

When she was delivering she grabbed my arm as I was trying

to support the baby's head. My eyes watered as she twisted my skin, digging in her nails.

'Let go!' the other midwife working with me instructed, to no avail. She wasn't relinquishing her hold of me.

Looking up, I caught her eye.

'Take your hands off please!' I told her in a firm voice. 'If I can't control the baby's head, you're going to end up with a really bad tear.' That did the trick and she pulled her hand away.

The whole atmosphere from start to finish was menacing. She made everything difficult and it was very uncomfortable. She lashed out with her legs constantly and it was hard to avoid getting kicked.

The prison officer interjected whenever she could.

'Do what they tell you to do,' she barked. 'Stop lashing out.'

She was coping well with the pain but I got the impression she liked lashing out. There was an uncontrollable rage simmering inside of her, most likely because we all knew there was a child protection order on the baby and she wasn't going to get to keep it.

For that reason I did feel really sorry for her. She'd gone through her entire pregnancy and labour just to have her baby taken away.

Once I'd freed the baby's head, she delivered the body quickly and, scooping up the little girl, I placed her in her mother's arms. As she held the baby for the first time I saw a glimmer of emotion. Her eyes definitely softened.

'Can you take her?' she said, after a minute or two.

Carefully taking the baby, I placed her in the cot next to the bed. Although she glanced over occasionally, she lay back with her arms folded, looking at the ceiling. It was clear she did not want to get attached.

In a cruel twist, the child protection order can only be served once the baby is born. Within an hour a social worker arrived. As a midwife you do think, 'Oh, let her have a cup of tea and get cleaned up!'

As the social worker read out the order the prisoner refused to look her in the eye.

'Do you understand?' the social worker asked.

'Yeah, yeah,' she replied in a dismissive fashion.

Although she feigned disinterest as the social worker carried the baby out of the room, I saw a flash of distress on her face and she bit her lip.

'Are you OK?' I asked.

'Yes,' she hissed, her face immediately hardening again.

I never did get a conversation out of her. She stopped you every time by firing back hostile one-word answers. It was a strange experience. The midwifery seemed like such a small part of the process when there were so many outside influences: security, police, social workers and the prison's plan of action.

As soon as the woman was physically able to be transferred back to the prison she was removed and when I started my shift the next day she'd gone. I never asked why she was in prison in the first place but to have that level of security it must have been for a very serious conviction.

Most of the prisoners I looked after were incarcerated for things like drugs and prostitution and I even met one who was imprisoned for not having a TV licence. In terms of privacy they were in a highly vulnerable situation. Unless you talked extremely quietly people could hear everything, and of course once they got wind of the situation they were naturally very interested.

I remember one black girl from Nigeria – she was only about twenty-four years old and thirty weeks pregnant. She had been arrested on a drugs charge for being a drugs mule and was waiting to go to court.

While she was in hospital she had to go to court but when they transported her there she somehow managed to escape. She was heavily pregnant so we were all very concerned but they did find her the next day.

She came back on the ward with two prison officers and was now having contractions on and off. While I was looking after her she told me that she'd been terrified about what would happen to her so she'd managed to get out of the police car and had run off and hid. What she did was wrong but I felt very sorry for her.

She went back to court soon afterwards, where she was given a custodial sentence. When her baby was born she didn't get to keep it, which was often the case in these situations.

I found it sad. A lot of these women were so vulnerable and we saw many drugs mules. It was so distressing to think they were doing that when they were pregnant. They'd arrive nervous, shaking and crying – far removed from the stereotype of hardened criminals.

At that time there wasn't much structure in place for the hospital to work with the prison to improve facilities for these women. They didn't have access to all the services they should have. A nurse worked in Holloway Prison but she wasn't a midwife.

And if a woman in prison had a problem with her pregnancy she would have to speak to a prison officer who would phone the hospital for advice. Eventually they might get to see a doctor or nurse if it was deemed serious enough, but by the time they got transferred it would have taken a fair few hours.

The system changed gradually and in later years I was pleased to see a project underway that addressed the inequalities for pregnant prisoners and gave a more structured approach to their care. When I got a job in the community later in my career I realised that a lot of women reoffended to get back *into* prison, as it enabled them to get away from violence and drugs at home. The mother-and-baby units had really good support by then and the care for the prisoners was a lot better.

But back in these early days it was a weird dynamic having the prison officers there at all times. I didn't really like approaching the bed and seeing two of them there. My core belief was to treat everyone the same and I wanted to make sure that I didn't treat prisoners in a different way to other women on ward. I would find myself really thinking about what I was saying. I wasn't sure to what extent the prison officers needed to be involved and when they'd be present. Would they sit at the end of the bed when you drew the curtains or did they need to be inside? Would they witness the birth? In the end it was often down to what the officer was like and whether they felt it was appropriate or not. I was really quite naïve and soon realised they wouldn't move unless you asked them to move.

I actually got to know a few of them quite well but while some were good and stuck by the prisoner they were allocated, others would unwittingly cause problems with the other women on the wards while they hung about.

One day I was called over by an anxious-looking mother.

'Is my baby jaundiced?' she asked. 'That woman over there says she is.'

It transpired that the warden opposite, clearly considering herself a bit of an armchair midwife, had pointed out that her baby was quite yellow.

Jaundice is a normal physiological process that a baby goes

through. Babies usually get it when they are three to seven days old. In the womb a baby has a very high red cell blood count but once it is born it doesn't need them all so they are broken down in the baby's liver. The liver takes a little bit of time to go through this process and in the meantime bilirubin circulates into the blood, giving the baby a yellow colour. As long as the baby is alert, well and passing urine it's absolutely normal.

But you tell a new mother her baby is jaundiced and she'll absolutely fear the worst. It makes life very difficult for us when people start interfering with our role and I had to spend a good ten or fifteen minutes with the woman reassuring her that there was absolutely nothing wrong with her baby.

Afterwards I wandered over to the officer.

'Hi,' I said. 'I was wondering if you could tell me, what does jaundice mean?'

'Well,' she said, looking a bit puzzled, 'it means the baby is yellow.'

'And what does that mean?'

'Um, it means the baby is yellow and needs to be kept an eye on . . .'

'Well, the lady you told that to was actually quite frightened – yet there is nothing wrong with her baby.' I replied. 'Please don't give women advice on jaundice. I'll stick to my job and you yours.'

She looked very affronted but I never saw her giving patients advice again.

As well as the vulnerable prisoners you got the ones at the other end of the spectrum who were very loud and manipulative and would play the midwife and hospital off against the prison staff. They'd make claims such as saying that their waters had gone and the prison staff hadn't believed them. Over time I learnt how to deal with them. I didn't make any comments and tried to remain professional.

I never asked the women why they were in prison but it was often almost the first thing they'd tell you.

'I'm in for drugs,' they'd tell you matter-of-factly.

Then there was a small, scrawny woman with dark, straggly hair.

'I murdered him, you know,' she said as I took her blood pressure.

I immediately acted unfazed even though I felt very different inside.

As time went on she told me a bit about her circumstances. She'd experienced appalling conditions with a violent partner who had raped her on numerous occasions. He had come in one night and she had grabbed a knife and stabbed him. She'd had a horrendous life and now she was paying the price and going to be in prison for a long time.

'I hate being in prison,' she told me. She was doing everything to get out and had previously even tried to break her own waters with some kind of hook.

Visiting hour could be very difficult when we had prisoners in. They had a strict visiting system in prison but in hospital anyone could come and see them – a privilege that was often abused.

One prisoner we had was a young black girl aged about twenty-two, who had given birth to a premature baby who was in special care. She had no officer with her as the prison felt her risk of absconding was low due to her baby being in special care.

However, that didn't take into account the chaos her presence caused on the ward. She must have had about fifteen to twenty people turn up to see her. There were no locks on the wards then and they just wandered in.

Suddenly a crowd of noisy and threatening-looking people stomped around demanding to go into special care to see the new arrival. They didn't seem remotely interested in the rules of the hospital that deemed the special care unit a no-go to visitors because of the risk of infection.

With no baby to see they paced the ward, looking at all the other babies and making loud, rude comments about the other women on the ward.

After I'd already explained that they couldn't see the baby, the news that the rule was two visitors to a bed was also met with hostility. As I tried to tell this to the motley-looking crew the verbal abuse was incredible.

'Look, we can't have this amount of people!' I said. 'You have to go out.'

As I stood my ground, trying not to shake, I heard a commotion behind me.

'What you looking at?' a scruffy-looking female visitor shouted, gesturing aggressively at an Asian woman in a bed opposite. 'Don't you look at me like that!'

The woman in question had just had a C-section and, sleepy and sore, she couldn't look in any other direction. She'd just come back from the theatre.

In that moment, something inside me snapped.

'Get out, get out now!' I barked, pointing towards the door.

Looking completely affronted, the woman walked up to me. 'I want to speak to the person in charge,' she said.

'I am in charge,' I replied. 'You're not speaking to patients like that. Get off the ward now!'

Finally one of the other relatives took hold of her and pulled her away. To my relief they all left. The ward was so silent. You could have heard a pin drop.

Afterwards I felt quite shaky. By reacting like that I'd put myself in a vulnerable situation. They could have been violent. On another occasion I did hear about a midwife who was actually hit by a male relative.

The Asian lady was in a terrible state after being screamed at and it took me a long time to calm her down.

After a while the prisoner came over to apologise.

'I am so sorry about the behaviour of my friends and relatives,' she said. 'My cousin is very quick tempered.'

'OK, but I have to protect the women on the ward,' I told her. 'I would protect you!'

On the positive side, incidents like these gave me huge experience in dealing with difficult situations and all through my career I've pulled on those early lessons. Instinctively I'd stand up tall and try to protect the women. Of course now I would be calling security but it wasn't really the done thing then.

Chapter Six

Just after 4 a.m. on one night shift I watched as an unkempt woman, about twenty-six weeks pregnant, continually paced the ward.

She had thin, bedraggled hair and a very gaunt and pale complexion, with dark circles under her eyes. She was dressed in leggings and a T-shirt and, apart from her bump, she didn't appear to have a scrap of meat on her. She must have been about twenty-eight or twenty-nine but looked a lot older, having been a heroin addict for many years.

'Can I have my methadone?' she asked, catching me studying her.

'I'm sorry, I can't give it to you until 6 a.m.,' I told her. 'Why don't you try and get some rest?'

As she continued to pace up and down in an agitated fashion, she reminded me of a frustrated animal in a zoo enclosure. I made her a coffee and tried to have a chat with her. But nothing was working. As dawn arrived I continued with my duties. With just one midwife and an auxiliary on overnight you didn't stop from one moment to the next.

We had women in labour, those who needed transitional care, women in with antenatal problems . . . and then there was this woman pacing up and down relentlessly.

At 5.58 a.m. she came over to me. 'I need my methadone now!'

'OK,' I replied, turning round and walking back to the desk.

Suddenly I was aware of her looming towards me and was shocked when she came right up into my face, backing me against a wall.

'I said, I need my methadone now!' she growled.

Extracting myself from her, I headed quickly to the phone to request another midwife to come and check the dosage, which is standard procedure for this controlled drug. When she arrived, I then went to the medicine cupboard and tried not to shake as I measured out 30 mls of methadone, with the other midwife observing. The woman knocked it back immediately, then licked every last drop from the container.

I learnt a valuable lesson that day. After seeing the state of that woman before she got her methadone I made it a priority to make sure I had summoned the other midwife beforehand so the drug was always ready on the dot. In my naïvety I had wasted five minutes waiting for the other midwife to arrive, which for an addict is unbearable.

The desperation of an addict was always really sad to watch. And it was important to remember that as intimidating as she was, that mother was actually fighting to do the right thing.

On another occasion I remember taking a dose of methadone over to a woman only to find her in a deep slumber.

Waking her gently I offered it to her, only for her to mumble incoherently and roll back over to sleep. When I approached another addict on the ward she also seemed sleepy and uninterested.

Heading over to one of the other midwives I expressed my confusion.

'I don't understand why these two women are asleep and not that bothered about taking their methadone?'

My colleague stared at me with an incredulous look.

'Think about it, Maria,' she said. 'They've probably had something else!'

'Oh,' I replied, as the penny suddenly dropped. Naïve or what?

When I examined them more closely both women were flat out and zonked, clearly having managed to get a hit somewhere. As it turned out, one of their relatives had dealt them both the drug.

A couple of days later I was looking after someone in labour when a woman burst through the door and literally grappled with my patient for the gas and air.

I recognised her as one of the girls on the methadone programme who'd been suspiciously sleepy two days before. She just rushed over and pulled the tube off the wall while the woman was holding it. Then she put her mouth over the opening on the wall. When I tried to put my hand over it she looked like she was going to bite me.

Thankfully one of the midwives from the postnatal ward appeared ten seconds later and took the woman back to the ward where she was prescribed diazepan to calm her down. She was such a poor, vulnerable girl and sadly we heard that six months later she was found dead after a drug overdose. It seemed such a waste of a life.

Of course the problem with drug-addicted mothers is that the babies are born addicted themselves, having received the drugs via the placenta while they are in the womb. Horrifically, the babies would have to withdraw after they were born. Those mothers who were addicts were kept on the ward under observation so we would witness the babies having withdrawal symptoms. It was a harrowing sight. The babies have the most high-pitched screams and seem jittery, agitated and very sweaty, as their respiration is faster.

When they were born we had to give them oromorphe, which is a type of morphine, and then over time they'd be weaned off the drug. The most astounding thing of all was seeing the reaction of the addicted mothers. They gave you such hassle when you were administering the drug to the baby.

'What you giving my baby?' they'd snap. 'I don't want the baby to have that!'

Yet trying to explain that the baby was withdrawing and we needed to keep it comfortable proved taxing.

I don't know if it was the reality check or the guilt. Sometimes they got quite aggressive. Almost like the midwife giving the baby the drug was the evil person.

When they are pregnant and take drugs they don't realise they are also giving them to the baby because they can't see it. When the baby is in front of them in the cot they get really upset about it. As a midwife you're not there to judge but you have responsibility for both the woman and the baby. If you can work with the women and get them to see what is happening it is very rewarding when the penny finally drops.

Of course, dealing with drug-addicted mothers was one of the more unusual and upsetting things I had to learn to cope with at the Whittingon. But it was by no means the only strange sight I witnessed there. One week at work a woman aged about twenty-five, who I'd previously seen during her antenatal care, came in during labour to deliver twins. Everything was going well and we had two midwives and two paediatricians at the ready.

As soon as the first baby was born it was handed over to the paediatrician and meanwhile the other doctor set to work, feeling the abdomen and making sure the second baby was head first, which it was.

There is normally thirty minutes between twins so the mum had the joy of holding her first twin for a short break before she had to do it all over again.

It was only when the second twin arrived that a clear difference between them became apparent – one was black and one was white.

The paediatrician had taken note of it but, saying nothing, he handed the baby to the dad. Unless you are certain you should not make judgments or assumptions.

But of course the parents did notice and got very upset. The mother was adamant that no one else could be the dad but the father clearly didn't know what to think. At first he refused to have anything to do with the black baby so we took blood from both of them to find out what had happened. What transpired was that the black baby was a genetic throwback from his family, which was extremely rare. With that information the father was able to finally accept his son.

Of course, there are occasions when you just know that something is not quite right. Like the time I was teaching a student midwife about blood groups.

Keen to help other young midwives, I'd completed my mentor study day and was now taking one of the students round the ward. I took her to see a couple who by coincidence started talking about blood types.

'What blood type is the baby?' the father asked.

'Blood group O,' I confirmed.

'Oh, that must be what you get with an A and a B!' the mother trilled.

Eek! I immediately adapted my poker face but I could see the information processing in the student's mind. I shot her a look that said in no uncertain terms: 'You do *not* say one word!'

Once we'd left the room she looked puzzled.

'Maria,' she said, 'how do an A and B make an O?'

'They don't usually,' I confirmed. 'But in that situation you say nothing at all!'

In amongst those lighter moments there were some days when the pressure was absolutely relentless. One very hectic afternoon a woman aged about thirty-two came in. She had a really long labour that lasted over eighteen hours ending with a forceps delivery and heavy blood loss. She had already been put on a drip to keep her womb contracted.

I was just in the middle of the postnatal checks when an auxiliary shouted to me.

From where I was standing I could see across the room, and it was clear even from a distance that the mum from earlier was flat out on the bed. She had collapsed. Seeing another midwife run to her, I grabbed the crash trolley and rushed over. Someone else had put an emergency bleep out to summon doctors.

In that time I had three women shouting from their beds for my attention.

'Can I have some more water, please?'

'I need some more cotton wool for the baby.'

'Can you show me how to bath the baby, please?'

I couldn't even answer them. Rushing to the bed I saw that the woman had lost a lot of blood and we needed to put another drip in her other arm to give her more fluid.

My colleague held her chin to make sure nothing was obstructing her breathing, and maintained her airway by tilting her chin gently upwards. Although she was breathing it was quite shallow and, pulling back the covers, we realised she was trickling blood vaginally. I sped up her hormone drip and rubbed on her abdomen to make the womb contract. With the problem identified she was immediately whizzed off to theatre to manage the situation in a more controlled area.

After seeing her off and ringing her partner I came back to a bombsite. When we'd wheeled the woman across the ward to the theatre there had been an eerie silence but now everything was back to bedlam.

'I know you were a little bit busy there,' a woman acknowledged. 'But can I get that water now please!'

Sometimes we'd get medical students coming in to observe births as part of their obstetrics training.

One day as I helped a woman in her thirties with her labour I was joined by quite a timid male medical student aged about twenty-two, who was dressed very smartly in a shirt and tie. Despite his shyness he'd built up a good rapport with the couple and was now waiting anxiously to witness his first-ever forceps delivery.

As was the norm we put the woman's legs into the lithotomy position, in which the legs are supported by stirrups and part of the bed is taken away.

'In order to deliver the baby and get access we need to remove the lower half of the bed,' I explained.

While we were getting set up, the very glamorous female registrar came in, wearing an expensive skirt, high heels and a designer top. Putting on a white coat she explained how she was going to help the baby to be born with forceps.

As I continued to set up, organising the forceps tray, the woman's partner stood at the top of the bed supporting her.

'Everything is fine and the heart rate is being monitored,' I reassured the couple. 'What do you think it'll be?'

Meanwhile I placed a chair behind the registrar, as I knew she had a finely tuned routine where she always stood up to deliver the baby's head but sat down to deliver the baby's body.

Moving back to the woman, I placed my fingertip lightly on her abdomen to feel her womb contracting.

'OK, I can start to feel a contraction,' I confirmed. 'So take a deep breath in and push right down into your bottom.'

The baby's head was advancing and as the woman pushed the registrar pulled. Within about three contractions the baby's head was delivered.

'Well done!' I said. 'You'll see the baby in a minute.'

With the head out, the registrar went to sit down – but the chair was now mysteriously absent and she promptly fell backwards onto the floor. The baby came shooting out and landed on top of her. It was covered in meconium (sticky newborn poo) and slid down her body and went under the bed.

Immediately I hit the floor, scooping up the baby and grabbing the cord to stop it from bleeding. (Until the cord is clamped the baby can still bleed through it.)

'Where has the doctor gone?' the mother questioned, oblivious. The dad, who had seen everything, burst into tears.

The registrar immediately scrabbled to her feet and clamped the placenta cord. Thankfully the baby was fine and immediately started screaming.

'It's a boy!' I said. 'Now I'm just going to take him over to the baby doctor.'

Saying nothing, I handed the baby to the ashen-faced paediatrician who had seen it all, having been stood at the back of the labour room.

When I turned around I saw the medical student biting his lip as he tried unsuccessfully not to cry. It seemed that in his naïvety he'd thought the chair was in the way, so he'd 'helpfully' moved it.

'I'm really sorry,' he said, his voice shaking.

'We'll talk about it when we come out,' I said quietly.

With the baby none the worse for wear and safely in his mother's arms, we walked to the office with the registrar who luckily had a good sense of humour, despite the fact that her clothes were now covered in green poo and she had to go and change.

'I'm sure you'll never do it again,' she laughed.

Bless him, the poor student was so distressed he went to apologise to the parents as well. The mother was in hospital for four days and he went to see her every day.

After that I learnt a lesson as well, and whenever we had a medical student present I made a point of saying, 'I'm putting this chair here. It has a purpose!'

This wasn't the only time we had a surprise at the point of delivery. After a long, slow labour it can be quite a shock how quickly things can progress at the end, and one thing every midwife knows is that you should never take your eye off the baby.

I can remember one woman who was breech with her second baby. Everything was absolutely fine and the baby's heart rate perfect, so a junior doctor had come in to deliver the baby, observed by a registrar.

Everything was going well. I was encouraging the woman to

push and, in a textbook breech, the baby's bottom was coming first followed by one leg, then the other. In these circumstances the weight of the body brings the shoulders to the perineum and the baby does all the manoeuvres itself.

As the body appeared, the junior doctor held a towel over the baby's back and pulled a loop of cord out, gently bringing it downwards so it wasn't tight. The baby's body was hanging out with the head still to emerge, and the registrar was busy explaining to the junior doctor how to put the forceps on top of the baby's head to ease it through. Meanwhile the baby was kicking and moving and almost dancing.

'Um, excuse me, this baby is moving quite a lot,' I interrupted, putting my hands underneath just in case. Suddenly the baby shot out and I caught it.

Just at that moment the junior doctor turned to me, forceps in hand.

'I think it's a bit too late!' I confirmed, raising my eyebrows.

Turning to the mum, I lifted the baby up so she could see. 'Congratulations, you've had a girl!' I said. The junior doctor cut the cord and I handed the baby to the parents.

That's the thing about midwifery: you have to constantly observe everything. Never take your eyes off the baby's body! Things can happen so quickly.

With all this activity my time at the Whittington sped by. After six months a promotion came up on the internal vacancy board. It was the same job I was doing but moving up a grade.

I hadn't been there very long and the talk on the hospital floor was that another midwife, Tracey, who was older than me and had been there for a year longer than me, had the job in the bag and there was little point applying. Tracey, to be fair, gave off a super-efficient air.

But I decided that I wanted to show them that I was willing to go for a promotion. Plus it was good experience to be interviewed. Even if it was a foregone conclusion I wanted to demonstrate what I could do.

Unfortunately before my interview I had to go into the maternity unit and sit on a chair in the corridor where everyone could see me. There were certainly a few knowing glances that seemed to imply, 'Well, that's a waste of time!'

When I got called into the meeting room, I was interviewed by two senior midwives, Mrs Jones and Mrs Hope. One was from the labour ward and the other worked in the community.

I was very nervous but answered the questions as best I could. The interview felt like it was over in a flash and then it was time for me to start my late shift.

'We'll call you or someone will be along later to tell you,' they promised.

Although I'd tried to keep it quiet, obviously the word had spread, and during my shift everyone kept asking me, 'Have you heard anything yet?'

Then I got a call saying, 'Can you nip along and see the senior midwife?' Off I sloped on the walk of dread. I went in the room and sat down.

'You did really well,' said Mrs Jones.

'Oh, here we go,' I thought. 'Let me down gently.'

'We actually have two jobs instead of one,' she continued. 'And I'm very happy to say you've got one of them!'

I was gobsmacked.

'Please don't say anything to anyone yet, though,' she instructed.

Well, that wasn't easy. Of course everyone was asking. Even the women on the ward were talking about it. 'Oh, I hope you get it!' my colleague Sarah said.

Then Mrs Hope rang and said I could tell people. Just at that moment one of my friends, Jane, came running in saying she had got the job too. We knew then that Tracey hadn't.

It taught me a lesson not to listen to what everyone else says, as often you have as much chance as anyone.

With my new promotion under my belt, my job remained as hectic and as varied as ever, with constant new challenges to face. With the 1992 Winterton Report encouraging women to attend antenatal classes and know about their choices, a new surge of very well-informed pregnant women were flocking onto the wards extremely sure of what they wanted. As a result we were getting a lot of women who wanted water births.

We didn't have a water birth pool on the unit but women could bring in their own pool and the father would set it up. However, the number of women who actually saw the process all the way through was surprisingly small.

On one occasion I watched a father-to-be looking more and more stressed as he struggled to get to grips with the instructions to inflate the pool. Eventually, he stepped back with a triumphant look, having finally managed to set up the thing. He duly filled it up with water and together we helped his wife towards the pool. Sticking one toe in, she turned up her nose.

'I've changed my mind,' she said. 'I don't like it.'

His face just fell.

'You can't have!' he cried.

'I have,' she said.

'Will you just get in the pool for five minutes?' he pleaded. 'It took me ages!'

'Steve, I don't want to!' she snapped.

'Um, I'll just leave you for a minute,' I said, retreating out the room.

When I came back the pool was abandoned in the corner and she was leaning over the bed. He looked at me, crestfallen, and I just gave him a sympathetic look. There's no chance of winning against a woman about to deliver!

Another father made an even more vivid impression on me when his wife came in for a water birth. I settled the woman in and popped outside to get some equipment.

Returning to the room, I was horrified to see her partner had also stripped naked and was now floating around the pool too, happy as Larry. Shocked was not the word.

'I'm sorry,' I began. 'But it's just not appropriate for you to be in there. Can you get out and put your clothes back on please? I really don't want to run into danger while cutting the cord!'

I turned on my heel and left again. When I returned he was fully clothed and looking sheepish but nothing more was said.

Water births weren't the only new development that was becoming fashionable. Another strong-minded lady arrived having gone to an alternative class where she'd been taught different types of breathing.

I'm all for women using natural techniques but unfortunately somewhere along the line she'd lost sight of the fact that she needed to allow me to do my job. She would not listen to anything I said; it was all about what she wanted to do. It was her experience, she insisted, so she wanted to control it herself. She was aged about forty-two and very articulate.

'I don't want to be induced or restricted in any way,' she told me matter-of-factly.

She wouldn't even let me listen to the baby's heart rate with the pinard (the fetal stethoscope).

'It's for the wellbeing of the baby,' I explained, but she just wasn't listening, no matter how much I attempted to build a rapport.

She wouldn't communicate with me at all. She didn't want to get on the bed and refused to change out of her trousers and shirt into a more comfortable nightdress or long T-shirt.

After disregarding all the advice I was giving her, she got down in the middle of the floor in a fetal position and opened up a book about giving birth. She was completely focused on the book.

It's so difficult when women become tunnel-visioned and will not deviate from their idealistic view of what their birth will be like. Sometimes it's not like it is in a book. Everyone is different and copes in different ways.

It isn't that we want to go against anyone's wishes – it's just that as midwives we are trained to be in tune with what is normal and what is not. Occasionally we have to give advice and intervene.

As I sat down, trying to work out how to talk her round, I was distracted by a strange noise: 'Oooowwwwooot!'

I nearly fell off my chair.

Then I heard it again. I realised the woman was shouting 'Out!'

I was about to say something when her partner started bellowing as well. But he was yelling, 'Shout!'

Again I opened my mouth to protest and off they went again. 'Ouuuuuuut!'

'Shouuuuut!'

Inwardly I cringed. It was gone 10 p.m. and there were mothers and babies upstairs trying to sleep.

There was a knock on the door and I opened it to find Sister Poppleworth looking at me quizzically.

'Maria,' she asked, 'what's going on in here?'

'I'm just assessing what is happening,' I stammered. 'They're both shouting.'

'Well, I can hear that!' she replied.

'Give me ten minutes to see what's happening,' I asked.

After trying unsuccessfully to listen to the baby's heartbeat again I attempted to broach the subject of the noise.

'Can I ask, why are you shouting?' I enquired.

'It's what I've been taught,' she snapped. 'It's what I want to do and it is what it says in the book.'

'OK,' I replied. 'I have to tell you that it is important for me to listen to the baby's heartbeat . . .'

Immediately she scowled.

'I'm desperate to go to the toilet,' her partner interrupted.

'Don't go anywhere,' she snarled.

He looked pained and hopped from foot to foot.

'Oh, just go now then!' she snapped. He was back within a minute.

After about half an hour of persuasion, she finally let me do an examination to see if she was in labour or not. To my dismay she was only about two to three centimetres dilated. So all the shouting was about twenty-second tightenings. She was not even in labour!

I couldn't move her because of how she was behaving and besides she was forty-three weeks pregnant. I needed to keep a close eye on her as she was so overdue.

As I feared, when the next 'tightening' occurred she went back to the noise. The wards upstairs were ringing down to ask what the commotion was.

When her contractions actually started, the shouting increased to every ten minutes.

Sister Poppleworth knocked again.

'Maria?' she said, raising her eyebrows.

'I can't get her to stop!' I whispered.

'OK, you go for your break,' she said. 'I will sort this out.'

Gladly, I went upstairs to get a cup of tea. But all the way through my break I could hear the distant sounds of 'Ooouuuut!' and 'Shoooout!'

I came back after my break to find Sister Poppleworth scratching her head. The woman and her husband were still shouting.

Despite it being pointed out that it was the middle of the night, other people were trying to sleep and that all her bawling was doing was giving her a sore throat, she still carried on. In fact it went the whole night until the end of my shift – at which point a midwife who was also an antenatal teacher came in to listen. 'Isn't it wonderful how women can express themselves so much in labour?' she trilled.

I looked at Sister Poppleworth and our jaws just dropped.

'Well actually, it's been a really difficult night,' I said. I was physically and mentally exhausted looking after her and very relieved to be off home. During the handover the next night I heard from some weary day staff that she had not delivered until 3 p.m. that afternoon.

When women get tunnel-visioned about what they want it can be very difficult. Another woman's birth plan went to pot when her baby got early jaundice because some of the mother's antibodies had passed through the placenta to the baby and had caused a problem. With early treatment this can be resolved but, if left, the baby is likely to become very ill.

Immediately the consultant advised that the little girl should be kept in for phototherapy using ultraviolet light, until she was fully recovered.

'But we want to go home,' the mother protested. 'Can't we just hire a light and do it ourselves?'

Despite all our protests they just weren't listening so we got the consultant paediatrician to come and talk to the mother and her husband. In the end the consultant got tough with them, explaining that once born a baby has rights.

'You will not be taking this baby anywhere,' he said, getting more irritated by the second. 'She could be brain damaged if she doesn't get the right treatment. If you don't agree then we will be getting social workers involved.'

So off the baby went to special care where she also needed to be on a drip because the mother refused to breastfeed, saying she was too tired. She just seemed to think everyone was against her and although I tried to sit her down and explain, she wasn't having it at all. I wondered how on earth she was going to cope with a baby. Everything about her was about being in control.

I heard later that she'd been diagnosed with postnatal depression and I was glad to hear she was getting help.

One of the strangest cases on the ward was a woman aged about twenty-two who remained paralysed from the waist down after an epidural. For three days she had everyone terrified as she was unable to move her legs.

We had numerous doctors out to see her but they just couldn't identify a physical problem with her. We'd even sent her to another hospital for an MRI scan but no one could work out why she was now bed-bound.

To our dismay she kept telling the other women on the ward that she'd been paralysed by an epidural, which as you'd expect was causing quite some concern.

On the third day of her mystery condition I was on the evening shift, busy doing my night round before lights were turned down, when suddenly the ward doors flew open and seven firemen ran through with a clattering of heavy boots.

They ground to a halt at the bottom of the ward in the sluice area where they huddled together, peering through the window and looking outside with very serious expressions.

'Um, hi,' I said, interrupting. 'My name is Maria and I'm in charge of the ward tonight. Is there something I should know?'

'Oh sorry,' one said. 'We didn't stop to look where we are!'

'Is there something wrong?' I asked.

'You see that huge tank over there?' he said. 'It's full of oxygen and we think it is leaking and could explode.'

My jaw dropped. The tank was alarmingly close.

'We're going to have to evacuate the whole ward,' the fireman confirmed.

'Please tell me this is not true,' I thought. It was just me and an auxiliary nurse looking after twenty-six women, mothers and babies.

'OK,' I said and immediately went to call the senior midwife on the night shift who was on another ward. Together we called staff from other parts of the hospital to help, and rang round to find where we could evacuate the women to. It was decided that we'd go for another ward upstairs. Anyone who could walk would set off on their own and the rest we'd wheel.

Bed by bed we got the women up and going. Then out of the corner of my eye I caught sight of a woman rushing along the ward – it was only my paralysed friend! Having seen the women going past her pushing their babies in cots she had been out of bed like a shot and was scurrying along, pushing her own baby to safety.

'Oh my goodness, you can walk!' I cried. 'It's a miracle.'

She looked down at her legs, feigning surprise.

'We were going to push you,' I said. 'But now we can see you can walk . . .'

Then off I went trying to get all the other women organised.

It was 4 a.m. before all the women and babies were safely in the other ward and calm was restored.

At 6 a.m. the phone rang again. It was the night sister.

'The ward is no longer at risk,' she said. 'It's absolutely fine for you to move the women back.'

'You are joking!' I said. 'I am not going anywhere. They've just settled. I'll leave that for the day shift!'

From then on in the paralysed woman was mysteriously fine with no side effects. Now when women ask, 'Have you ever seen anyone paralysed from an epidural?' I always remember that story and firmly say: 'No.'

As if we weren't busy enough delivering babies it was amazing the number of people who appeared to think midwives were their own personal skivvies too.

Like the man who buzzed to say his child had poured a carton of Ribena all over the floor.

'Can you clean it up?' he said.

'No, I can't,' I replied. 'But if you wait one minute I'll get you a cloth and you can do it!'

He looked disgusted but he did it in the end.

There were times I'd find teenagers messing around with

wheelchairs and kids aged eight or nine would give me mouthfuls of abuse. Then there were the grown adults who were sometimes very intimidating.

One particularly fraught night shift I found myself constantly running around after lots of women in labour – and their extended families.

I didn't have time for a break and an hour before my shift ended a woman deemed to be in early labour arrived on the ward with her boyfriend. She was having a few contractions but seemed to be coping very well.

'I'm the only midwife,' I told her. 'But I will soon be handing over to the day staff.'

I left her for five minutes to get another woman a glass of water, but hearing her huffing and puffing I went back to see her.

'Are you OK?' I asked.

'I'm very uncomfortable,' she said. So I sat with her for ten minutes, talking her through what she was experiencing and setting her mind at rest. Her partner was in the room but didn't say anything.

'Now you are feeling a bit more comfortable I'm going to ring the labour ward and ask them to collect you and look after you,' I said. Walking just a few metres out of her bed space I headed to the telephone.

As I put the phone down and started to walk back up the ward I was confronted by a man, who squared up to me. It was the partner of the woman who'd just come in.

'I'll tell you what,' he yelled, as I reeled in shock. 'If I just break your f****** legs then you'll know what the pain feels like.'

He was right up in my face and my heart was pounding but somehow I collected myself and stood up as tall as I could.

I felt like jelly inside but I knew he'd hit me if I showed any emotion.

'I've just come off the telephone and someone is coming for her,' I said, trying to stop my voice from shaking. As calmly as I could, I followed him back into the cubicle to collect the woman. Then, attempting to avoid his glare, I walked her to the door of the ward to meet the other midwife. The woman herself was oblivious to what had happened; her partner had been out of her line of vision when he had threatened me. I wondered how she would have reacted if she'd heard him.

Afterwards I headed straight to the office and closed the door. My whole body was shaking and I could feel tears prickling in my eyes. I concentrated on breathing for a moment. I knew that if I started to cry I wouldn't stop.

'I don't have time to cry – I have a whole ward to hand over!' I thought.

I was interrupted by the auxiliary nurse who opened the door, making me jump.

'Are you OK?' she asked.

'I'm fine,' I replied unconvincingly.

I took another deep breath and started my walk around the ward, checking on another couple of women who looked at me anxiously, clearly having heard the situation unfold. Gradually the ward started to buzz again and the day staff arrived. Before I left I phoned down to the labour ward.

'When that patient comes back after her baby is delivered, please make sure she comes back to another ward,' I requested. Then I headed home. I felt totally shaken up and I really didn't want to go to work that night in case I bumped into him again.

That night, as I started my shift at 8.30 p.m., I was surprised to see six men sitting with their partners in various parts of the ward. They all seemed to be distracted, busy staring at each other rather than fussing over their wives, girlfriends and babies.

Eventually, as I checked on one woman and her baby, her husband leant over.

'Which one was it that was really nasty to you this morning?' he whispered.

Suddenly the penny dropped.

'Is this why you're sitting here?' I asked.

'Yes,' he confirmed. 'My wife was telling me how awful that man was. He won't get away with that tonight.'

A big smile spread across my face. So all these men were hanging around to keep watch! The word had obviously got round.

'I appreciate your concern,' I said. 'But honestly he's not here and he's not going to be on this ward. It's after visiting time and so you should really make your way home.'

It was very touching and reminded me that generally it is quite unusual for someone to threaten a midwife and that when it comes to the crunch your patients generally will look out for you.

Other days at the Whittington sometimes found themselves taking a surreal turn. With a regular influx of immigrants, refugees and asylum seekers, we often faced a huge language problem, especially when we first tried to book women in and get their pregnancy history.

One day I faced the daunting task of trying to communicate with a Kurdish woman aged about thirty-four.

It was important to me to be able to communicate and make asylum seekers part of the process so they know the focus is on them and that the hospital is not just a baby conveyor belt. These women have fled horrendous situations and you can often see the fear. Many have never been in a western hospital and if you can't understand anything then it must be frightening. We wanted to try to give everyone quality and decent care so we regularly called upon interpreters to translate.

On this afternoon in quite a farcical situation I was using two interpreters – one who could speak Kurdish but couldn't speak English then another woman who could speak Turkish and English. So one interpreter was translating what I said into Turkish and then the other was translating from Turkish into Kurdish.

Bit by bit I began to discover that the Kurdish lady had previously had other babies but not in the UK. You can only imagine how long the interview was taking as I asked her about her health and when her last period was.

Sometimes I would ask a question such as, 'Did you have any problems in your pregnancy with your other children?' only for the conversation to go on for ages and ages in the various languages. Then the final interpreter would turn to me and state, 'No,' like nothing else had been said.

Finding out about her last birth took quite some time as we asked what year her baby was born, in which country, in which hospital, how much it weighed and whether it was a normal delivery.

Throughout we smiled at each other and despite the language barrier I felt like I was building a rapport with her. After finally getting to the end of this section of the interview I asked how many other children she had.

I watched, confused, as a lot of discussion went on. Then she started counting on her fingers. Oh Lord, I thought, as she moved on to her other hand. Finally she stopped at nine.

'I'll be here all night if I go through details for every one,'

I thought. So in the end we did a summary to check if there were any premature births or any problems. The answers all came back, 'No.'

Finally, we went through health info, discussing what she was eating and also establishing that she was living in a two-bed flat in London with all nine children.

After an intense two hours I finished up, aware that there was a lot of noise going on outside. Hearing a woman shouting I headed to reception to see what was happening. There I found a woman aged about forty who was not at all happy and appeared to be demanding a scan. Ushering her into a room, I asked her what was wrong.

'They said I'd get a scan at this appointment,' she said, clearly very agitated.

I explained that seeing as it was her booking appointment it wasn't the norm to do a scan at this point.

'But I want a scan!' she said. 'My GP said I could have one. I'm not leaving without one.'

'Can I ask you is there any reason you are desperate for a scan?' I said.

'Well,' she snapped, 'I don't know who the father is.'

'OK,' I said. 'Shall we go through your period history and work out how pregnant you might be?'

She calmed down a little.

'OK,' she said. 'If I'm ten weeks pregnant then it'll be James.

'If I'm about twelve it'll be Rob.

'If I'm about fourteen it'll be Gerard.

'But if I'm sixteen weeks it'll be Miguel.'

Unfortunately it wasn't clear how many weeks pregnant she was because of her cycle.

'Well, can I just ask is there anyone you'd particularly like it to be?' I enquired.

'Yes, I've got a fiancé,' she said. 'James. I want it to be the ten weeks one.'

She was clearly suffering from huge anxiety so because of that I agreed to a scan. 'It might make you feel less anxious,' I said. 'But you also need to be prepared that it might not be the news you want.'

'OK,' she agreed. 'There's just one I really don't want it to be.'

After sending her for the scan. I went into a room with another lady to book her in.

We were about halfway through when I heard more yelling: 'MARIA! MARIAAAAA!' By the tone of her voice I could tell the result wasn't the one she wanted. I had to come out and get someone to take over with the woman I was dealing with.

'I'm twelve weeks pregnant,' she huffed. 'That's what they're saying. That's not the one I wanted!'

How that was our fault I had no idea.

'In view of the information you've been given, do you feel you need to speak to a counsellor?' I suggested. 'I can refer you.'

'No, I am not speaking to any counsellor,' she barked. Then she marched out.

I next met her when she was thirty-six weeks pregnant and she had been admitted with high blood pressure. We had to send her for a Doppler scan at the Royal Free in Hampstead then she was transferred back with her notes.

When I opened the notes I was surprised to see red pen everywhere. She had written all over them, including on my record where I'd stated that she had been offered counselling.

'I WAS NEVER OFFERED COUNSELLING,' she had

scribbled in capital letters. I didn't know what to make of it. But the oddness didn't end there.

'I'm not maternal,' she announced when I asked her how she was feeling about giving birth. 'I'll have one but that will be it. I'm going straight back to work immediately after I've had it.'

It felt like she was deliberately attention-seeking so I make a conscious decision not to react.

On the Sunday after she'd been in for five days, with still no sign of the baby arriving, she came out of the room and marched determinedly up to the desk.

'I need to go out today,' she said. 'I need to have sex.'

It was clear she was going to go out whether the doctor allowed her to or not, so reluctantly we agreed as long as she allowed us to check the baby over when she got back.

When she returned a few hours later I popped my head round the door.

'I need to monitor the baby,' I reminded her. 'I'll give you a few minutes to get organised.'

'I don't need that,' she said.

So I walked into the room trying my hardest not to react to the fact she was lying on the bed in her best underwear!

'You don't want to get covered over?' I asked.

'No.'

So, putting the monitor on, I did all the tests and left.

'If you have to go into that room don't get a shock,' I warned the other staff.

When she eventually went on to have her baby she did have trouble bonding at first. You just got the impression that she felt inconvenienced by the whole thing. But after a few days she did soften quite a bit towards the baby and was really quite maternal.

I don't know if it was fear or being out of her comfort zone that made her so cold but she came round and actually did say thank you to me.

She was also lucky to have a nice partner supporting her, so it worked out in the end. But she really was one of the strangest mothers I have looked after – and there have been many candidates.

On Christmas Day 1993 I was scheduled to work so had to stay in London rather than going home to Newcastle. I duly woke up on Christmas morning feeling very sorry for myself.

Heading into work I went onto the ward to find we had just three patients being looked after by a student midwife, an auxiliary nurse and me, as quite a lot of women had been discharged over the course of the morning.

Not much was going on but then after lunch I noticed that one woman, who was in her late thirties and had a premature baby in special care, was starting to act oddly.

All of a sudden she was all over the place. She was up, she was down, and she seemed very restless. I was busy writing up a report when out of the corner of my eye I saw her heading over to the Christmas tree, which she promptly fell into with a clash of baubles. Rushing over, I hauled her up and led her back to bed. Her eyes were all over the place and her speech seemed slurred.

After quickly reading her notes the penny finally dropped. She had a history of alcoholism and she was also on diazepam for panic attacks. When I went back to check on her I could definitely smell alcohol.

'Where did she get it?' I asked the auxiliary.

'There is a box of wine in the day room,' she said.

It turned out that unbeknownst to me a box of wine had been

placed in the day room so the women could have a glass with their Christmas lunch. When I went to look, sure enough it was drained dry.

After I'd tucked her up like a baby I left her to sleep it off. When the night staff came in and saw her snoring they assumed I'd had a lovely peaceful afternoon.

'You must have had a great shift!' they exclaimed.

'Hmm,' I replied, with raised eyebrows.

Suffice to say the women were never given wine with their lunch again.

Chapter Seven

Sitting at my desk I studied the overnight report. Suddenly there was a huge noise and the whole place rocked. My heart was in my mouth.

'Oh my goodness, what was that?' I thought.

Everyone was looking around anxiously on the ward, trying to fathom what was going on.

Then a father arrived to see his wife and baby.

'A bomb has gone off in Highgate,' he revealed. 'All the roads are blocked off.'

I felt physically sick. Just ten minutes before the ward had been rocked I'd driven my usual route through Highgate Village on automatic pilot. I'd parked up at the hospital and made my way to the maternity unit completely oblivious to the danger I'd just put myself through.

I learnt later that the bomb we'd heard was one of five IRA incendiary devices that had gone off at intervals just after 6.30 a.m. Two exploded near a YMCA in Crouch End, two more about a mile to the west on the main A1 into London at Archway and the fifth a few hundred yards away near an art gallery in Highgate High Street. A sixth was found nearby outside an estate agent's and was defused. The IRA seemed relentless in their attacks on London and now I was frightened.

Later on my break I managed to catch the news on the TV in the day room. As I saw burnt-out buildings in Highgate it really brought the situation home to me. But as usual the ward was busy so I had to get on with the day ahead. Meanwhile any visitors who came in brought updates and descriptions of the scene, telling us that they'd seen windows all smashed and shops completely blackened. That night I had to drive home a different way as the road was blocked off due to bomb damage.

Taking stock that night, I couldn't stop thinking about the day's events. The bombings could happen anywhere and it was affecting my life. I was starting to get edgy being in London.

A few weeks later I had just begun to forget about the incident and was busy finishing off on the night shift when the sister came up to me.

'I'm going to tell you this now,' she said. 'It's a hoax, but we've been told a bomb is going to go off in this hospital at 7 a.m.'

My stomach lurched as I looked at the clock. It was five to seven. I felt physically sick.

'Why are you telling me?' I said.

'I'm telling you because you are in charge of the ward,' she replied. 'Look out that window and you'll see all the police. But they've said they've got the wire and it is definitely a hoax.'

It was not exactly reassuring considering what had happened a few weeks before.

Those five minutes were the longest minutes of my life. All I wanted was to get everyone out. As the second hand ticked up to 7 a.m. I just stood still, my heart in my mouth. Then I watched as it ticked on. Slowly, 7.01 came, then 7.02 and 7.03. Gradually I stopped shaking and carried on doing my rounds.

But sadly that wasn't the last time I was affected by the bombings.

One night I awoke at home to the noise of a huge distant explosion. A plant pot fell over in the hall and we all came out of our rooms.

'What was that?' Tracey cried.

When we turned on the TV the news began to filter through that the B&Q in nearby Brent Cross had been bombed.

'Not again!' I said, despairingly.

I was already very aware of going into central London and now my route from home to work seemed to be fraught with danger as well.

To make matters worse whenever I went out with my housemates we found ourselves being eyed suspiciously because of their Irish accents and my 'northern' one.

One Saturday night my housemates accompanied me to the birthday party of a girl I worked with at the Whittington. It was in a pub in East London and it was only when we got there that I realised it had quite a hostile vibe to it.

I was just getting the drinks in at the bar when I became aware that the man next to me, dressed in a leather jacket and jeans, was staring at me.

'You're from up there, aren't you?' he growled.

When I turned to look at him I found him extremely threatening. He was probably in his late twenties and had a huge scar down his face and quite menacing dark eyes.

'Sorry?' I stammered.

'You're from up there, aren't you?' he repeated.

'Yes,' I squeaked. 'Newcastle.'

'What are you doing down here?' he grilled.

'I work here,' I said, handing over the money for the drinks and planning a sharp exit.

'I better go,' I said.

'I'll see you later,' he said, his eyes still boring into me.

When I got back to the table I was shaking.

'That bloke is really scary,' I told the girls. 'You have to make sure he doesn't come anywhere near me.'

'Well, you're not going for the drinks again,' Jane quipped. But joking aside all of us were feeling uncomfortable, particularly with the girls being Irish, so after a while we decided we should leave.

But when Jane went up to the bar and asked if it was possible to order a taxi she was met with hostility. The landlord flatly refused to help her. In the end my friend's mum ordered us one and we congregated outside to wait.

When the taxi arrived we all piled in.

'How are you doing?' Susie asked the driver.

'Are you Irish?' he said. 'Get out.'

'Ha!' we all laughed.

'I am serious,' he spat. 'GET OUT.'

Despondently we clambered out and he drove off.

At that moment who should come walking out the pub with three equally menacing-looking friends? My mate, waltzing scarface.

They all looked so hostile that I really felt as if he was going to run over, pick me up and put me over his shoulder. I could feel every beat of my heart.

Luckily, at that moment, the pub door swung and out came the birthday girl with her mum and dad.

'SANDRA!' I bawled. She turned round and we legged it over to them.

'Did you not get your taxi?' they asked.

'No, he kicked us out for being Irish,' Mary said.

'I am mortified that you've been treated like that!' Sandra's mum said. Then she took us back to their home and got us a taxi from there.

Funnily enough, I always seemed to have a lot of connections with Irish people. When I'd moved back south I'd taken up once more with the on-off Irish boyfriend I'd met while working at St Heliers.

My job was so busy that we generally struggled to see each other more than once a week but I liked him a lot and enjoyed being with him. I had even been over to Ireland to meet his family and had been welcomed with open arms, but as it turned out it was just not the right time for either of us.

After a while he moved to Germany to work. He asked me to go with him but it just didn't feel right. I was happy to have a long-distance relationship, but inevitably the distance took its toll and after a few years we called it a day. I did feel sad as we got on very well but I knew it was the right decision for both of us.

I was upset for a while after we split but as soon as I walked in the hospital I knew I had to leave my personal life at the door. There was no time for emotional fallout on the labour ward. I just had to get on with my job. And inevitably no matter how sorry you felt for yourself there was always something going on at work to take your mind off it.

One day I came into work only to find myself plunged into a sinister, almost nightmarish drama, which certainly helped to immediately banish any thoughts of my romantic troubles.

The woman I was attending to had been brought in by ambulance just thirty minutes into full labour in a terrible state.

A neighbour had heard her crying in the next-door flat and phoned the ambulance when she realised she was having her baby.

As the paramedics wheeled her onto the ward she had pushed everyone away from her and had started making strange howling noises like a wolf. When I tried to settle her she got up out of the chair and started running around in circles, clawing my arm away.

'Can you help me get her into a labour room?' I appealed to her husband, an odd-looking, gangly man. He didn't even acknowledge me; instead he just stood there doing nothing.

Somehow I got her into the room and up onto the bed where her baby was born. He was in a very poor condition and needed to be resuscitated. Scooping up the baby, the paediatrician immediately sprung into action. 'He's not breathing,' he told me quietly so as not to alarm the mother.

The doctor had just begun to resuscitate the baby when the father tried to barge him out the way.

'Breathe, breathe,' he whispered, putting his hand over the baby like he was performing a magic spell and continuing to block the doctor's access.

'Can you get someone in here now!' the paediatrician shouted.

I pressed the emergency call button and in ran Sister Poppleworth. She quickly pulled the father out of the way and outside into the corridor.

With the baby thankfully breathing I turned my attention to the mother, who had already hopped off the bed. The placenta was yet to be delivered and she was trailing blood all over the floor. Immediately she looked a bit faint and as she started to wobble I helped her back onto the bed where she promptly delivered the afterbirth. Meanwhile the paediatrician whisked the baby off to the special care baby unit. The baby was stable after two hours and was returned back to the mother.

'Just take it easy,' I instructed her; she seemed very agitated and not at all with it.

With the afterbirth delivered I'd just turned to get something off the trolley when I saw her reaching for the placenta. I then looked on in horror as she did the unthinkable. She lifted it to her mouth and took a bite out of it.

For the first time in my midwifery career I thought I was going to be physically sick. I'd heard of people wanting to eat placentas before – Vietnamese and Chinese tribal communities fry it to prevent postnatal depression – but seeing her with blood dripping down her chin was far from pleasant.

I quickly got it away from her, passing it to a shocked student midwife and asking her to take it off.

Of course she would have been within her rights to do whatever she wanted with it. Placentas belong to the patient and quite often women request to take them away for burial. In places like Kenya, Malaysia and Nigeria the placenta is thought to have its own spirit and is buried in a special ritual. I'd always warn people to bury it at least six foot deep otherwise you'll likely have all the neighbour-hood dogs in your garden trying to dig it up.

When I tried to clean the woman up she refused to wash and remained with blood specks on her face for the rest of her stay. Happily her baby made a full recovery so eventually she was allowed to take him home.

Before she left the building she went into the toilets and began howling like a wolf again, which echoed down the maternity ward. She came out in a trance-like state. It was just weird to watch and it made me very uncomfortable to see her taking a baby away but I couldn't do anything about it. I had her address so I sent a community midwife round later to check on her and I also highlighted her strange behaviour to my seniors.

As I watched her sloping off to the car park, wearing her dressing gown with wild hair and blood still on her face, I caught sight of a newly arrived heavily pregnant woman who was being helped in by her partner.

I'll never forget the look of fear on their faces as they spied her. What on earth could I say to reassure them?

Another harrowing case came when a woman arrived by ambulance, huffing and puffing and seemingly about to deliver a baby at any minute.

'She's been pushing for a while,' the paramedic hurriedly explained. 'We gave her gas and air.'

Immediately we whipped her into a room. 'Make sure you get her on a monitor quickly,' the sister advised.

Safely in the room I headed over to her side.

'Can I feel your tummy?' I asked.

She nodded, her face contorted in pain.

But placing my hands on her abdomen I was shocked. I couldn't feel any sign of a baby. It just felt like she was pushing her abdomen right out.

'Am I missing something?' I thought. 'There is no baby in here.'

At that moment the sister came and asked if I'd checked the baby's heart rate.

'Do you want to have a feel of her tummy?' I said, trying to keep my tone light.

She glanced at me with a questioning expression but did as I asked, throwing me a knowing look almost immediately.

Meanwhile I asked the woman how many weeks pregnant she thought she was.

'Forty-one,' she said.

'Can you feel the baby moving?' I enquired.

'Yes, it's pushing. It's going to come out.'

You've got to be so careful in these situations. Outside we quickly got the doctor in for a second opinion.

'There's no baby in there,' he confirmed quietly once we'd left the room.

So very gently I had to sit her down and break the news.

'Are you definitely pregnant?' I asked. 'Because I can't feel that there is a baby at all.'

She burst into tears and started crying hysterically.

'Do you have other children?' I asked.

She revealed that they were in care and it was clear she was desperate to have another baby. She'd gone through the whole process of believing she was pregnant out of sheer desperation.

'Please, please can I look after this one?' she pleaded. It was just heartbreaking.

As it was a phantom pregnancy we had to get her seen by the psychiatry team and a social worker. It was clear she didn't have the skills, support or ability to look after a baby. She had nobody. It was terribly sad. Patients like these made a lasting impression on me – how did they get through life with the dice loaded against them like that?

Alongside the more 'problematic' patients who suffered from emotional or social issues, we also saw some very well-heeled types who expected nothing but the best for themselves and their babies – no matter what the cost. In addition to looking after its NHS patients, the Whittington also offered private care, with some mums-to-be paying to have their babies delivered by a consultant.

I'd been at the hospital just a few weeks when I'd had my first introduction to this two-tier system. At the time I was quite naïve and didn't realise how it worked. In fact I'd been really quite surprised when Sister Poppleworth intervened with a woman I was looking after.

'Joyce, you know you're going to call the consultant for the delivery?' she instructed in her Bajan drawl. 'You don't tink you're doing it?'

'But I've been with her the whole time!' I said, surprised.

'No, you call the consultant when she ten centimetres dilated,' she said. 'He deliver the baby because she a private patient. That's what she pay for!'

I have to admit I felt a little put out. Why was it assumed that the consultant would be better at delivering when I'd probably already delivered more babies than he would do in a lifetime? But I had to respect that was what she wanted, so once she hit ten centimetres I duly called for the consultant.

'Can't *you* help me have my baby?' the woman asked about a minute later.

'Um, I can, but the consultant is on his way in,' I said.

'I feel awful because you've looked after me all the way through,' she said.

'Ah, it's OK,' I said.

Well, the consultant did come in but by then the baby was almost being born and the head was visible. He immediately took over delivering the baby then I was left to deal with the afterbirth and clean up. I couldn't help but feel a little deflated.

But then I tried to see it objectively. When booking in for their first babies these women just wanted to do everything they could to ensure their baby was born safely. They thought by booking the consultant they were paying for the best but once they had received competent care from a midwife they understood that they were already in the best of hands.

In time I learnt that the unwritten rule was that if the woman seemed to be changing her mind and wanted you to deliver her baby then the call simply went out a bit later. That way the consultant would just miss the birth and it worked out best for everyone.

It was one of the ironies of my job that one minute you would be tending a well-off, well-educated private patient, then the next you would find yourself dealing with women who were socially disadvantaged, economically deprived, or even suffering from some previous trauma. You never knew who you were going to be dealing with next, or what their 'back story' would be.

I felt like I was constantly learning new things about human nature – especially as the patients at the Whittington came from all over the globe, so I was witnessing different cultural practices at work too.

For example, at the Whittington we saw a lot of Somalian women who had been subjected to female genital mutilation (FGM) or circumcision.

Up until then I had no idea that it is carried out by the elder women in the family. In some cultures FGM is considered by its practitioners to be an essential part of raising a girl properly – girls are regarded as having been cleansed by the removal of 'male' body parts. It ensures pre-marital virginity and inhibits extra-marital sex, because it reduces women's libido. Women fear the pain of re-opening the vagina, and are afraid of being discovered if it is opened illicitly.

It is generally performed by a traditional circumciser, usually an older woman known as a 'Gedda', without anaesthesia or sterile equipment, though richer families may pay instead for the services of a nurse, midwife or doctor, using a local anaesthetic.

It may also be performed by the mother or grandmother, or in some societies by the local male barber. In Somalia the operation is normally carried out between the ages of four and nine years old.

In may have been an age-old tradition but the problems these women then faced were immense. Not only was the procedure extremely painful but the women could have urine and menstrual problems for the rest of their lives, and a bleeding complication could be fatal. Other immediate complications included acute urinary retention, urinary infection, wound infection, septicemia and tetanus.

Some women even had to have elective Caesareans as they had so much scarring from the mutilation. I always found it very upsetting looking after young girls who had to endure the pain and trauma of living with the scars from this horrific practice.

I also regularly met women who had had multiple terminations (one who'd endured eleven) after being repeatedly raped. Many were from Serbia or Bosnia.

It was nothing short of barbaric hearing how these women had been treated and the horror stories of the suffering they'd endured will always stay with me.

Working at the Whittington I sometimes felt like I'd attended a crash course in multicultural issues. The catchment area for the Whittington spread over very diverse districts of London and I soon learnt which women you could put next to each other and which you couldn't.

The African women didn't seem to like the Asian women, then you'd find the Nigerian women arguing with other African women next door. The Serbian and Bosnian women refugees were also not happy next to each other.

But the nice thing was that generally women did speak to each other and become close, despite their different nationalities and religions. If another mother had just arrived the other women would often familiarise her to the ward by giving her a run-down of the routine. It was quite endearing at times to see that women will help each other out despite their differences.

With the hospital located very close to an affluent part of London called Golders Green, we also had a large orthodox Jewish population to care for. By meeting women from this community I was to learn a lot about their faith and all the rituals that went with it.

Often these women would arrive with their heads covered with wigs or a headscarf, as it is common Jewish practice to shave the head during pregnancy. Hair is considered unclean. Consequently I got used to wigs being kept on a figurine on the bedside locker.

As the labour progressed the husbands would sit behind the screen reading the Bible and chanting. They wouldn't get any nearer, as it was custom not to touch their wives when there is blood.

There were also strict rules about Shabbat, the Jewish Sabbath or 'day of rest', which begins on Friday evening and ends on Saturday evening. This could sometimes cause difficulties. For Orthodox Jews, any sort of physical work is forbidden during this period.

For example, if a woman went into labour on a Saturday the husband would not be allowed to drive her to the hospital, so it was not unusual to get a panicked call. Then sometimes on the postnatal ward we could have up to six women on a Saturday who were not allowed to pick their baby up or turn a light switch on, and could only breastfeed if you took the baby to them.

It was making a lot more work for everyone else so in the end we had a chat with a local Rabbi, who came in and confirmed that women who have just given birth are exempt from this rule on the Sabbath day.

Later when I worked in the community in Gateshead I really saw how the Jewish community rallies together to help when a baby is born. When the woman goes home she only has to look after the baby as the community takes all the other children in for a week. New mothers are brought food so they don't have to cook and they really do get the chance to rest. There is a lot we can all learn from these traditions.

However, while we tried to accept and work with all types of religious beliefs, there was great concern on the ward when we were faced with a female Jehovah's Witness who needed a C-section.

At the last minute she stated that she wouldn't accept any blood products due to her religious beliefs. Unfortunately, there was no record of this in her notes and she had left her directive at home. I quickly informed the anaesthetist and the doctor who would be performing the operation, once I understood what she was telling me.

Meanwhile, her husband was saying, 'But she will have it if it means life or death.'

'No, I won't,' she replied firmly.

'But what about our children?' her husband pleaded. 'Surely you would agree if the alternative was them growing up without their mother?'

But she was adamant that she would not accept a blood transfusion at any cost. We had to get her to theatre but as we wheeled her off she was still refusing. He just sat there with his head in his hands.

I tried to console him as best as I could.

'Have you ever discussed the subject before?' I asked.

'No,' he said, then he started to cry.

It was with immense relief that later I was able to tell him that his wife had come through the Caesarean with no complications and bleeding and that she and his new baby son were doing just fine.

He looked like a huge weight had been lifted off his shoulders but his eyes were still sad. I think they had a lot of talking to do once they took their baby home.

It wasn't just religious beliefs that sometimes stopped us from doing our jobs. One day a lady came in for investigation at about thirty-four weeks pregnant, as her GP was concerned that her baby bump was a lot smaller than it should be at this stage of her pregnancy.

When I put her on the monitor to check the baby I was alarmed to hear a lot of decelerations in the baby's heartbeat. Immediately I called the registrar who decided quickly that she would need an emergency C-section. But when we told her she refused to consent.

'I can't have a Caesarean. My husband is not here,' she said.

'We can contact him,' I said. 'The baby is distressed so we need to do this right away.'

Shaking her head, she refused again. She seemed really upset.

'No, I can't do it without him,' she said.

Quickly we arranged for her to call him but although she told him to come straight away she didn't say why.

'He's three hours away,' she said.

Concerned that her baby's condition could be going rapidly downhill we called the consultant to talk to her.

'If you don't have it soon I don't know if the baby will survive,' he told her.

'No, I won't consent,' she said. 'I'm not having my baby without my husband!'

It was an impossible situation. She just didn't seem to get it!

Huddled outside the labour room, we discussed what could be done.

'We could get an injunction,' the consultant suggested. 'But that will take time.'

It was so frustrating knowing that her baby was distressed but there was nothing we could do. If we did it without her consent she could sue us for assault. Eventually it reached the point where I was pleading with her and the consultant was saying, 'Your baby might be dead if you wait.'

In the end we had to write it all down and get her to sign it, saying that she understood everyone's instructions and was still refusing.

Then after two hours her husband arrived. Quickly we gave him all the information.

'Why are you waiting?' he asked in disbelief. 'Just go now and have it.'

Immediately we went into overdrive, whipping her off to theatre where her baby was delivered within ten minutes. The little boy was born in a very poor condition and needed resuscitation, after which he was put on a ventilator and taken off to special care.

She was taken to recovery and then back to the ward where I think the gravity of her actions began to hit her. Her husband just could not understand why she'd waited and went down to special care to see the baby.

He came back distraught, clutching a photo of their son. She just lay there, staring at it in disbelief.

'Can I go and see him?' she asked. So after warning her that her baby wasn't very well and she should expect him to be very small with lots of tubes attached, I took her round to special care.

When she clapped eyes on him her face just crumpled.

'He's so tiny,' she said, tears streaming down her face.

Thankfully the baby started to make progress but it was clear he was going to be in special care for a fair while.

A few days later she started to talk to me about her decision to delay consent.

'You know that poster over there,' she said pointing to a photo on the wall of a bouncing baby. 'That is what I thought my baby would look like. I've done everything right; I've eaten everything I should. When you told me all the information I just thought he'd be OK because he would look like that. Then I had him and he looks like a skinned rabbit. I can't believe it.'

I felt so upset for her. It's very true that women often have an image of what a baby is like in their head and sometimes the reality can be quite shocking.

She knew she couldn't justify her decision and she felt very, very guilty but she also felt betrayed by all the things she had read and all the images she had seen. In her head she saw a big, bouncing baby that would be fine. I didn't think she'd ever get over the guilt.

Dealing with such circumstances was emotionally draining and after a hard day's work all I'd want to do was go home and flop on the sofa. I loved my job but, boy, did it take it out of me. However the thing about midwifery is sometimes the highs are so amazing too.

One morning at the Whittington I came in as usual for the morning verbal report. It had been a quiet couple of days and one of the midwives had previously warned me that there was a practical joke doing the rounds that involved the head sister making up a report of a woman with loads of complications to give you a scare.

'I reckon the joke will be on you soon,' she said.

Karen, the head sister on the labour ward that day, had a very dry sense of humour that she imparted with a deadpan face, so you often didn't know whether to take her seriously or not. So when, after giving the general report, she had an unusual instruction for me, I was on my guard.

'Maria, if you could just go into room five and look after the women having quads . . .' she said.

'Ha!' I thought to myself. 'They think they've got me but they haven't.'

'OK,' I said with a knowing smile. 'I'll go and see the woman with the quads.'

'Yes, the woman with the quads . . .' Karen replied.

'Yes,' I confirmed loudly. 'I'M GOING TO LOOK AFTER THE WOMAN WITH THE QUADS.'

Walking into room five I smiled smugly and waited for the joke to unfold. But to my surprise, there on the bed was a woman with the hugest bump I'd ever seen. Her partner was stroking her head.

'Excuse me one minute,' I said, before backing out the door hastily.

Darting into the office I collared Karen.

'Quads!' I said. 'I thought you were joking!'

'No,' Karen confirmed. 'Get back in there!'

Composing myself I headed back into room five to meet the quads' mum, who had incredibly managed it all the way to thirty-four weeks pregnant. Most women would go into labour earlier because of the sheer size of carrying four babies.

Shelley and her husband Rav were a lovely couple. Unusually,

Shelley had conceived naturally (not via IVF which is often the case with multiple births). The odds of it happening are 1 in 730,000.

She was having a few contractions and because there was a high risk of miscarriage she was very grateful to get this far.

'Have you found out the sexes?' I asked.

She shook her head.

'No,' she smiled. 'It'll be a really nice surprise.'

I rushed on with the observations. In order to monitor the heartbeats I had the novel problem of sourcing two lots of twin monitors, which I managed to find after scouting round the ward.

At this point Shelley was about three centimetres dilated and going into labour but because you can't deliver quads naturally she needed a Caesarean. The call had already been made to theatre so meanwhile I arranged for four cots to be made available in special care. Then I sat down to explain everything that was going to happen and who would be there.

'As the midwife in charge of your care I'll be looking after you when you go in for your Caesarean,' I said, at the same time mentally planning for how I would be coordinating with a consultant, a registrar, an SHO, four paediatricians and two medical students.

Before we took her down I headed to the theatre to make sure everything was in place. We had four resuscitaires and I carefully wrote out labels for Quad 1, Quad 2, Quad 3 and Quad 4. The paperwork was incredible – four sets of notes.

'Right,' I said, addressing the two medical students in turn. '*You* need to take the time of the first baby then the third and then *you* take the second and fourth. Each time you need to say loudly, "Baby born at time blah blah . . ." Then I will record the information.'

Back on the ward I smiled at Shelley.

'Ready to go?' I asked.

'Ready as I'll ever be!' she giggled nervously, glancing at Rav.

In the theatre the surgeon immediately got to work, making an incision. Within a minute he was holding up the first baby.

'Congratulations, it's a boy!' he said.

'Oh, that'll be Tom!' Shelley smiled.

Next came a baby girl, then another girl and then a third one.

It was the best experience to witness quads being born. I'd never looked after quads before so it was very special and exciting. All four babies came out crying and in good condition but we sent them off to special care just to be observed.

Sticking by Shelley's side I congratulated her and watched, almost shedding a tear myself, as she and Rav shared their sheer delight that all their babies had arrived safely. I was thrilled when she agreed that I could take a photo of the placenta the quads had shared to show student midwives.

'I doubt I'll see one again in my career,' I said, thanking her.

I saw a lot more of the couple after that as the quads were kept in special care for six weeks. It was a special day when Shelley and Rav eventually took them home. They had to borrow someone else's car to fit all the car seats in!

It was such a privilege to witness that birth and when I went on to qualify as a midwifery lecturer one of my teaching subjects was multiple births.

In another touching moment in maternity I met a woman who, despite numerous attempts at IVF, had not been able to carry a baby to term – that is until her sister stepped in to help her.

Rachel and her husband were desperate for a child but their specialist had pretty much said there was no point them trying again. Not able to handle any more disappointment they had sadly given up.

Then Rachel's younger sister Natalie offered to be her surrogate.

Natalie had two children of her own and had no intention of having any more of her own but she really wanted to help. So she went to see the couple's consultant. It was agreed that a fertilised egg would be implanted in Natalie's womb and if it worked Rachel would pretend she was pregnant. The procedure would be kept secret from the wider world as the sisters wanted it to be kept a private, family matter, though of course the child itself would be told of its origins when it was old enough to understand.

The procedure worked and as Natalie disguised her expanding stomach with loose clothing, Rachel began to wear prosthetic bumps.

When I met them I was really quite amazed by how stoical Natalie was in hiding her pregnancy symptoms and I often wondered how the younger sister coped with her elder sibling getting all the attention while she didn't get a look in. Thankfully she sailed through the pregnancy and the elder sister was involved in every step of the process.

I did see Natalie on her own a couple of times throughout the pregnancy. 'Can I ask you how are you feeling emotionally?' I asked her. 'Are you OK?'

'I'm absolutely fine,' she said.

When Natalie went into labour I was ready to deliver the baby.

'I admire everything you're doing but my focus has to be on you as a pregnant woman,' I told the pregnant sister.

'OK,' she agreed. 'But afterwards I don't want too much of a focus on me.'

It was clear she viewed it as her sister's baby. She was just the carrier.

The birth, which her sister was there for, thankfully went fine. Natalie was five centimetres dilated when she came in and gave birth to a little girl a couple of hours later. She immediately asked me to hand the baby to her sister who cried tears of joy.

Natalie too had tears in her eyes but you could see that she was just delighted that she could do it for her sister. It was a real labour of love and it made me emotional too.

Natalie could have stayed overnight in hospital but said that she wanted to go home so she left after six hours. They all went to their mother's house to recover and adjust to the situation. Amazingly, there were no problems and no one else found out about the surrogacy.

When I visited Natalie after the birth I took her aside once more.

'How are you feeling?' I asked.

'Fine! It's not my baby!' she said. 'I'm just so pleased I could do it for her.'

She was an incredible lady.

Chapter Eight

Stepping into the bedroom I was alarmed to see Anita, a new mum who had been discharged from hospital four days earlier, curled up in a ball on the bed. Her eyes were wild and she was whimpering.

As I approached she visibly shook, pushing up onto her knees and putting her hands out defensively.

'Stop, stop! Get away! You're an alien!' she screamed. 'You're coming to take my baby away!'

'Anita, it's Maria here,' I tried to reason. 'I've come to help you. You're doing really well.'

But she wasn't focused on me. She was staring past me and my words weren't registering. She had no sense of reality and thought everyone was working against her.

After four years at the Whittington an opportunity had arisen for me to take a job in the community. The area we served was a vast patch spreading across the whole of north London, covering districts such as King's Cross, Highgate, Hornsey Rise, Archway, Holloway Road, Finsbury, Islington, Highbury and down to Shoreditch.

Now I was working as part of a team of eighteen midwives doing a high amount of home births and so-called 'domino' deliveries, whereby the community midwife does all the antenatal care right through to the birth. When you go into labour the community midwife can go into hospital with you and help you deliver your baby. It was all part of a drive for continuity of care, but it was also a lot more responsibility for me in my role as the midwife, as it meant I would be making a lot of the decisions on my own.

When I visited women in the community I'd have a set of questions to ask. But it was not just about ticking boxes – it was about making sure the women were OK physically and mentally and making sure the baby was well cared for and healthy.

Now, at Anita's house, I needed to take stock of the situation. I'd been concerned about Anita for a few days and now I was extremely worried.

It hadn't always been this way. When I had first met Anita she couldn't have been more prepared for her impending baby's birth. She had everything decorated beautifully in the baby's nursery. There was the best cot money could buy, a Moses basket with white drapes and a matching changing table with cotton wool changing balls laid out in a little dish.

She had given birth to a baby boy in hospital with no complications and everything appeared to be fine.

When I first saw her at home a few days later she was admittedly tired and seemed anxious, having struggled a little with the breastfeeding – but she didn't seem any worse than other new mums. However, when I visited again a few days later, I found her crying.

'I feel like I'm not breastfeeding him properly,' she said. 'He wakes up all the time and I'm so exhausted.'

'But this is all normal for the third day,' I said. 'You've got to stop being so hard on yourself!'

I spent a lot of time reassuring her and helping her to breastfeed – like a lot of women she had a huge fear the baby wasn't getting enough milk. I explained that as long as the baby had had at least six to eight wet nappies and the poo had changed from being black and sticky (having been in the bowel since the sixteen weeks mark) to being a bright yellow colour, then everything was fine.

She was obsessed with cleaning the baby so I showed her how to bath him and explained that you don't have to bath the baby every day, as the soap and chemicals used in some bath products – which are easily absorbed into the skin – will just wash away the baby's natural oils and the bacteria that are used to fight infection.

'Is there anything else you are worried about?' I asked.

'Well, my mum is coming to stay soon,' she said. 'I don't want to look like I can't cope.'

Seeing as she was so anxious I decided to go back later in the day to see how she was doing. By now she'd had something to eat and got some sleep and her husband had taken the baby round the block. But she still seemed very agitated about her mother arriving.

I arranged to go back and see her the next day. This time I was met at the door by her husband.

'She's saying odd things,' he said.

When I saw her I felt significantly concerned as well. She wasn't giving me any eye contact at all and looked like she had completely retreated into herself.

'Mum is going to monitor me,' she mumbled. 'I can't even hold my baby properly. He doesn't like me.'

I stayed for an hour and a half, during which time she was getting more and more anxious.

'If she gets worse you need to call the hospital or your GP,' I told her worried husband.

The next morning at 8.30 a.m. I visited again to find her husband very traumatised. He explained that her mum had arrived the night before and she'd just gone berserk the moment she'd come in.

'She wouldn't let her mum in the room and screamed at me to "Get her away!"' he confided. They'd had the GP out but he had been dismissive, putting her behaviour down to tiredness.

'But she's even worse now,' he told me. 'Maria, I don't even recognise her.'

Seeing Anita in such a terrible state in her bedroom I knew we had to act fast.

'I'm seriously concerned about her behaviour,' I said. 'We need to get the GP out again.'

Immediately I rang my manager to say that I couldn't leave her. Then I rang her GP. 'I've seen her and she's anxious,' he said, sounding a bit put out.

'No, it is a very different situation,' I said firmly. 'She is behaving in a psychotic way.'

He referred me to an emergency psychiatric team but when I rang they said they couldn't get anyone to come that day. So we called the GP out again who confirmed that Anita was having a psychotic episode that could be potentially dangerous for her and baby. But without anyone else able to come out that day we were at a loss. Thankfully the referral system is a lot better now with more structured services available to all women.

'Do you have private health care?' the GP asked.

Luckily they did and within an hour a male psychiatric nurse arrived. By this stage Anita had run outside and was cowering at the bottom of the garden in a fetal position. When anyone went near her she started howling and screaming.

The nurse believed she was suffering from puerperal psychosis – a rare form of postnatal depression that can cause paranoia, delusions and hallucinations – and that she should be sectioned.

Normally that would have meant being separated from her baby but because of Anita's private healthcare the nurse managed to find her a place in a local mother-and-baby unit. In the unit she was treated for acute psychosis and they gave her medication. As time went on she improved very slowly but she was in the mother-and-baby unit for five months.

When she came home she couldn't remember a lot but after counselling she was able to realise that childbirth had triggered her feelings of not being able to cope. It made me think what would have happened if she hadn't been able to take the baby with her – she would have missed out on five months.

To see something so acute was shocking and I'm pleased to say I have only seen one other case in my career and that was hospital-based. However, it emphasised to me how important it is to have community midwives. The UK is one of the only countries in the world that has them. My brother Christopher lives in Norway with his wife Katharina and his daughter Ellea, and no one visits the women afterwards. If anything happens they hope it will be picked up in clinic but there must be lots of cases where women slip through the net.

But being out in the community on my own at all hours brought its own dangers. It was before mobile phones were common and at times I did feel vulnerable.

I remember going into a block of flats on one occasion and out of the darkness of a stairwell came a homeless man, dishevelled, drunk and staggering.

'Do you have a light?' he asked, looming over me suddenly.

'No,' I stammered, ducking past him and carrying on up the stairs.

Luckily he didn't follow me but looking back I can see how exposed I was going out into the community on my own like that. At the time – perhaps fortunately – I didn't really think about the safety aspect. I just focused on getting on with the job.

In order for the hospital to communicate with me I had a radio pager. I'd get called at home or I'd get a text on my radio pager telling me to call in. It didn't matter what time of day it was, I was expected to go out. I would quickly drive to the hospital to pick up my gear and venture out.

Then, often in the dead of night, I would drive to dodgy areas all by myself, aware that the two or three cylinders of Entonox I had in my car, along with my home birth bag containing various drugs, could be viewed as valuable commodities on the street.

I drove everywhere in my little Astra, who I'd nicknamed 'Katie Potty' because of her registration 'K . . . PTY'. She was my pride and joy but didn't escape community life unscathed.

Over a series of months I had my window smashed, a tyre let down and the side scratched with a key. Unfortunately I didn't get money for wear and tear.

Mam was understandably worried about my safety so my Christmas present that year was a mobile phone, which was one of the first models and looked like a brick! It made my life a lot easier but sadly the calls I made weren't reimbursed so I had to pay for them myself.

My patch began in Archway and went down into King's Cross and as far as the East End of London. I would see all walks of life and society, visiting millionaire houses in Hampstead and Highgate and then travelling just down the road to huge blocks of council flats in ghetto-like areas, which even the police wouldn't go into by themselves.

Funnily enough the working-class homes were the ones where you were most likely to be offered a cup of tea and a biscuit. The general rule was the posher the house the fewer the perks. You got the impression they thought, 'You're here to do your job.'

As for the job itself, if I'd thought I was busy before then this was something else!

My day began at the hospital at about 8 a.m., where around nine community midwives would meet in the community office. There we would be told who had been discharged the day before and who we had to go and visit.

It wasn't unusual for me to be allocated ten visits before 1 p.m., which I managed with great difficulty. I'd be whizzing around London going from high-rise flats to mansions and I'd regularly skip lunch.

Twice a week, on top of all the home visits, I'd have a clinic in a GP's surgery where I'd see between twelve and fifteen women.

If I hadn't seen all my home visits before the clinic started, which often was the case, then I'd have to go back to them following the clinic at 4.30 p.m. When you go to someone's house they don't see or know about the other women you're looking after, and they can be put out if you're late. I learnt not to give people a definite time, instead opting for a loose time slot so they wouldn't feel so inconvenienced.

At any point on top of all this you could get called to a home birth. If this happened while I was in the clinic then I'd ask the GP or another midwife to come and take over. If there was more than one home birth to attend it was allocated on a first-come, first-served basis and all the community midwives would frequently help each other out.

Babies don't work nine till five, so inevitably I could start work at 8 a.m. and then end up at a home birth that evening that kept me out for the rest of the night.

We did get paid overtime but when I look back on it, it probably wasn't a safe way to work. I constantly suffered from severe sleep deprivation and midwives are only human.

I remember one evening when I'd worked all day then had to attend a home birth in the evening. I'd got into bed completely shattered just after midnight only for the phone to ring at 1.30 a.m. I'd been asleep for barely an hour and was being called out again! With the next home birth completed I got home at 6.30 a.m., but just as I'd put my pyjamas on the phone rang . . . You've guessed it, another home birth! By this time my eyes were practically rolling back in my head from the tiredness. Phoning the office back I asked them to send someone else.

'I am so tired I cannot physically do this,' I said. 'I am not safe to drive or deliver a baby. I have to go to bed.'

Of course not all home births were at antisocial hours and generally I enjoyed doing them. One of my favourite home-birthers was a Cockney lady called Jackie who already had four children. I did her antenatal care at home and liked her a lot. The fact that she was going to have a home birth was creating quite a buzz in her street.

'The neighbours keep telling me, "Ooh, I wouldn't do that! It's dangerous,"' she laughed. 'When I have the baby they'll all be twitching their curtains.'

Previously she'd had quick labours with no problems but

because she'd already had four kids her abdominal muscles were lax, which had resulted in her having what is known as a pendulous abdomen, like the Jamaican lady I'd encountered at St Helier. This meant that towards the latter part of the pregnancy, the baby would move around a lot, known as an 'unstable lie'. One minute the baby was lying across, the next it would be lying breech. It was fine until she was thirty-six weeks pregnant at which point the baby really needed to be head down for the home birth.

Jackie had her heart set on the baby being born at home and I'd do checks on a daily basis to see which way it was positioned. At thirty-nine weeks it was breech, then at forty weeks it was head-first again. When she started contracting I got a call during the afternoon.

As I arrived on her doorstep, Jackie met me at the door with her four boys snapping at her heels.

'Mummy says she's going to have her baby today,' the youngest shouted excitedly. When I walked inside, Jackie's mother was there and also her husband. I quickly established that her contractions were coming every ten to fifteen minutes and she was four centimetres dilated.

'Come on, Maria, put me out of my misery!' she pleaded.

'Well, looks like the head is still down,' I smiled.

Now, good to go, I set about getting everything prepared. She was having the baby in the sitting room and the kids had been dispatched off with their granny as they were getting a little worried. Her husband was pretty agitated too.

'Shall I go and get some milk?' he suggested.

'No, there's two cartons in the fridge. You're staying put!' she told him in no uncertain terms.

When she got to six centimetres I called for a second midwife. As the labour progressed Jackie pushed in a standing position and in no time at all out popped the baby's head. At that point my second midwife arrived to help. Then the landline rang. The husband immediately started dashing across the room.

'Don't get the phone!' I advised. 'Now is not a good time!'

Seconds later I'd scooped up a beautiful baby girl.

The phone rang again and this time I didn't intervene when the new dad went to answer it. It was Granny, who immediately headed back round with the children. It was wonderful to see all their faces lighting up as they caught a glimpse of their new baby sister.

Then the knocking started, as one by one the nosy neighbours came to investigate.

'Cooey, has she had a baby?' one woman in her fifties asked me, all the while trying to peer around the door.

Jackie gave me a look that said in no uncertain terms, 'Please get her out!'

'She'll let you come in when it's the right time,' I said, before practically having to push her foot out the door to close it.

I know that afterwards Jackie was very proud of her home birth. However, they weren't for everyone and some couples seemed positively terrified at the prospect – especially the husbands, who felt the need to drive like lunatics to make sure their wives got to hospital.

Bundling a labouring woman into the car one day, I pulled her husband aside before we set off.

'I'll be following behind but if there are any problems pull over and I'll stop,' I said. 'We've got time. You don't need to drive like a maniac.'

He nodded but was completely distracted, hopping from one foot to another in an agitated fashion.

'Now listen to me,' I continued. 'Don't go driving off at sixty miles an hour.'

With my pep talk over he went flying around to the driver's seat and practically wheel-spinned down the road.

'For goodness' sake,' I muttered to myself, accelerating to keep up with him. 'Happens every time . . .'

As we approached a junction I cringed. He hadn't seen the red light and as he ploughed across the road a car coming the other way had to swerve sharply with an angry hoot and a screech of brakes.

The driver jumped out shouting and waving his fist. 'WHAT ARE YOU DOING?' he bellowed.

The man wound down his window with a look of desperation.

'Sorry, my wife is in labour!'

Having pulled up behind, I jumped out the car.

'I'm the midwife,' I said loudly to the growing crowd of onlookers. 'I thought you were going to go slow?' I hissed to the husband.

The other guy backed off quickly but by now a passing police car had stopped.

'Oh great,' I thought.

'She's in labour!' the father-to-be shouted, clearly still panicking.

'I'll give you an escort!' the policeman responded.

'Thanks!' the dad agreed breathlessly, jumping back into the car.

'But she's only two centimetres,' I muttered under my breath.

So there we were with the police leading the way with a flashing light, the man and his wife in the middle and me bringing up the rear and cringing inside.

Arriving at the hospital, the dad and the policeman quickly grabbed a wheelchair and dashed her inside to the maternity unit.

'Thanks,' I said to the policeman once I'd caught up. 'I'll take over from here.'

Of course she didn't have the baby for another six hours.

For the rest of the day I was the butt of everyone's jokes.

'Did I hear the rumour right?' they laughed. 'You came into the car park led by a police escort? Ooh, get you.'

However, there were times when the panic was justified. A few weeks later when I was called out to a woman in labour with her second baby it became clear that even the speediest of drivers would not be able to get her to hospital on time.

When I arrived she was already at the eight centimetres mark. I immediately called for a second midwife and informed the labour ward at hospital.

'I'm afraid you're too far on,' I told her. 'If I start moving you now, you're probably going to deliver on the way. You're going to have to have your baby here.'

Her husband looked at me.

'You're going to deliver the baby here?' he questioned. 'In the house?'

'Yes,' I confirmed, before heading out to the car to get my bag and all the equipment.

When I came back the woman was showing signs of wanting to push and her husband was running around in circles.

'What shall I do?' he said. 'Shall I get you some hot water and towels?'

'What's that for?' I teased.

'I don't know!' he exclaimed. 'But that's what they tell you on the telly!'

She pretty much delivered there and then.

At the time the husband was like a headless chicken but later he seemed to love telling the story.

'I helped organise the equipment,' he told his friend.

Each time he told it, the story evolved.

'I was helping the midwife!' he told someone else on the phone.

I couldn't help interrupting.

'Just remember, *I* delivered the baby,' I joked.

'Yeah, I know that!' he laughed.

My rounds in the community came at a time before the trusty sat nav so I would constantly find myself blindly driving around with a map clamped to my steering wheel, as I tried to get to where I needed to be. Driving in London was not a pleasant experience with impatient drivers hooting at you or cutting you up for even a second's hesitation.

Then there was the traffic! At the weekends if I was working anywhere near Highbury when there was a match on I could pretty much expect to sit stationary for hours as the roads around the ground became gridlocked.

So on match days I'd set off at the crack of dawn to get in and out before the traffic began.

Over time I got to know all the back areas but I still ended up in all sorts of trouble. One day, as I travelled to an address with a student midwife in the car with me, I was puzzled to see a couple of cars coming the other way flashing at me.

Pulling over so we could eat our lunch I thought nothing more of it until there was a tap on the window.

'You do realise you are facing the wrong way on a one-way street?' the man said. Oops.

On a daily basis, trying to park was horrendous. I had a British Medical Association badge which in theory should have allowed me to park in restricted areas. But for some reason the local traffic wardens didn't recognise it. I used to get so many parking tickets a day. It must have cost a fortune in fines for the local health authority.

On the plus side, with parking spaces like gold dust, my reverse parking was soon second to none.

I actually got to know a lot of the traffic wardens but frustratingly they were constantly being shifted around, so along would come a new one and another parking ticket would arrive. Generally I'd park the car and wait for a few minutes and a warden would appear.

'I'm a community midwife and I'm going in that house,' I'd say. 'Are you going to give me a ticket?'

'I won't, but I can't guarantee someone else won't,' they'd say.

'Can you tell me anywhere I can park where I won't get a ticket?'

'No' would come the reply, with shrugged shoulders.

'Every day this happens to me!' I'd sigh. It was a huge problem.

I also learnt the hard way that I should hang on to my car keys at all times.

One day I'd just finished visiting a woman when I noticed my car keys were no longer on the bench where I'd left them. When I looked outside my car had gone too.

'Er, where's my car?' I asked.

'Oh, Dave just nipped to the shop,' the woman's other son told me casually. 'You were busy but he didn't think you'd mind.'

'But he's not insured!'

At that moment the son arrived home and just handed me the keys back. 'There you go!'

Travelling around on my own brought other problems too. Although in theory we would see women through the whole process from first booking to labour, at one time we had so many home births that we could not guarantee it would be the usual midwife who would attend. So sometimes you'd be desperately rushing to a home birth without being familiar with your final destination. This could lead to mix-ups: on a few occasions I was given the wrong address and turned up at a house to find no baby. And on another occasion I was left tearing my hair out as I spent ages going round the streets of King's Cross, looking for an address just off York Way for a postnatal check-up.

When I rang the ward they laughed.

'How can you not find her?' they said. 'She lives on a barge!'

'I didn't know that!' I replied.

Wandering down to the canal I made my way along the towpath, stopping to ask barge owners along the way if they knew where it was.

'This is like a wind-up, this!' I thought.

But finally a man called out to me: 'Hello! Are you the midwife?'

'Please tell me you are the Woodcock family?' I sighed breathlessly.

'Come onboard,' he grinned.

Stepping down into the barge I was immediately struck by how nice it was. You could clearly only have the basics but they'd done it out beautifully. The mother was bathing the baby in the sink and she had a little Moses basket for him to sleep in.

After they'd handed me a glass of elderflower cordial we sat up on deck to chat about how they were getting on. It was all very relaxed and I was interested to see how she was going to manage.

'We're just going to dock here for six months before moving on somewhere else,' she explained. They seemed really happy and self-sufficient.

The set-ups I encountered weren't always so agreeable. One Saturday at 2 a.m. I got a call for me to attend a home birth at a trendy house in Islington. When I arrived at the address a thirty-something man opened the door.

'If you just go up the stairs she's there,' he said.

Walking to the end of the corridor I was confused to see no stairs.

'Excuse me, is this not a flat?' I said, beginning to worry that all was not what it seemed.

He came along the corridor and pointed to a corner on the left where there was a narrow iron spiral staircase going up into the attic.

I looked at him and I looked at the steps. 'Oh Lord,' I thought. 'Please don't tell me she's up these cramped stairs!'

'The pool is up there?' I said.

'Yes,' he replied.

'Right,' I nodded. 'I'll just leave my bags here.'

I started to walk slowly up the steps to a gap where one of the ceiling tiles was pushed through. I popped my head through like a meercat.

There was a woman in the pool with two other women supporting her. I could tell she was in labour as she was breathing heavily and making a guttural sound. Above her was a low, sloped ceiling with a huge skylight revealing the night London skyline.

My eyes must have looked like saucers.

'Oh my goodness!' I thought. 'I can't believe she is up here!'

Immediately I checked her over but all the while I was mentally assessing the situation. 'If there's a problem how are we going to get her out?' I wondered. 'We'll have to call the fire brigade!'

I went down the steps and called for the second midwife. The woman wanted her birthing partners to do most of the assisting so when the second midwife arrived I was sitting on a chair beside the pool sipping on a tropical fruit drink. I got the full view of her face as she popped up. Her expression was just the same as mine had been. We didn't have to say a thing to each other; the eye contact said it all.

Thankfully everything went well: the baby was born in the water and she seemed delighted with the birth.

But I did feel the lady had slightly taken advantage of us. In the office on Monday my colleagues revealed they'd told her she had to get a surveyors report to say the attic had been checked and would take the weight of the pool. But when they hadn't got the report they'd advised her against it, as structurally we didn't know if it was a safe area. It worked out well but it could have been disastrous.

I learnt a lesson after that. When discussing home births the first thing I always asked was, 'Where will the pool be?'

There was never a dull moment and one morning as I was visiting a woman who lived in a townhouse in King's Cross, I had to fall back on all my old nursing skills too.

On my way into the woman's home I'd been greeted by a man in his fifties who was on a ladder painting the railings.

'Hello,' I replied before pressing the bell. A friendly looking lady opened the door and I showed my identification.

'Hi, Sophie, I'm called Maria and I'm your midwife,' I said, introducing myself. We'd just sat down with cups of tea when the doorbell went and Sophie got up to answer it. Within a minute there was a panicked shout.

'Maria! Maria!' she called.

Running to the door I found Sophie outside, bent over the workman who was bleeding from a wound below his chest. He'd fallen off the ladder and impaled himself on the railing on the way down. There was paint everywhere and he was gasping for breath.

'Phone 999!' I instructed.

Then, turning to Sophie's husband who'd come outside with all the commotion, I asked him to collect the oxygen cylinder from the back of my car.

'You've injured yourself but we've called an ambulance,' I tried to reassure the man as he fought for his breath. 'Now I've got some oxygen. Put this over your head and breathe shallowly.'

A small crowd had formed so when a passing policeman arrived I asked him to keep everyone back. A paramedic arrived on a motorbike, bending over to assess the injury before radioing for further help.

'It looks like he punctured a lung when he impaled himself,' he said.

An ambulance turned up ten minutes later then suddenly I heard the echoing sound of helicopter rotor blades. They'd sent the air ambulance. It landed nearby and the man was placed on a stretcher and airlifted to hospital.

After seeing him off I stood there completely shellshocked, my dress now covered in white paint. Going back into the house we sat down once more.

'Sophie, I don't know what to say! I can't believe that happened!' I said.

'Neither, can I! I'm so glad you were here!' she replied.

'So where were we?' I joked. 'Oh yes, I'm called Maria . . .'

Then after finishing our chat I had to go trotting off to another house. Having already lost the best part of the morning I knew going back to the hospital to change would take too long. So swallowing my pride I arrived to my next appointment still covered in paint.

'Are you all right, Maria?' the lady asked, looking me up and down. 'You're covered in paint!'

'I know,' I sighed. 'You wouldn't believe the morning I've had.'

I did the rest of my rounds and then headed back to the hospital.

'Maria! What on earth has happened now?' my manager asked.

'Well . . .' I began.

I knew that working in London I had to take all the opportunities that came my way so when the chance arose to do an advanced diploma in midwifery at the age of twenty-six I jumped at it.

It was a big commitment. Not only did it mean travelling to Watford General Hospital for a study day once a fortnight and lots of studying in between, I also paid the £1,000 tuition fee myself in monthly installments.

At the same time I was sent on a 'Bloomsbury workshop' on the theory of breastfeeding. I was very interested to learn more as so far the information I'd gathered about teaching women to breastfeed had come from older midwives and was not that comprehensive.

Over the years I'd seen midwives almost grabbing at boobs to help women, which I was pretty sure made some patients very uncomfortable. I tried my best to assist women without being that invasive but I was working it out for myself, not having been formally taught.

The objective of the Bloomsbury workshop was to educate midwives and give them the practical skills to go on to teach and help mothers without touching them. All the midwives I worked with had had to do the course, which taught us how to run breastfeeding classes to help women to feel confident about doing it.

It was amazing. Now that we could impart our newfound knowledge, the difference it made with the women was extraordinary. You could see their confidence soaring.

However, while the breastfeeding courses grew in popularity, there was a clear social divide in who was attending. The places were often snapped up by 'Yummy Mummies' but, as was often the case, the vulnerable women just didn't source the information unless you made it easier for them. My dream was to involve vulnerable women and make it multicultural as well.

So when I was out in the community I offered the classes to everybody I met on my travels. The more vulnerable or younger women were often intimidated but I would encourage them.

'I'm running it! Come along!' I'd urge. 'You won't be on your own!'

It was something I thought I'd definitely like to develop at another hospital in the future. I hate discrimination. Why should people not have equal opportunities? Everyone should be open to the best available advice and care.

That's what I really enjoyed about working in the community. You got to really know women and when you visited them you could see if they were living in difficult circumstances and immediately work out what their needs were.

I remember one lady who was living on the seventeenth floor of a huge block of flats not far from King's Cross. She was in her early twenties and was from Kurdistan.

As I made my way upstairs in the lift I covered my nose with a scarf. I had never got used to the stench of urine that often accompanied council flat lifts so I now carried a scarf sprayed in perfume in my handbag at all times.

Worse than urine were the discarded syringes. It was awful to think that mothers with newborn babies had to tiptoe around them.

But at least the lift was working . . . I couldn't count the number of times I'd had to climb the stairs, huffing and puffing, when the lift was out of action.

On the seventeenth floor the door was answered by Ariya, a woman aged about twenty, and as she ushered me in I was immediately struck by how very bare her flat was. She had a pan to boil water and a few basic plates and cups but nothing to sit on. She had hardly anything for the baby – just a blanket but no real clothes.

Despite the stark surroundings, however, she clearly took pride in her home, as every inch of the flat was squeaky-clean. Everything was handwashed and you could almost smell the cleaning agent. She was doing the best with the little she had.

Yet there was a real sense of loneliness about her. Her husband went out and did everything, as he knew a little bit of English. He would meet with other men from Kurdistan, whereas she was home with the baby and the radio all day and never left the flat apart from antenatal visits. What she needed was to meet other women in a similar situation.

The NCT (National Childbirth Trust) has been going for a long time but it was very middle class. Yet there were pockets of women like Ariya who felt completely isolated.

After discussing it with other midwives we decided we would try and get the new mothers in the local Kurdistan community to come to a little hall in a local health centre to meet each other. When I went round to tell Ariya her husband was also home.

'If you bring the baby we can go through some things,' I said. Although of course the real reason was to get the women together to chat and form a bond with each other.

'I speak with my husband,' Ariya agreed, before turning to him to talk in their native tongue. It looked like there was a bit of resistance from him about how she'd get there but finally he appeared to give her permission.

When the women met at the health centre they were initially shy but after a while it was great to see them chatting to each other. They were clearly enjoying being able to speak in their own language and looked so at ease instead of being tense and unsure. The outbursts of laughter were heartwarming.

I'd also arranged for a link worker and translator to be there so we could find out what practical help they needed. In Ariya's case it was apparent she needed a pram or a Moses basket for her baby and through asking around I was able to source her both. Often women who had finished their families would donate their old things so I would take stuff and pass it on. It was important to me to do all I could.

'I can't let these women down as they have no one else,' I thought.

However it wasn't just the underprivileged who felt isolated.

Not long after I went to a millionaire's house set back from the road in Highgate, where I met a mother who had all the material things any new mum could dream of.

The baby had a wardrobe full of clothes, a Moses basket with all the frills, a huge beautifully crafted handmade wooden cot and charming stencils on the wall. There was a rocking feeding chair, a chest of drawers and a changing station and matching curtains and lampshade. When you walked in the nursery you sank into a plush carpet – it was pure luxury.

But the lady's husband worked away all the time and she was completely isolated.

'George isn't going to be back for another week,' she confided. 'I feel like I am going crazy.'

'Can I ask you something?' I said. 'Do you know anyone else who has had a baby?'

'No, I don't,' she said.

'If I knew someone in the area in a similar position would you be interested in meeting up?' I asked.

She agreed that she would.

As it happened, my next visit was with the woman living right next door who, unbeknownst to her neighbour, had also just had a baby. Due to confidentiality I had to tread carefully, but afterwards I quickly went round to see this woman, who also complained of feeling isolated.

Immediately I asked her if she would be interested in meeting another new mum in the neighbourhood.

'Yes, yes I would,' she agreed.

'Well, how would you feel if I told you that your next-door neighbour has just had a baby and is in a similar position?'

'I don't even know my next-door neighbour!' she said. 'But yes, that would be brilliant.'

So a few days later I got the two of them together and they got on like a house on fire. Like the Kurdistan women all they needed was support and companionship. It happens in all circles, no matter what your cultural background.

However, being out in the community did make me aware of both the similarities and the differences between the different cultures I encountered, even more so than when I was on the maternity wards. I had to quickly learn the traditions that various religions have regarding newborn babies.

For example, on the seventh day after birth, Jewish boys are circumcised by the Rabbi. Whereas day seven for followers of Islam means that the baby's head should be shaved.

This was all well and good but I can still recall the chill that went through me as I walked into a house to see an aging grandmother shakily holding a razorblade to shave a baby's head. Yes, you respect other people's cultures but when you are seeing things like that it is really hard to watch. I've consequently seen babies with nasty injuries to their heads.

One day, as I visited an African family, I absentmindedly picked a thread off the baby's head and put in on the settee.

When I looked up the whole family was looking terrified.

'Oh, Maria, that is supposed to be there!' the mother said. She then explained that it was an African tradition to put a piece of thread on the head and do a ritual to name the baby.

As I got wise to it I never went to see babies on the seventh day. You don't want to be disrespectful but you have got work to do.

As well as visiting women in homes in the community we were also responsible for visiting the new mums in Holloway Prison's mother-and-baby unit.

The first time I went was quite daunting and I really didn't know what to expect. Reporting to the little reception area I waited nervously for someone to collect me. I was duly given a security pass and then guided through various doors. Each time we went through a door the warden got a big key out and locked the door behind us. It was unnerving and as we went from one door to the next I felt very claustrophobic.

En route we passed the long-stay women's area and I felt very self-conscious as I was eyeballed by prisoners locked up for crimes such as murder and manslaughter. The thought that Myra Hindley was in there somewhere was just chilling.

But during the tour I got to see more of the facilities available. I was surprised by all the activities on offer. There was a huge area where the prisoners could do pottery and art and two big sports halls. I can't believe how large the gyms were. It was clear there were lots of opportunities to learn, opportunities that many of these women wouldn't get in the outside world. They could do any kind of course or qualification, learn to read or sit exams.

Suddenly I could understand why a lot of women did reoffend. I imagined that for some women this would seem so much safer and nicer than home.

Finally we reached the area where the pregnant prisoners were. I was really taken aback. Each woman had a cell with a hard bed in the middle and a shallow mattress. There was a basin and a sink to get washed in. It just looked very bleak. I'd assumed because they were pregnant they would be staying in more comfort and it made me feel uneasy.

The pregnant prisoners were walking around wearing casual clothes like tracksuits or leggings and T-shirts. Some of them looked at me with suspicion but despite being intimidated I started to speak to them. Once they knew I was a midwife they relaxed and started asking me lots of questions, just as any other mums-to-be would.

Once the prisoner had had her baby, she would move to the mother-and-baby unit in a separate block. This actually struck me as being a really supportive environment. There was a lot of camaraderie and I figured that these women were getting a lot more support than they would in their own communities.

The warden explained that they could keep the babies up to the three-year mark. But if they were going to be in for longer then the children would have to go to their family or be adopted.

In contrast to the main prison, each room here had a comfortable bed, toys and a Moses basket and the prisoners were allowed the use of a communal area. The only thing they didn't have was the access to services to speak to midwives. Instead everything went through the prison officers.

Some time later my colleague, Jane, who did a lot of work with prisoners, managed to organise a mobile phone for the mother-and-baby unit that would allow prisoners to speak directly to the midwife. It was a big lifeline and it made a huge difference.

It actually took a long time to get people to listen and understand that there was an inequality at work there.

Despite all the progress I'd seen in my profession and the many personal highs I'd had working in north London, after three years as a community midwife I did start to feel it was taking its toll on me.

I'd had tremendous opportunities to make a difference, which I loved, but it went alongside sleep deprivation and the constant worry of 'Am I doing enough?' When you know people are really vulnerable there is always that thought in the back of your mind that you should be checking to see if they are OK. You feel constantly guilty, especially if you get caught up or delayed. One way or another I was giving so much of myself that I didn't have room for anything else in my life apart from work. I couldn't imagine doing that job long-term or with a family. You work so hard but constantly feel torn.

In the second half of 1995 I started to get itchy feet. After eight years in London it was time for me to head back north . . .

Chapter Nine

'Now tell us, pet,' the woman said leaning forward with a glint in her eye. 'I bet there's loads of mischief going on here. Just like on *Casualty*!'

'Oh no,' I replied. 'There's nothing like that at all!'

'Get away, man!' she exclaimed. 'You need to open your eyes.'

'What do you mean?'

'Well, that bonny lass there is definitely having a flirt with that doctor . . .'

Laughing, I shook my head. It was good to be back in the North East.

After applying for a few jobs I had been pleased to get a staff midwife job at the Royal Victoria Infirmary in Newcastle.

It was a lower-grade job but I knew that the further you went up north the fewer jobs there were available. I felt that it was better to go into a new hospital at a lower grade to suss everything out then – with luck – work my way back up.

Moving back home to Mam and Dad I took up residence in my old room, complete with all my posters and trinkets from my teenage years. It was good to be back in my old bed again but at first I didn't unpack. I just felt a bit disjointed.

I started at the RVI as a staff midwife at the beginning of 1996 and my first morning passed by in a flurry of paperwork and occupational health checks. I was given a tour of the unit but I didn't see any familiar faces. I didn't know any other midwives in the area because I hadn't trained there. I found it all quite unsettling.

To be honest it felt like walking back in time – the pace was a bit slower and while I was glad of the change in environment I was unsure whether I would settle in.

At the time I started they'd just created a new labour unit to deal with 5,500 deliveries a year and had amalgamated staff from two local hospitals – the Princess Mary and the General Hospital. Everybody was out of their comfort zone and people would intro-duce themselves with, 'Hi, I'm Margaret, I used to work at the Princess Mary . . .' I found it weird.

The unit was very medically focused compared to London where it was more midwife-led. The RVI was a regional unit for women with high-risk pregnancies and women were often referred there from other parts of the country. It had a specially developed fetal medicine unit and facilities to care for high-risk babies in the special care baby unit. Perhaps as a result of this, I felt that low-risk women sometimes had more interventions because the unit was so medically managed. I am sure it is very different these days as they have opened a state-of-the-art birthing unit, but when I was there it was quite different working on the labour suite.

Every morning doctors did rounds on everyone, even low-risk women who hadn't been able to go to the midwifery led unit as it was either full or they didn't meet all of the criteria, and there was quite a lot of intervention that I found difficult to get used to. I didn't think I could work in an environment where it was completely medically orientated.

During my first week, for example, I was looking after a lady in labour with her second baby who was about seven centimetres dilated.

We were interrupted by the sister knocking on the door.

'Have you broken her waters yet?' she asked.

'No,' I replied.

'You need to break her waters,' she instructed.

'Can I just ask why?' I said.

'The consultant will go mad if she hasn't had an ARM [artificial rupture of membranes] by the time he comes round.'

'I'm sorry but I'm not doing it,' I said, cringing at the thought of using an amniohook. 'She's seven centimetres and she's coping really well with the pain. If I break them she will be in pain and won't be able to cope.'

Lots of people think if you break the waters the birth will happen quicker. But all the evidence I'd seen suggested it makes no difference to the time of delivery, even though the myths suggest otherwise. The membranes can also act as a form of pain relief during contractions and I had witnessed a woman changing from calm to hysterical when she had artificial rupture of the membranes in advanced labour. As far as I was concerned it went against normal midwifery practice.

'But you just have to do it!' the sister replied.

'I'm sorry,' I said. 'I'm not doing it. If there's a problem I will speak to the consultant myself.'

As it happened her waters broke naturally and by the time the doctor came round she'd already delivered.

'That was a close one!' the sister warned. 'He would have gone mad.'

A couple of days later I was put into the induction room, a four-bedded bay area where women were induced and then observed.

One induced lady was there for the second day. I was quite surprised she'd been induced as she was only two days overdue and at the Whittington it would be standard practice to wait twelve days after the due date before we did it. But when I chatted to her she revealed that because she was anxious her consultant had agreed she could be induced.

It was 7.45 a.m. and as I continued with the observations the doctor from earlier in the week, who insisted women had their waters broken, came in on his round. He was trailed by the labour ward sister, a junior doctor and a couple of medical students. I introduced the woman, explaining it was her second day of induction. He completely ignored her and addressed me.

'Why has she been induced?' he said.

'Well, you had a conversation with your consultant, didn't you?' I began, drawing the woman into the conversation.

'No,' he said. '*You* tell me why this woman is being induced.'

The question really got my back up. He knew that I knew there was no reason for it.

'I've actually just taken over the care,' I said.

He gave me a withering look, turned on his heels and continued on his round.

'He was horrible to you!' the woman said. 'Why was he being so horrible?'

'Ah, it's OK,' I shrugged. But inside I was seething. 'I've only just started working here and I'm trying to keep my head down,' I thought. 'Why is he trying to show me up?'

I went up to the sister afterwards.

'Can I ask you who was that consultant? Do you not think he tried to humiliate me?'

'Oh, he does it all the time,' she said.

'All right,' I replied. 'I'm not going to get used to that. I'm going to have a word with him.'

'You are joking!' she said. 'Don't! He will go mental if you challenge him.'

But later that day when I saw him I tapped him on the shoulder and asked to have a word.

'Hi, we met earlier,' I said. 'My name is Maria Joyce and this is my first week. I am unfamiliar with the way things work here . . .'

'Yes, that's good,' he replied.

'Can I ask you what were you trying to get me to say in that room?'

'You know!' he replied incredulously. He had obviously wanted me to somehow apologise for the fact that she was being induced early, despite the fact that it hadn't been my decision.

'Listen,' I said. 'I'd only just met that woman and found out she was on her second day of induction. What you tried to do is undermine me in front of her. I'm sorry but I'm not going to be undermined.'

He just looked at me.

'I'm not causing trouble,' I said. 'But I will not be spoken to like that.'

As he paused again I had no idea how he'd react.

'Thank you,' he finally said.

'Sorry?'

'I like it when midwives come and speak to me,' he said. 'Nobody tells me what they actually think. I am so glad. We are going to get on well!'

Then for the rest of the week whenever I saw him he'd greet me with: 'Hello, Maria, are you OK?'

Although there was a lot for me to learn about the ways of the RVI I did begin to settle down and really enjoy the good old Geordie humour again. The sense of fun from the women on the ward was very entertaining and they were always gossiping.

'Oh it's like being in *ER*!' they'd comment, eyeing a handsome junior doctor appreciatively. 'He's a nice-looking one! Who's that?'

I also started to enjoy the banter with the other staff. Despite me having worked at the RVI for some time they seemed to be having trouble getting to grips with my name, repeatedly calling me 'Marie'.

Each time I'd reply by saying 'a' pointedly.

I didn't realise but I must have been doing it all the time, as one day a colleague called Amy said, 'How you getting on, Marie?'

'A!' I replied in an exasperated fashion, only for several of my colleagues to shout 'AHH!' in unison.

'We know your name's not Marie,' another colleague, Claire, said. 'It's MARIE-*AHHH*!'

They had a good laugh at my latex allergy too. Within a couple of weeks of being in the job it became apparent that I was having an adverse reaction to the regulation gloves. My hands were becoming very sore and red and the skin was breaking. They were making my lips swell up too and one day as I came in, coated in my usual red lipstick, I was met with laughter.

'That's not a good look!' Amy said. 'What's wrong with you? You look like Mohammed Ali!'

In the end I had to go through seven pairs of gloves, which was rather embarrassing. Typically the only ones that didn't affect me were the most expensive ones.

Of course the other staff took the mick.

'Here she is, posh gloves!' they'd laugh. 'All right for some, isn't it? Too posh for our gloves, aren't you, Marie-ahhh? Did they have fancy pairs in London?'

The fact that I was completely baffled by some of the expressions the women used greatly amused my colleagues too.

'I'm having a dry labour, pet,' one mum-to-be told me. 'I had a dry labour last time n'all.'

'Does that mean the waters have gone?' I quickly questioned Amy.

'Aye!' she confirmed.

'Well, I've never heard that!' I said.

'You've got a lot to learn!'

A few days later I grabbed her again.

'I've got another one!' I said. '"Me colours have gone." It's not to do with washing, is it? Does it mean she's had a show?'

A show is when the browny-red mucus plug that blocks the cervix comes away.

'Aye, you're catching on!' she smiled.

One of the senior midwives was very funny and I noticed, much to my amusement, that she put on a posh voice when she was addressing staff.

'Now staff midwife Joyce, could you go and look after the woman in room four please?' she asked me, sounding distinctly like she had a plum in her mouth.

Just at that moment one of the porters interrupted.

'Man, whatya doing?' she exclaimed in broad Geordie. 'Ah'm talking!'

It was the funniest thing.

* * *

Working in such a big unit meant that I was to gain a lot of experience working with high-risk women – but with all of that came huge ethical dilemmas.

There were babies with gastroschisis, a condition in which their abdominal organs were on the outside, and others born with missing limbs due to gene factors or environmental issues such as drugs and alcohol in pregnancy.

There were also issues with very premature babies. Legally a fetus is not 'viable' until twenty-four weeks gestation. In other words if it is born at this age it has a chance of survival with intensive care treatment. There is a legal right to resuscitate a baby at twenty-four weeks but not at twenty-three.

One day I was looking after a woman going into labour at twenty-three weeks and six days, meaning that her baby was one day away from the viability cut-off. If we were going by the law then the baby was not viable but this was a couple who were desperate for baby. The thought of not resuscitating seemed barbaric.

Behind the scenes I was having a big debate about whether the paediatrician would attend.

'It's not a viable baby,' one said.

'But what about the parents?' I argued. 'What if it is? I don't want to be in this position!'

'We're not giving them false hope!'

Eventually one of the paediatricians agreed to come and speak to the parents.

'If your baby shows signs of life we will resuscitate,' he promised.

Well, their tiny baby girl was born weighing 800g and although she cried briefly she was struggling to breathe. The paediatrician swooped into action, resuscitating and taking her to special care.

She had only a five per cent chance of survival but remarkably she did live. It made me think, how can you ethically not do something? I did reflect on it and speak about it to a paediatrician afterwards.

'We don't want to resuscitate babies that are disabled and difficult for parents to look after,' he reasoned.

'My point is, how can we make that decision without involving the parents?' I said. 'We can't be playing God.'

It is the same with IVF pregnancy, when all of a sudden a couple find out they are having triplets. Many are offered a 'fetal reduction', where one fetus is terminated to increase the chances of survival of the other two. How do you choose?

The trauma and dilemmas continued and on one occasion a mother sadly died in theatre after her baby was born. She'd had a heart problem and years earlier she probably wouldn't have had the opportunity to have a baby.

She'd been under the care of the local hospital a few miles away but had been transferred to the RVI after experiencing complications all through her pregnancy. At thirty-seven weeks she was admitted for an emergency C-section but she became very unwell afterwards and didn't survive. It was a terrible situation.

It wasn't me that broke the news but I was there with one of the doctors. I'll never forget the husband's face. He was sitting holding the baby and just staring, completely shell-shocked. I don't think he was taking in what anyone was saying.

It was so strange going back onto the ward afterwards with everyone else celebrating new life. Some of the staff and I went to the funeral to show our respects. We wanted him to know we cared.

* * *

Three months into the job I was allocated a student midwife called Lynne to mentor. She came to me a bit by default as she kept being passed from pillar to post.

She was the same age as me and had a four-year-old and a two-year-old. She was such a hard worker and being the first person I'd mentored who had two young children it was a real insight into the juggling act she had to do. For that reason I was a little flexible if necessary. I knew she'd make up her time.

She was in her second year of her training but I was shocked that she'd never been taught to use a pinard. I made it my mission to teach her as much as I could. Still, she often remarked that I didn't let her make any mistakes.

'You're really tough!' she said. 'I cannot get away with anything with you!'

'Well, you've got to learn to look after people to a high standard,' I laughed. 'If it's not the best I'll tell you!'

She worked really hard and was an excellent student, so we had a very good relationship. Over the years we worked together often and became firm friends. And when I eventually got married, her children Rachel and Beth were my bridesmaids at my wedding.

All that was still in the future though. I might have had more time on my hands now I was at the RVI but I was still resolutely single. However, I did seem to have an unlikely admirer on the maternity ward.

When a Russian doctor, aged about fifty-five, who was very tall with heavy-set features started, he quickly singled me out.

'I think you are Russian,' he said. 'You must have Russian blood.'

'Oh no, I'm not Russian,' I said.

'But your eyes – I can feel you have Russian blood,' he insisted.

He was quite flirtatious with a lot of the midwives but then he asked me out for a drink.

'We could go out,' he said.

'No, thank you,' I replied.

He asked again a few more times but I always declined.

Then one night I was out in Newcastle when I spotted him across the bar having a drink with another older guy.

'Right, don't say one word,' I instructed my friend Lesley.

'What?' she asked.

Before I could say another thing he was over.

'Hello, Maria! Who is this?' he said. 'I will buy you a drink.'

'I'm sorry, we're just leaving,' I said, despite the fact we had two full drinks.

Lesley was eyeing me with a pained expression. She'd just got the drinks in and they weren't cheap.

'I cannot believe you did that!' she declared on the way out.

'I had to get away from that man!' I said.

'OK, but you're buying the next drinks,' she told me.

At work the next day he came over to the big desk.

'Hello, Maria! Did you have a good night?' he said.

'Yes thanks,' I replied.

'I have to say I am convinced you are Russian,' he started again.

Well, I couldn't help myself.

'The only time I am Russian is when you are coming in my direction and I am rushin' the other way!' I declared.

The other midwives present looked at me aghast and then dashed out the room as one, clearly about to howl with laughter. But after that he seemed to get the message and moved on to someone else.

* * *

209

Newcastle is a football-mad city and inevitably the beautiful game had its influence on the maternity wards at the RVI.

The hospital was located near St James' Park, meaning that it was a nightmare to park on a match day. Yet the buzz that filtered into the hospital was infectious. Every room had Sky TV and when Newcastle scored you could hear all the cheers from the grounds.

We even had farcical moments during international tournaments where women who'd had epidurals were glued to the screen.

'Can we not push after the penalties?' they asked.

The football-inspired names were also hilarious. We had baby girls called Ginola and boys called Alan after Shearer or Kevin after Keegan. One baby boy even had all eleven Newcastle football team names as middle names.

But more than once on a match day I'd get women in who actually weren't in labour. It was always the same old story . . .

'My husband is at the game,' they'd say. 'Can you call him at St James' Park and get him out the match?'

'Shall we just see what happens?' I'd reply, knowing full well that magical football-induced contractions weren't always on a par with the medical variety.

Then there were the women who'd already summoned their husbands back from the game. They'd come rushing in at a million miles an hour and I'd have to break the news.

'You're not really in labour. I think you should go home.'

'You are joking?' the husband would pipe up.

'I thought I was in labour,' she'd insist.

'You called us out the match and you're not in labour!' he'd storm. 'Well, I might just go back in if they'll let me re-use my ticket!'

'You're going back to the match?'

'Well, you're not in labour . . .'

'What if something happens? What's more important? The baby or the match?'

At that point I'd discreetly leave them to it.

However, all things considered, the football-mad husbands were better than the ones with roving eyes. We had some very pretty midwives and one day Keeley, a petite brunette, complained of a father who was acting inappropriately.

'He keeps flirting with me and I don't know what to do,' she said. 'I'm really embarrassed!'

For the rest of the labour process she did her best to ignore him but once his son was born he followed her outside.

'Can I ask you something?' he said. 'Do you fancy going out for a drink?'

At that moment all politeness went out the window.

'No,' she snapped. 'I've just delivered your baby. I think you should get back in that room and be with your family.'

Sometimes it felt like an episode of Jerry Springer.

I built up a great rapport with one woman yet her husband kept avoiding my eye contact, almost like he was trying to hide something . . .

'Do I know you?' I questioned. 'I feel like I know you!'

'No, you don't know me,' he replied.

Yet he seemed quite nervous watching me. Normally people chat and ask where you are from but he seemed to want to say as little to me as possible.

Then the penny dropped. He'd been in three weeks ago when his girlfriend had a baby.

'Now you're here with your wife!' I thought. 'And she has no idea!'

The realisation must have registered on my face as suddenly he gave me a pleading look as if to say, 'You're not going to say anything, are you?'

If I'd asked that man to stand on his head he would have but of course I would never have let on.

This wasn't the only time I got caught up in complicated domestic tangles. A few weeks later I walked in to find another woman who'd just delivered completely inconsolable.

'Just go!' she was telling her partner, although judging by her face that was the last thing she wanted.

'I do have to go . . .' he said, miserably.

'But I've just had our baby, when am I going to see you again?' she pleaded.

'I don't know,' he muttered, then he kissed her on the forehead and left.

'Are you all right?' I asked.

The poor girl wouldn't stop crying.

'He's gone home to see his wife,' she said. 'It's a really complicated situation.'

So he'd been with his girlfriend all day and now he'd gone back to his wife and children.

'Gosh, that is really sad,' I thought. It was also quite frightening to see such deceit in progress.

Then there were the dads who couldn't do right for doing wrong.

One woman was about to deliver and her husband was flapping around her in a right panic.

'What can I do? What can I do?' he asked.

'You could get me a wet flannel and put it on my head,' she said. 'It's in my bag.'

He immediately rushed over to the chair to a perfectly packed bag and started pulling everything out. He literally looked like a cartoon character as he scrabbled frantically to locate the flannel.

'Where is it?' he asked.

'It's in the side pocket,' she snapped.

'I got it! I got it!'

He rushed to the sink and then just as she was in the middle of a contraction and before I could stop him he slapped it on her face. It was absolutely soaking wet. Her look of fury said it all.

She took a big intake of breath and grabbed the flannel and threw it back, slapping it in *his* face.

'Wring it out! Wring it out!' she shouted.

He went running over to the sink then back again just as another contraction hit.

'Wait!' I instructed.

'Now?' he asked hopelessly. It was all I could do not to laugh.

On other occasions I'd be guiding women, telling them they were doing really well and helping with their breathing, when well-meaning partners would try to help too.

'You're doing great!' I'd enthuse.

'Yes, really well done!' the husband would gush, rubbing his wife's arm in the process.

'Get off me!' the women would holler. Largely because women in advanced labour don't want to be touched at all.

At the other end of the scale are the knuckle-crushers: the women who grab their partners' hands with an iron man's grip. You should never underestimate the strength of a woman in labour.

'Aagghhh!' the bloke is suddenly screaming. Long nails are even worse and at times as guys were having their hands gorged mercilessly I wondered if this was a form of revenge.

My advice is just let your partner hold two fingers – no matter how hard she squeezes she won't be able to crush them.

We had lots of fainting dads too, all extremely embarrassed when they got back up.

However, the balance of power wasn't always on the woman's side. Sometimes you'd get an unpleasant vibe from a couple that made you wonder just how much control the man exerts over her day to day. I found in those cases it's better if the husband or boyfriend goes outside and you ask questions to the woman directly.

I can remember one woman who was not far off birth and was really struggling with pushing, using the gas and air like it was going out of fashion.

'I need an epidural,' she gasped, eventually.

'Now, darling,' her husband began. 'We had this discussion and remember you said that if you want an epidural I was to say no.'

'I've changed my mind.'

'No, you said that as well. You don't really want one.'

In parenting lessons beforehand I warn the women never to say you definitely don't want one, as you never know how you'll feel when the pain really hits.

So there I was stuck in the middle.

'Do you want one?' I asked.

'Yes,' she growled.

'No,' he said.

'Get me an epidural!' she yelled. 'And you be quiet and shut up.'

'OK,' I said. 'I have to go with what you're saying.'

Well, the husband started chasing me down the corridor and got really quite aggressive.

'I'm telling you if you get her an epidural she will totally regret it.'

'She made that decision when she wasn't in any pain,' I explained.

'Imagine you'd made a decision and then were in a lot of pain? Imagine if you were crying out and everyone held that to you. People change their minds!'

Childbirth is such an emotional time. If you are in a lot of pain and you have a partner who is disrespecting you or not being attentive enough it can be very upsetting.

As a midwife I would feel very protective of the women in my care but I would always remind myself that it was important to work out what was going on without being judgmental.

Take the big biker-looking bloke who was lying flat on a bench in a labour room with his jacket on. His wife was huffing and puffing with contractions and he was lying with his back to her with his head propped up, reading the paper. It was insulting. Like he had better things to do.

After asking how she was, I walked over to him.

'Are you OK?' I said.

'Yes, I'm fine,' he replied.

'Then what are you doing lying on there?' I said, keeping my tone light.

'I'm tired.'

'You're tired already? Why have you got your jacket on? It is so hot here! And it's just going to get hotter. I recommend you take your jacket off.'

'I'm all reet,' he shrugged. 'How long will it be?'

'Five or six hours at least,' I confirmed.

'*What?*' he said.

'I think you should take your jacket off, turn round and come and talk to your partner. There's no point looking at the wall. You'll miss everything. I've got a chair for you here.'

Reluctantly he moved over and when I chatted to him he

admitted he was terrified of hospitals. He had been acting distant because it was his way of coping with being in hospital.

Over the course of the next three hours I kept engaging with him. He was really shaking. He desperately wanted to be there but he was genuinely suffering. It stemmed back from a parent being in hospital and him visiting them as a child.

'So you're in charge of drinks,' I said, trying to keep him focused. 'Then how about you choose a channel on the radio?' When fathers feel involved their anxiety levels drop and they feel useful.

You pick up the vibes very quickly about whether it's good for the partner to be there or not. Some academics say partners shouldn't be in the room at all and it is true that sometimes women are less focused and don't push as well when their husband is present.

The key thing to remember is that you don't have to have a partner or a husband there if you don't want: a sister or a friend can be just as good. It's just best to have the right person.

As the months passed I quickly made friends at the RVI.

There was Kirsty, a girl who arrived just before me. I had already worked with her at the Whittington hospital when she was a student midwife there. Then there were Claire and Ashleigh, funny characters who always added humour to the twelve-hour shifts. Another woman who was always friendly to me was Gillian, a senior member of staff who always seemed to have the same break as me. Over time I realised this wasn't just a coincidence. I just thought she was being friendly but then people started making comments.

'Oh, you've got a friend!' they'd say mockingly. 'I see she's looking after you!'

She certainly did seem very interested in my wellbeing – and also my personal life.

Gillian was nice enough but then I started to feel she was being *too* friendly. In fact, she seemed to be coming up with any old excuse to pop over to the antenatal ward to speak to me, even though the ward she worked on was a good five-minute walk.

'Oh, Maria, can I borrow your pencil?' she'd say.

'Sure,' I'd reply, feeling quite puzzled that she'd come all the way just for that.

An hour later she'd be back.

'Have you got a red pen?'

Next it was, 'Are you wanting to change your shift?'

Then, 'Are you going out tonight?'

One day she came to see me about five times. It was almost obsessive. I was getting a bit agitated about it but because I was new I was reluctant to say anything.

'Are you all right?' another midwife, who'd clearly been observing it all, asked. 'You're very quiet.'

'Yeah, I'm fine,' I lied.

'She's done it before, you know,' she said quietly, as we tidied away our equipment.

I said nothing.

'You know what I'm talking about,' she whispered. 'You need to keep away.'

Confiding in my manager, I eventually made a complaint. She assured me that I wouldn't have to work in the same area as her again.

Before I worked at the RVI I'd never really seen drunk pregnant women but in Newcastle they seemed to rock up to the maternity unit on a weekly basis.

I really didn't know what to say when I was first faced with a young woman stood in high heels and a bright Lycra dress that emphasised her bump. She was giggling and clearly intoxicated.

'I'm having a few pains – what does it mean?' she said. I could smell alcohol on her breath.

'Have you been drinking?' I asked, trying carefully not to come across as judgmental.

'Aye,' she replied, twisting her hair.

'You shouldn't really be drinking,' I said softly.

'It says in me book I can have a couple,' she said. 'In moderation, like!'

'What is moderation?'

'Well, I only had six bottles of WKD.'

I soon discovered that on a Friday and Saturday night in Newcastle you'd have at least one or two pregnant women coming through the doors thinking they were in labour or that their waters had broken. Sadly, it was all a big joke to them.

'I can't believe how many pregnant women are coming in drunk,' I exclaimed to Amy.

'Yes, that's Friday neet!' she sighed.

The worst case I ever encountered was when I delivered a baby where the women was so drunk she didn't know where she was. She came in by ambulance and it transpired she was an alcoholic. When the ambulance went to pick her up they found her front room strewn with about twenty cans of Carlsberg.

She was pushing, but trying to get any response was impossible. The baby was born in a bad way. It had fetal alcohol syndrome.

When women drink in their pregnancy there is a set of characteristics that can occur, including low birth weight, protruding eyes, low-set ears and a narrow face. The child can be disfigured and have huge developmental problems. It's very difficult when you know the only reason the baby is that way is because the mother is drunk. Yet women always assume it is not going to happen to them.

The fact the guidelines are always changing doesn't help.

'Well, nobody is telling me I shouldn't drink,' women always say. 'It never did me mother any harm.'

But even a small amount of alcohol can affect the baby and I always recommended no alcohol at all during pregnancy.

This wasn't the only cultural difference I noticed between London and Newcastle. I'd been at the RVI for a few months when I got talking to one of my colleagues, Gwen, about breastfeeding and how I'd done the Bloomsbury workshops in London.

I'd just come from an area where the percentage of mothers who were breastfeeding was almost seventy per cent. I thought it was a real shame that just fifty per cent of new mums who came through the RVI gave it a try.

Gwen was very encouraging and together we organised a breast-feeding workshop for the midwives at the RVI. Over time we integrated the mums-to-be as well.

There was room for twelve to fourteen women at each workshop on a monthly basis but we soon had to run them more frequently because of the demand. To my delight the number of women breastfeeding began to increase.

As the months went on my persistent friend Gillian was clearly not planning to back off.

Sometimes she would follow me around saying nothing and other times incessantly asking me questions that were not very relevant to anything to do with work.

Then when my twenty-ninth birthday came round, she left me

presents and a card in my locker. I hadn't told anyone when my birthday was so clearly she'd looked it up on my file.

I made a conscious decision to write every single thing down and my manager agreed I should record any inappropriate communication.

I'm quite an open person but I felt like I was restricting my personality. Every time I saw her it made my stomach lurch. Determined to distance myself from her until she got the message, I asked my friends on the ward not to speak to me about my personal life in front of her.

Meanwhile my career was progressing and I was as busy as usual. Not long after I joined the RVI, I registered to do an honours degree in midwifery. I also had the option to do a higher ENB (English National Board) award alongside the degree. Any time at university was over and above my working week so I worked three shifts and studied the rest of the week.

There were new developments at work too. At the time the RVI had just opened a midwifery-led unit alongside the maternity wards. To go to the midwifery-led unit women had to be viewed to be completely low-risk in their pregnancy.

The women were falling over themselves to get a place there. You would step through a door and find yourself in this plush unit, totally different in feel to the rest of the hospital. I'd never seen such lovely big rooms – there were four, decorated in different colours, with stenciling around the walls.

In the unit the midwives wore their own clothes and the idea was that it was like a home from home. The one problem was the huge, low double beds: they might have been comfy but were not very practical for delivering babies.

When the midwifery-led unit first opened there was some tension. On the labour suite midwives were running around looking after three women at once but if you pushed through the door into the midwifery-led unit it was almost one on one. You did twelve-hour shifts in both units but it was a completely different experience depending on which side you were working – you would get regular breaks in the midwifery-led unit and there was a maximum number of women who you would be looking after, whereas on the labour suite you were generally flat out.

It was absolute luxury to look after one person in labour and they were not stressed at all. It felt like an elite place to work. I worked a couple of shifts there and found it fantastic, not least because you had time to spend with the women and that is what it should be like in an ideal world.

However, back in the thick of it I carried on working on the labour suite, thinking on my feet as the daily dilemmas unfolded.

One day a woman came into the delivery suite with her partner, looking very worried. Excusing myself from the women I was already attending to, I went to talk to her.

'I'm forty weeks pregnant and I haven't felt my baby move for two days,' she said. A chill went through me. It wasn't a good sign.

Taking her off to a room I got her lying down and then quickly tried to listen to the heart rate of the baby.

When I felt the abdomen I just got a horrible sense that the baby wasn't alive. I could see the stress in the parents' faces. Then I couldn't get the baby's heartbeat at all.

I listened for about a minute while all the time the woman and her husband were desperately looking at me.

'I'm having a bit of difficulty getting the baby's heartbeat,'

I confirmed, as gently as I could. 'So I'm going to get a doctor so we can do a scan.'

Outside, I immediately called for a doctor then I wheeled a scanner in and started to set it up.

'When did you last feel the baby moving?' I asked.

When the doctor came in and we did the scan, it was evident very quickly that there was no heartbeat and the baby had died.

'I'm so sorry,' she said. 'There's nothing we can do.'

The lady just screamed – it was an agonising cry of pain. She was completely inconsolable.

'If only I'd come in earlier,' she cried. 'I should have come in.'

It was so heartbreaking to hear and the husband just looked pale and distraught.

'There is really nothing you could have done,' I urged. 'Please don't blame yourselves.'

They were clinging on to each other. Part of me just wanted to cry with them but that doesn't help.

'What's the next step?' the husband asked.

'If you can just give me one moment I will explain it all to you,' I said, guiltily remembering the woman just down the ward who was in labour.

Nipping out to ask a colleague to check on her I went back into the room with a doctor.

'How am I going to get the baby out?' the woman asked, her face etched with panic. I knew that like many women who lose their babies late into their pregnancy she was probably feeling sick at the thought of having a dead baby inside her.

'We recommend you deliver the baby naturally,' I said, gently. This was because psychologically women cope better when they deliver a stillborn baby themselves.

With the couple agreeing, the woman was given a couple of tablets and had the option of going home or staying in hospital. She decided to stay and her contractions started within a couple of hours.

As she went into labour we set about doing all the checks. Without the baby's heartbeat the silence was eerie.

Meanwhile, as normal life resumed outside the room, I went to check on my other patient who was progressing well. I felt really guilty when I headed back to the devastated couple.

The lady who had the stillbirth delivered first, and the silence when the baby was born was just heartbreaking. There she was, a little girl who just looked as if she was asleep.

Carefully I wrapped her up in a blanket.

'Would you like to hold her?' I asked.

'Yes,' she said.

As I gently passed the baby over, the mother let out a choked sob. I don't think she truly believed the worst until she held the baby in her arms. Leaving them to have a quiet moment I stood outside and rummaged in my pockets for a hanky to wipe my eyes. I was unable to stop the tears from falling. It was just so sad.

Half an hour later as I delivered a live baby from the other lady I felt absolutely drained. Everyone was really happy but all I could think about was that poor, devastated couple.

Having worked fourteen hours solid, I headed home, my stomach churning with hunger. During my break I'd only had a quick glass of water; I'd just felt too guilty about leaving the mother of the stillborn.

'Hello, Maria,' Mam greeted me.

'Just give me five minutes,' I asked. Then I poured a cup of coffee, got the paper and just zoned out.

My family knew when I'd had a hard day. They didn't ask too many questions and knew to leave me alone.

I sent a card to that couple a few weeks later to say I was thinking of them and that I hoped they were getting the support they needed.

Tragedies like stillbirths affect everyone in different ways but in my work I am often astonished how people manage to turn terrible events into positives, just through sheer force of personality. Many years after this episode, in 2011, I met a lovely couple up in Scotland called Susan and Andrew, who had been through tremendous heartbreak.

Their first daughter, Charis, was born by emergency C-section in 2005. Susan bled heavily and needed further surgery after the birth.

The couple were elated when Susan fell pregnant again in 2007 but sadly at twelve weeks no heartbeat was found. After grieving for their baby, Susan discovered she was expecting again the following year. Once more her pregnancy was not without complications and when her waters broke at thirty-five weeks, her daughter Niamh was delivered four days later, again by C-section. She was transferred straight to SCBU where thankfully she made good progress.

Susan's final pregnancy came in 2010 but was blighted with problems from the start. At twelve weeks the sonographer noticed a thickness on the baby's neck that could be an indication of chromosomal abnormalities. As the weeks passed it was concluded that Susan's baby probably had Down's Syndrome, but was otherwise strong and healthy.

Then at thirty-two weeks a scan showed that the baby had developed hydrops fetalis, a condition where fluid builds up inside the body. Susan was admitted to hospital two days later to have an amniocentesis and some fluid drained off. After much discussion between obstetricians and paediatricians in Glasgow and Inverness, it was decided that the baby would be delivered by Cesarean section as soon as possible. Sadly, before the procedure, the baby's heart stopped and Susan and Andrew's daughter Eilidh Beth was stillborn on 24 September 2010.

The couple were absolutely devastated but immediately started to think about how they could use their experience to make a difference. Susan joined an Edinburgh-based charity, SiMBA (Simpson's Memory Box Appeal), meeting with midwives at the hospital and organising the supply of memory boxes containing a teddy, blanket and a certificate recording the baby's birth, which would be given to parents whose babies were stillborn.

Susan is still working tirelessly alongside midwives at Raigmore Hospital to support other parents who have experienced tragedy and her latest venture is to set up a Tree of Tranquility – a life-sized tree with leaves bearing the names and dates of babies lost before, during or after birth.

I have met a few 'Susans' throughout my career and the strength and kindness that some parents manage to find within themselves, despite having endured the worst of circumstances, never fails to amaze me.

Chapter Ten

Leaning back in the pew the woman in front of us at church turned to Mam and me.

'Have you heard?' she said. 'Princess Diana is dead.'

With the priest starting the mass almost seconds later I couldn't ask any more. I spent the rest of the service in complete disbelief.

I like to attend when I can, as I feel it gave me strength when times were tough or sad. When I'd met couples like the ones whose baby was stillborn I liked to go to church and light a candle for them.

Back at Mam's, we turned on the telly to have the terrible news confirmed. My dad, a huge Princess Di fan, was devastated. In stark shock, I recalled the time she'd come to visit my ward, all dressed down and unassuming.

On the ward that evening the atmosphere was sombre and everyone was talking about it.

'Oh my goodness, I can't believe my baby was born on the day Diana died,' women who'd given birth on that day were exclaiming.

'I don't know what all the fuss is about,' a few anti-royalists would retort, prompting daggers from everyone else.

There were some big Diana fans on the ward and some midwives even swapped their days off to go down to Kensington Palace to mark their respects. The rest of us huddled around the TV on the ward to watch it. I found the whole thing extremely sad.

As 1997 drew to a close I bit the bullet and bought my own place: a two-bedroomed flat in Low Fell, a nice part of Gateshead four miles from my parents.

I'd first gone to view it on a miserable October night when it was lashing down with rain and when I walked in the door to see the dilapidated state of the flat I thought it was really no surprise that it had been on the market for nine months. Everything was really old, rotten and filthy. As I walked around I was overcome by the stale smell of damp.

'What do you think?' the owner asked.

'Er, will you be leaving anything as part of the sale?' Mam enquired.

'I could lose the settee,' the owner replied.

'What?!' I thought, looking at them both incredulously. 'You won't catch me sitting on that!'

However, despite the state of the place I could see past the grime. It was quirky and it had a good feel about it. All of the rooms were an unusual shape; there wasn't a square room in the place. It needed a huge amount of work but it could shape up very nicely, I thought.

So I feigned indifference then called up and put in an offer much lower than the asking price. The estate agent called back thirty minutes later.

'I can't believe I am saying this, but they have accepted,' he sighed.

And so began a mammoth project . . .

Thankfully I had Dad on hand to help me. Bless him, I think he was just really glad to be helping me with my first step on the property ladder.

Our first job was getting the carpet rolled up.

'Right, come on, get the other end,' Dad instructed, clearly forgetting that I was a 5ft 7in female, as he marched ahead leaving me running after him, straining from the weight. Then I felt a sharp pain in my foot.

'Daaaaad!' I protested.

'What's wrong?' he asked.

'I've got a nail in my foot!' I cried. 'Don't stop, whatever you do!'

'It's not that bad!' he said dismissively. 'Have you had a tetanus jab?'

The next job was the damp proofing, so I engaged a building firm to strip the flat down to its bare bones.

When I walked in it was quite a shock. 'Am I inside or outside?' I thought.

The builders who came to work on the flat were far from enthusiastic. None of the electric tape measures were working because of the obscure angles of the walls.

'Did you not think about buying a house with square rooms?' one workman asked sarcastically.

'No, no, I really like it!' I said.

'I'm sure it's got lots of potential,' he humoured me.

I might have smiled back but for six months I did wonder, 'What on earth am I doing?' The money I'd allocated to spend soon dried up and somehow I had to finance a whole new kitchen and bathroom suite. I scrimped and saved until I could afford it all.

Finally we got to the point where we could decorate. But there was one thing always guaranteed to distract Dad – the footie. It didn't help that there was a pub at the bottom of my road and if

Dad was helping out he'd often nip down for a pint and then head back again.

One day he mentioned that he'd like to watch the Newcastle game.

'Oh, Dad, we need to get on!' I sighed. 'Can't you listen to it on the radio?'

He reluctantly agreed and in the meantime I popped out to buy more paint. When I came back half an hour later nobody was in.

'Hmmm,' I thought, and promptly headed down to the pub.

As I marched determinedly down the road I caught sight of Dad through the window, clearly as he'd just spotted me. As I walked in the front door of the pub he bolted out the back. I caught up with him as he was speed-walking back up the road.

'Excuse me! And where have you been?' I chastised mockingly.

'I was just nipping in to see the score, love,' he insisted.

'Get back!'

'I'm going, I'm going!'

We got there in the end, with the flat decorated from top to bottom with different colours in every room.

'That'll do,' I thought to myself as I walked around admiring each room.

It was such a relief to get into my own flat. I moved in during October 1998, twelve months after I'd first bought it.

Meanwhile I was having new complications at work.

Despite keeping Gillian at arm's length, she continued to make a nuisance of herself. Having realised I was giving her the cold shoulder she got her revenge – by hiding my gloves!

I was looking everywhere for them one day when one of the other midwives piped up.

'You know who'll have them!'

So then I had to go and ask her directly.

'Have you seen my gloves?' I asked.

'Oh yes! I've got them,' she said, as if it was the most normal thing in the world.

'Where are they?' I asked.

'Oh, I just put them away for safekeeping,' she said. 'In my locker.'

At that moment I decided to bite the bullet.

'Do you know I feel really uncomfortable with this situation,' I told her. 'I feel like you're following me everywhere!'

'There's nothing funny going on,' she said defensively.

'It's not funny to me either,' I said. 'I feel uncomfortable and I'd prefer it if you just kept away from me. I'll be professional but don't ask me anything about my personal life please.'

Well, after that she changed and suddenly she turned nasty. She'd do her best to put me into difficult situations and would say things to me when no one was around.

I was pretty sure she was calling my home too. There was a spate of incidents where the phone kept ringing and then was put down when I answered it.

I was getting really stressed. People were joking, 'You better make sure your tyres don't get slashed,' but I was no longer finding it funny. I was watching over my shoulder and getting panic attacks.

Then one day I went into my bedroom and immediately sensed that there were eyes watching me. As I turned around I saw someone hiding behind the door.

I shouted in fear – before realising it was just my little brother Christopher.

'Don't do that!' I screamed, which only upset him too.

Despite making numerous complaints it was difficult to prove she was harassing me. She did get an official warning for her behaviour and these days she doesn't work as a midwife. But back then I decided I couldn't work with her any more.

When a promotion came up at another hospital I was relieved. Finally it was a chance to escape.

Walking onto the postnatal ward I felt light and happy.

It was my first day back at the Queen Elizabeth in Gateshead, the hospital where I'd trained to be a nurse.

As the phone rang I decided to make myself useful.

'Hello, maternity?' I trilled.

No one answered for a moment and then a familiar voice filtered down the line.

'Hello, Maria,' she said. Then the line went dead.

Immediately I put the phone down and steadied myself on the desk. Gillian didn't have a legitimate reason to call; she was clearly just trying to make me feel scared. All I could do was pull myself together and carry on.

Thankfully that was to be my last unpleasant encounter with Gillian and she appeared to leave me alone to enjoy my new job.

When I'd originally handed in my notice everyone thought I was mad. The RVI was the place to be, the best place to work in the North East, but while I loved it there the reality was there were no professional opportunities for me at all. I hoped the QE would bring me fresh challenges.

I'd never worked at QE as a midwife so it was really funny to go back to the unit where I'd fainted in 1985. There were so many of the same people still there and a few even remembered me as a student thirteen years earlier.

'Oh my goodness, it's you!' Sue exclaimed. 'Aye, you weren't well that day, pet!'

Despite new roles being like gold dust, after six months an opening came up. One of the midwives, a team leader in the community, was retiring and there was a chance to take over her patch. It was a great opportunity.

Well, I got the job and started within a week.

As a team leader I was responsible for all of the GP practices in my area – of which there were about six – and it was my responsibility to ensure they were all offering the same service to pregnant women in that catchment area. I also had to organise parentcraft education classes across the area and if antenatal clinics weren't running efficiently I had to sort that out too.

There was a shake-up of the teams and the midwives allocated to me were great. Everyone was motivated and very nice to work with. For the first time in ages I felt really happy and fired up.

But as I got into my role I had a bee in my bonnet! The QE only had a twenty per cent initiation success for breastfeeding. I'd just spotted my next project!

However, when I tried to fire people up, I got a lukewarm reception.

'Women aren't interested in breastfeeding here,' one midwife told me.

'Well, have you asked the women?' I said.

'No,' she admitted.

Determined to at least try, I got the go-ahead to put out an information sheet in the Gateshead area, asking mums-to-be if they'd be interested in breastfeeding workshops. I was thrilled when the feedback was returned with a resounding yes.

Now all I had to do was put together a presentation to the staff and sell the idea to them. Yikes. It took a good six months.

The presentations went well but as with any change there were stubborn sorts determined to oppose it. I tried not to take it too personally. Instead I realised that the best thing to do was to speak to those who were most resistant first in the hope that if I got them on board others would follow.

Painstakingly, I approached each midwife on a one-to-one basis and explained how it would work, assuring them it would make their job easier in the long run.

Our community patch was very mixed. There were a lot of teenagers and it was a very working-class area. The cultural mix wasn't as extreme as London but there was a huge Jewish community from Bensham in Gateshead and a lot of refugees. Once again I encountered many vulnerable women who were very isolated in flats.

I wasn't given any funding or overtime to promote breastfeeding so the work I did was over and above my job. But I was prepared to put in the time and effort, as it was something I felt very passionately about. I really knew what the benefits of the workshops were and, as I hoped, they began to take off. Women from all over the community came along and we were getting on the map. Importantly, Gateshead was on a par with the public health agenda. At the time the government was trying to tackle health inequalities and promote breastfeeding. We had a budget to advertise the benefits of breastfeeding in the North East but we were missing one vital ingredient: a catchy slogan.

At one point there was some talk of using a slogan from a Scottish district: 'You can't get fitter than a breastfed nipper.' But it would have cost thousands for the copyright. It seemed like such a waste of funds.

As the money was discussed during a meeting, suddenly I had a flash of inspiration.

'Give your bairns the best. Feed them from the breast!' I piped up to ripples of laughter.

It had to go to the health action zone committee for consultation but eventually word filtered back that it had been chosen.

When I found out I was laughing so much. We had a huge launch at the Metrocentre, a massive shopping centre in Newcastle, with a big turnout of women and their babies. We all had our photo taken next to one of the buses with the slogan on and it made the local press.

A few days later I was on my way to see a patient with a student midwife in the car when suddenly she shrieked, 'There it is!'

As I saw my logo emblazoned on the side of a bus I almost swerved and I had to pull over. It was just so exciting.

For that month I was laughing every day, as it was on all the buses in the area.

'I seen one of your buses the other day!' the women in the community would tell me. It was an exciting time. Most importantly, to my delight the breastfeeding rate did start to increase and it became mandatory at the QE for the midwives to actively encourage it.

Unfortunately the downside of this was that bit by bit everyone's workload was increasing. We were all running antenatal clinics and none of us were finishing on time. Then when people went on the sick or left they weren't replaced. It was quite a dire situation.

To add to the work pressure the home birth rate was on the up and there were only four people in my team in one of the busiest areas. What's more I was voluntarily doing lots of one-on-ones for teenagers in the area to ensure they got the right parentcraft information. It was a real challenge but one I relished.

As always, working in the community I got to meet all sorts.

One day I was visiting a new mum in a big tower block when I found myself struggling to concentrate. My eyes kept wandering over to the windowsill.

'Sorry,' I asked eventually. 'But *what* is that?'

She followed my gaze over to a substantial-sized black creepy-crawly on the ledge.

'Oh, that,' she said. 'It's a tarantula.'

'*What*?!' I spluttered, getting ready to jump up on the sofa.

'It's OK,' she laughed. 'It's dead.'

Even so it made me shudder and I couldn't wait to leave.

It was always amazing the weird pets people would have in flats. There would be cages with lizards, snakes and rats in them. I just used to look at them and think, 'If that gets out, I'm gone!'

Another time I lost my pinard stethoscope after going out on my rounds. I searched the house from top to bottom and clambered around in my car, straining to see if it had fallen below the seats, all to no avail.

Then one day as I carried out a postnatal check in Gateshead I couldn't believe my eyes. There, on the mantelpiece, turned upside-down with dried flowers coming out of the top, was my pinard stethoscope!

'Um,' I said. 'That vase over there is actually a piece of equipment that belongs to me.'

'Does it?' the woman replied, red-faced. 'I said to me husband: "I cannae imagine where it came from but it looks quite pretty so I'll put it to good use!"'

Thankfully we were both able to laugh about it and it was returned to me, none the worse for wear.

Working in the North East there was no shortage of characters. One day after I'd finished my rounds I popped into the hospital to visit a lady I'd been looking after. As I walked along the corridor I bumped into another mum on my books who'd just given birth to her second baby.

'Maria!' she said. 'Have you heard? I had my baby. He was eleven pounds four!'

'That's brilliant!' I said.

'No, it's not,' she said, looking around to make sure no one was listening. 'I nearly had him on the bathroom floor! I'm so embarrassed!'

'Why?' I laughed.

'He was eleven pound four, I nearly had him on the bathroom floor and I've had NO STITCHES!' she exclaimed. 'Oh, the shame!'

I didn't half laugh.

That's the funny thing about big babies; women are obsessed with stitches. The minute they meet another new mum they put on this Les Dawson voice, fold their arms and demand, 'Well, how many stitches did you have?'

Once I overheard a conversation on the ward where two women were clearly getting very competitive.

'Oh, it was bad, it took her ages to stitch me up,' one declared dramatically.

'Yes, me too,' the other interrupted. 'I think I've had about thirty or forty.'

'Oh really?' the first added. 'I think I had about forty or fifty!'

At that point I popped my head around the corner.

'Hi!' I said. They both looked at me.

'That was an interesting conversation!' I said.

The first lady tittered nervously. She knew and I knew that she hadn't had any!

As usual, though, this job had its share of high drama. Two years had flown by with me working in the community when one night the phone rang. With a home birth to attend I hauled myself out of bed and grabbed my bag.

Jumping in my car I drove two miles to an area in Gateshead, stopping *en route* to pick up a student midwife who – despite it being the middle of the night – was very excited as it was the first birth she had ever observed.

The lady we were going to see was called Fiona, who was pregnant with her third baby.

When we arrived she was quite far on and it wasn't long before she was close to delivering. With the birth imminent I called a second midwife, Caroline, who arrived fifteen minutes later.

Everything seemed to be going well until the head delivered and it was apparent there was a problem. Whereas normally the baby's shoulders would rotate at this stage, in this case it just wasn't happening, meaning that the baby could physically not be born.

We are taught an emergency drill in the unlikely event of this happening and immediately Caroline and I set about pushing Fiona's legs right the way back until they were almost touching her ears. This flattens the mother's spine and allows the baby's posterior shoulder to drop into the right place. It solves the problem in 99.6 per cent of cases. The odds were clearly stacked against us this time though, as it wasn't working.

Exchanging concerned looks, we moved on to procedure two: trying to rock the shoulder to dislodge it from the symphysis pubis. This was done by putting our hands over the symphysis pubis and moving the shoulder from the outside. Again nothing changed. I tried internal rotation manoeuvres, to no avail. We then went through all the manoeuvres again. Still the baby wasn't moving. The situation was getting critical.

Caroline immediately went out to call for an ambulance and I set about guiding Fiona into the all-fours position. I was keeping my tone calm but inside I felt like jelly. I began to panic internally.

'If I don't get this baby out now we'll be in trouble,' I thought. I knew that if I didn't free it soon this baby was going to die.

Knowing I had about thirty seconds to get the baby out, I tried again to rotate the shoulder with my hand using internal manoeuvres. Suddenly the shoulder rotated and at the same time there was a snapping noise as my left hand crunched.

The dad looked at me with horror.

'That was my hand,' I said.

With the baby out the relief was incredible. Caroline and I sped into action giving the baby oxygen but thankfully he was fine. He weighed in at almost ten pounds.

As I passed Fiona her baby, her face lit up with joy. She'd been completely oblivious to the close call but her husband was as white as a ghost.

I got on with delivering the placenta and then headed into the other room, my hands beginning to shake.

'That was fantastic,' Heather the student midwife was enthusing with wide eyes. 'That was so amazing! Is that what you do every time you deliver a baby?'

'That,' I said, 'was a huge emergency! I hope you never see it again!'

'What about your hand?' Caroline asked.

'Oh, it's OK,' I shrugged. It wasn't sore at that point, probably due to the adrenaline pumping around my body.

With Fiona happily cooing over her baby I drove Heather off.

'In their eyes you're a hero!' she said.

'Heather, what would I have been thirty seconds later?' I said. 'The baby would not have survived.'

'Oh, I never thought of it like that,' she said.

'Always have that in your head,' I warned.

Meanwhile I hardly dared look at my hand. There was no denying it was getting bigger and bigger and blacker and blacker. In casualty they sent me for an x-ray. The news wasn't good.

'I'm sorry, Maria, it's broken,' the doctor said. 'You've got a spiral fracture just above the little finger.'

My break wouldn't benefit from being plastered so instead I was instructed to wear a tubigrip bandage and keep moving my fingers.

'You'll be back up to speed in six weeks,' the doctor told me. If only! What actually followed was five months of agonising pain and time off work.

Over the course of a week my hand just seemed to get worse, then one day when I was lying in bed I realised I couldn't pick up left arm. Panicking, I tried to move it but I'd lost all sensation. I had to pick up my arm with my right hand. I lay there, frozen with panic.

Eventually I called Mam and Dad who came straight over and took me to hospital. Over the next couple of hours I could feel the sensation coming back into my arm and I could move it again, but it was a scary time.

'Keep an eye on it,' the doctor said.

Six weeks passed and the pain was even worse. When I managed to get an appointment to see the consultant at the clinic three months later, I got to learn the truth. The fracture was healing but I had nerve damage. The consultant diagnosed chronic nerve pain.

'How long will the pain last?' I asked.

'It will burn itself out after about three years,' he said.

I was absolutely devastated. I didn't know how I could continue to work as a midwife with these symptoms and the horrendous pain.

Although my boss was good about it I found it very frustrating being off work. I did get basic sick pay but I couldn't get any compensation unless I sued the woman's pelvis! I logged it with the RCM as it was a work injury but there was no financial help from that route either.

To be honest that was the least of my problems. I just wanted the pain to go away. I tried every single remedy but no painkillers worked. So I learnt to manage the pain with acupuncture and Chinese herbal medicine. Anything that anyone suggested I tried.

'I'm not going to be beaten by this,' I thought.

Over time I learnt to manage. It wasn't painful constantly and over a period of three years it got less and less.

After five months I was able to return to work and continue a postgraduate diploma in education that I'd started at the University of Northumbria. When I went back to work there were times when it was extremely painful but I just tried to have a positive mental attitude. I worked through the pain and I did get used to it.

I also knew that however bad I felt at times, there was always someone worse off than me. And at least my pain had been caused by an accident, as opposed to someone who professed to 'love' me. Sadly, violence against women was something I'd encountered too often in my career so I welcomed a new drive to target it in our community.

I would never forget one time at the RVI when I heard a commotion going on behind a curtain. Inside was a young woman who had just given birth who was being visited by her partner. I didn't like the sound of it one little bit.

Walking nearer, I heard a whimpering noise. Pulling back the curtain I saw her curled up, shaking and crying, and him with a look of thunder on his face.

'Has he just hit you?' I asked.

Her look said it all.

'Sorry, sir, but I am going to have to ask you to leave,' I said. Thankfully he didn't resist and stomped off down the ward.

Although I reassured her I could get her help, sadly she was just too frightened. This was not an uncommon response, unfortunately.

In the community clinics I often instinctively picked up on vibes that all was not well. Take one girl, Kimberley, who I looked after at the clinic. She was about thirty-two weeks pregnant and had her boyfriend with her at every single appointment. He was smart but somehow a little *too* nice and helpful with the information I sought. I found him rather domineering.

When I asked how she was, I noticed she glanced at him.

'She's fine,' he said.

I would have liked to have seen her on her own at least once, but it was clear this guy was not going to let that happen. What was going on behind closed doors that he felt the need to keep an eye on her 24/7?

After lots of discussions about how to help women like this, the Women's Aid group had come up with a clever idea so that vulnerable women could alert us to problems at home without the fear of their partners finding out.

During the clinic we'd hand them a bottle and ask them to go to the women's toilet to give a urine sample.

There, in each cubicle on the back of the door was a poster saying that if you wanted to talk about domestic violence then you could put one of the attached red stickers on your bottle and the information would be passed to the community midwife.

Sure enough, when Kimberley handed the bottle back there was a little red sticker on it.

Aware that he was watching everything we carried on as normal and then behind the scenes I started to formulate a plan to protect her.

A few weeks later I went to see her in her house. As she answered the door he was behind her. I could tell she was desperate to say something but with him constantly around she was terrified. I noticed she had what looked like bruises on her arms.

I ran through all the other questions about her wellbeing and then in a stroke of luck the phone rang. He left the room to answer it.

'He is hitting me,' she whispered, the moment he left. 'I need to get out.'

'OK,' I said. 'I might not be able to do something right now but I can get you the right information.'

Within minutes he was back in the room and I saw her visibly tense.

'The baby is doing fine!' I smiled.

When he wandered out again I quickly asked, 'Is there anyone you can speak to?'

'I can't!' she said.

'I'm listening to what you're saying but we can't discuss it here,' I said, knowing that it was too risky to give her any leaflets. 'Come up to the clinic when he has a work appointment. Tell him we need to see you to speak about breastfeeding information.'

A week later she came up to the clinic and I called in a health visitor to help. Quickly we went through a plan.

'These are your options,' I said. 'There's a women's refuge not far away that you can go to. Are you feeling that you can do that?'

She nodded and we agreed that a social worker could take her there but she would have to go with the clothes she stood in. There was no going back in case he returned.

But although we set her up with a place at the refuge, at the last moment she changed her mind.

'No, I'm not going,' she said. Sadly that is often the case with abused women. They are so terrified that they think they can't do it. But if they can't protect themselves, how are they going to protect their baby?

Unfortunately, once the problem had been raised it did become a child protection issue.

'OK,' I said. 'I respect your decision but if your baby is born and your partner is violent towards it then it has to be protected. If you can't guarantee that then Social Services will intervene.'

Child Protection Orders are for women who do not make the right decisions for their children. If they don't protect their kids from violent partners then the children are removed from them, by law. It's difficult but I always had to think about protecting the children. As a midwife you have a huge duty of care.

It is also important to remember that child protection is everyone's responsibility. It cannot be ignored as it may have dire consequences. You only have to look at the Baby P case to see that.

Thankfully the system is getting better at acknowledging these kinds of concerns. Midwives have a definite child protection pathway of care and it must be followed and everything documented. It's always worth following up any concerns. And when you help get someone out of a bad domestic situation, you can see for yourself what a huge difference it makes.

Another girl, Eva, caused alarm bells to ring when she failed to turn up to the booking appointment for her second child. When I eventually got to meet her she came in with her husband. I ran through the usual questions.

'What about your diet?' I asked.

'Oh well, I've probably not been very good but I'll try . . .' Eva began.

'I told her she eats a load of rubbish,' her husband interrupted.

Every time she began to say something in her bubbly way, he would interrupt and put her down.

'She's fat but I still love her,' he said, while she looked at the floor. 'Nobody else would!'

'She's not fat! She's pregnant!' I protested.

There was no laughing and joking between them and from the non-verbal cues I picked up she seemed absolutely terrified.

I made an appointment for her to see me at clinic and once again he was in tow with their little boy. I just had this very uncomfortable feeling. Whenever he spoke their child moved away.

Then it started to become really hard to get hold of her. When I popped around to their home he would answer the door.

'She's not in,' he'd claim.

'Can I leave a note?' I'd ask. 'OK,' he'd reluctantly agree, but I just knew he wouldn't be passing it on.

Then one day she answered the door with a black eye.

'What have you done to your eye?' I asked.

Suddenly the husband appeared from behind her.

'Oh, she's so clumsy! She tripped over and banged into the door handle!'

'Is that what happened?' I asked Eva.

'Yeah,' she said meekly. As the pregnancy progressed she was becoming more and more subdued. But I couldn't get her on her own. When I raised my concerns with her GP he said the same.

So in the end I had to be clever about how I did it. One day when Eva was taking her little boy to have a check with the health visitor I managed to have a conversation with her.

'I'm concerned about you and I'm going to have to be direct,' I said. 'Has your partner been violent towards you?'

She gave a sad little nod.

'Is it something you want to get out of?'

She nodded again.

'I can give you a telephone number but I won't write any names,' I said. 'If you need to get out immediately you can call this number.'

She went off and the next time I saw her, the husband was away for the weekend. He had left his mam to keep an eye on her. When her mother-in-law was out the room I asked if she'd thought about leaving.

'I'm terrified,' she said. 'He'll kill us!'

At that moment the mother-in-law walked in the room.

'I've told her to get out of the situation,' she said. 'If she doesn't, he'll kill her.'

'Sorry?' I said, quite shocked by this turn of events.

'The only person he will listen to is me. He will destroy her,' she added. 'If she doesn't get out of it he will kill her.'

'Are you listening to what she is saying?' I asked the girl incredulously. 'This is his mam! We've got to get you help. You have another child here! I'm going to introduce you to the health visitor, a social worker and child protection.'

With the mother-in-law's support we managed to act straight away. I took her and her little boy to the women's refuge with all the clothes they could pack.

I visited her in the refuge a few times over the next fortnight. It's quite harrowing to see women there. It was almost like they were in prison. It was just a very basic house supported by charities and Women's Aid.

But in a great outcome, she got rehoused and never went back to him.

The nicest thing for me was seeing Eva find her confidence again. She went from being subdued back to her old bubbly self. She rebuilt a life and you could see her personality starting to come back. Her little boy came out his shell too.

In 1999 an advert came out that offered the opportunity to undertake training to become a supervisor of midwives.

This is a role created through the nursing and midwifery council, which had decreed that every midwife must have a named supervisor. The supervisor is there to develop and maintain safe practice, protect the public (the mother, baby and family) and work regularly with midwives to ensure a high standard of care is provided. If you wanted to apply to do the six-month course, you would put your name forward and you'd have to be elected by other midwives.

It's a role that you're not necessarily given any extra allocated time to do and the supervisor would be expected to carry out many of her duties in her own time. Yet it was something I was interested in taking on, as I liked the idea of supporting other midwives. I also thought it was a good opportunity to get further training, as the role gives you a lot of information about setting standards and a huge insight into the law.

I put my name forward and had to submit a 2,000-word assignment on what I felt I would get out of the role and how it would affect my practice.

Well, to my great delight I was given the placement. This meant I was able to attend lots of meetings within the hospital, which gave me great insight into management strategies to minimise risk in healthcare. I even got to ask the chief executive a few questions and inform him of the role of a supervisor of midwives.

With my training complete I faced my first week being on call as a supervisor. I was quite nervous thinking about all the potential things that could go wrong but my manager, Mrs M, told me not to worry.

'It's very unlikely you'll get called about anything,' she said.

Well, actually I got called out two times. Famous last words or what?

The first night I got alerted was the Friday, when a community midwife called to say she was at a home birth where she'd advised the mother to come into hospital but she was steadfastly refusing. So at 2 a.m., I quickly got dressed and headed out to try and mediate.

The midwife was concerned after the woman's waters had broken and there was meconium visible (from the baby opening its bowels), which indicated the baby could be in distress. But the woman didn't want to go into hospital and took a lot of persuading.

Home births are fantastic for low-risk women but when that safety is no longer guaranteed things have to change. Eventually she agreed to go to the hospital and when the baby was born it was discovered that it had swallowed some of the meconium and needed some resuscitation to clear the airway. In the end the mother was very grateful that we'd persuaded her to come in.

On the following night, a Saturday, as I settled down for a lazy night in, watching TV in my pyjamas, I hoped that was my lot. No such luck. The next call was about a woman with a high-risk pregnancy who had discharged herself into the community.

Afterwards I called Mrs M, my manager, to fill her in ready for the Monday morning.

'Hi, Maria,' she said. 'How are you getting on?'

'Well, remember when you said I would never get called out?' I sighed.

Although I had no more call outs that week it was certainly an indication of things to come. After that I was always being called. I had made a rod for my own back.

On top of being a supervisor I was on call twice a week as a community midwife for home births.

One cold evening I got a call at about 7 p.m. to a harrowing situation. A girl aged about sixteen had concealed her pregnancy and had given birth in her bedroom but she was only twenty-six weeks pregnant.

Just before she delivered her mam had called the family doctor because she could see her daughter was experiencing crippling stomach pains.

'These pains are coming on and off. Are you pregnant?' she'd asked.

The girl had insisted she wasn't but had promptly given birth. The baby was premature and breech, and didn't survive.

When I got there I was ushered in quietly, as the girl and her mum were adamant her father shouldn't know. He had a serious lung problem and they were terrified his condition would worsen if he were stressed. They did break it to him gently later that week. He was devastated and I think the girl's mother felt really guilty.

The girl had managed to hide her bump with baggy jumpers but looking back her mum said there were so many signs that she felt she hadn't picked up on. She was just really upset that her daughter had felt she couldn't tell her.

But the reality was the girl was just trying to protect her dad. The family had already been through a hard time and didn't want to cause him further problems. In the end they really pulled together and the girl was very well supported.

It was a heartbreaking situation and it was hard not to be affected by it. In theory, as a midwife you should remain professional and not cross the line of emotional attachment but inevitably it happens from time to time.

I remember a sweet girl named Malika, aged twenty-four, who was living in Gateshead having fled Pakistan with her four-year-old daughter.

In the most tragic set of circumstances her husband had committed suicide and his family, viewing it as her fault, had thrown her out onto the streets. They said she had brought shame on the family.

After living on the streets in a lot of danger she'd got help from a religious group who'd brought her over to London. She was a beautiful girl but very vulnerable, and when a man befriended her she thought she could trust him. Instead she'd been raped and had fallen pregnant.

She fled up to Gateshead with absolutely nothing and arrived at a homeless shelter. When I met her, at twenty weeks pregnant, she had been given a one-bedroom flat. It was clear when I arrived that she'd scrubbed that flat from top to bottom before my visit. She was really quite subdued but very pleased to see somebody.

She had the bare minimum: just a mattress on the floor to sleep on, two plates to eat off and a can to boil water and make rice. Yet she never complained.

There was something about her that really broke my heart. She'd been through so much and was such a vulnerable person.

She didn't have a thing for her baby so I went out and bought a load of stuff for her and collected some clothes from mums in the community who no longer needed them. Over time I became really quite friendly with her and helped to get her little girl into school.

Every time I saw her she was so optimistic and grateful for what she had.

'I have biscuits today, Maria!' she'd tell me when I arrived to check on her.

She had to go to numerous interviews with the Home Office to make sure she was genuine so she had to keep telling her story over and over again which must have been very gruelling. I used to call her to see how she was.

She would sometimes ask me, 'What if they send me back?' If that had happened then she would never have survived.

I can't tell you how overjoyed she was every time they said she could stay for a few more months. It put a lot of stress on her while she was pregnant but eventually she was granted asylum seeker status.

When I broached the subject of what she would do when she went into labour with her second child, she said she was going to walk to the telephone box with her little girl and call for an ambulance.

I wasn't very happy with that. It wasn't a safe area she lived in and I didn't want her wandering the streets late at night in labour. Eventually I managed to get a mobile phone with some credit on it through social services.

She was very concerned about what would happen to her daughter while she was giving birth so I also arranged to get her daughter into foster care for one day.

In the end she gave birth to a beautiful boy and was really accepting and delighted with him, despite the fact he was conceived in such difficult circumstances.

Two weeks after her baby was born, another flat came up in a better area, near a park. By now I'd managed to source her a pram and I also set about introducing her to other people in the area.

I think it was a big thing for her to try and forget the past and make a new life for herself. Some days she would get very quiet and seem quite sad and reflective but other days she was fine. It was really hard when the time came for me to discharge her but she was fine and happy. After that I still popped in for a cup of tea whenever I could and I saw her baby growing up.

Of course not everyone is as hard done by as they might suggest.

I remember visiting one refugee family who claimed they had absolutely nothing but something about them made me wonder if they were telling me the full story. They seemed to have a fair few things in their flat but insisted they couldn't afford to buy a cot. I said I would see what I could do and the health visitor and I left together, stopping outside the building for a chat.

Bidding each other goodbye, we both headed for our individual cars: I had my little Peugeot and she had her battered old Fiesta. At that moment the father we had just met came down and, clicking his keyfob, walked over to a big, shiny, souped-up BMW!

The health visitor and I both looked at each other. You should have seen his face. As he spotted us observing him, you could literally read his mind as he thought, 'There goes the cot . . .'

We were just laughing. The majority of people are genuine but sometimes you do wonder if you are being taken for a ride. Unfortunately some people really do work the system.

Chapter Eleven

Fireworks exploded in the sky, crowds cheered and cries of 'Happy New Year!' rang out.

The Millennium was here and it was time to make some serious vows.

'I'm not changing me for anyone,' I decided, as singing filled the air.

Just four days earlier I'd called it off with my latest boyfriend, a guy called Danny who I'd been seeing for six months. I'd decided there was no way I was going into the Millennium still dating him, so on 27 December I broke up with him! I'd had enough of going out on dates and being taken for granted.

Nights out in 'the toon' were also to be knocked on the head.

'I'm sick of always seeing the same people and going to the same places,' I thought. 'Maybe I'll take a job abroad or take a career break to go travelling.'

At work I still had so much going on. I was a leader for a community team with a caseload of women from five GP practices. I was a supervisor of midwives with eighteen midwives to oversee. I ran breastfeeding workshops and parentcraft sessions at the hospital. And as I had been studying for a postgraduate diploma in education to become a midwifery lecturer – or 'practice educator' as it is now titled – I was also teaching at the University of Northumbria and in a clinical setting. I even had an opportunity to work in a higher education institution for fifteen-year-olds. If I'd thought that teaching some of the midwives could be tricky, this was something else. The most challenging part of the lessons was to get them to stop reading the *Metro* newspaper.

There were big changes afoot on a national level too. While I was working in Gateshead a new initiative was introduced nationally under Labour known as the Sure Start programme. The goal was to address inequalities in access to healthcare services for vulnerable and disadvantaged women. It was all about providing better support for families and children who wouldn't necessarily have the means or the know-how to improve their health and life chances. It also aimed to promote childbirth as a natural process by educating women, teaching breathing exercises and other natural pain-relief techniques, and encouraging mobility during labour.

It was a really big success across the whole of Britain and suddenly a lot of money was injected into maternity services. It meant that the QE were able to fund another midwife who was specifically there as a support to other midwives. Now if we had a woman who needed extra help we could refer her to this midwife for help. If a mum wanted to quit smoking in pregnancy she would go and visit her at home, or she would provide extra support if the mum wanted to eat more healthily in pregnancy, especially if she was overweight, so as to reduce the complications associated with this.

There was a Sure Start maternity grant for women on benefits or low income where they'd be given £500 if they attended all their antenatal clinics. It made a lot of women attend when they wouldn't ordinarily and gave us a chance to promote things like healthy eating.

I remember one young girl of about eighteen I saw at the clinic. She was a tiny little thing, about twenty-one weeks pregnant, but I was concerned she looked a little scrawny.

'Tell me about yourself,' I said. 'What have you eaten today?'

'I've had two custard creams,' she said.

'Have you eaten anything else?'

'Um, a packet of crisps.'

'Anything for your lunch?'

She thought for a moment.

'Another couple of custard creams,' she finally said.

'What will you have later?' I asked.

'I dunno,' she said, shrugging her shoulders.

It was clear she really didn't understand about her diet but it was important that I didn't just dive in and criticise.

I repeated the food list back to her.

'Is that a usual day's diet?' I asked.

'I sometimes have bourbons,' she said.

'How are you feeling?' I asked.

'Sometimes I feel really dizzy,' she said.

'Do you think that might have something to do with what you're eating?' I asked.

'Oh, right,' she said. 'What should I be eating?'

I showed her a range of plastic foods on a plate to give her an idea: fruit, fish, potato and broccoli, and explained that you could cook that sort of food on a budget price.

The next time I saw her I asked her what she'd eaten.

'Um, custard creams,' she admitted. 'But a banana as well!'

With girls like her it was all about guiding her gently in the right direction.

Walking into one house to meet an expectant mother I was

greeted by a lady called Linda, who was about thirty-three years old and overweight with dark hair. Her boyfriend was tall and gangly, with a ready smile.

To my dismay the booking interview took more than two hours, as there were just so many issues to work through.

'We advise that you don't drink,' I said. 'Have you had any alcohol units recently?'

'Maybe a few,' she said.

'No no no, that's not right!' he piped up. 'What about the eight bottles of Smirnoff you had last night? Is that not alcohol?'

'What about smoking?' I enquired.

'I only have a couple. I'm trying to cut down,' she said.

She was interrupted by coughing.

'A couple of packets, more like!' he scoffed.

'Well, you need to try and quit if you can,' I said.

Moving on, I asked what type of birth they wanted.

'I was thinking I wouldn't mind a water birth,' Linda said.

'Oh, hold on a minute,' her boyfriend added, dashing out the room. He returned with a box with a picture of a padding pool on it.

'What's that?' I asked.

'I was thinking I could deliver in that!' she exclaimed.

'You cannae deliver in a paddling pool!' I told her.

Her face fell. 'Why not? I got it at the market. I thought that would be handy!'

'No.'

I got on really well with both of them: their hearts were in the right place but I was quite concerned about their ability to look after a baby. If it wasn't so serious it would have been funny.

The next time I went to see Linda I parked up to see her hanging out the window puffing on a fag like it was the last cigarette of her life. When it was done she was straight on to another one.

Walking up the path to the door I knocked.

She greeted me with a smile and we went through to the lounge.

'How are you getting on with your smoking?' I asked.

'I've not had any today.'

'But I've just seen you smoking two!' I said.

Her will was there but the fact that they both had slight learning difficulties worried me. I built up a strong relationship with her and with her permission I did incorporate social services into her antenatal care. We got them onto this really intense programme teaching them parenting skills and she was given support to give up smoking, although it had to be spelled out that if she didn't stop smoking and drinking then she would not be able to take her baby home.

When she went into labour she had her baby really quickly but she was kept in hospital for a week so that her parenting skills could be observed and she could get the help she needed. This was a very positive outcome, as before Sure Start she would almost certainly have had her baby taken off her.

I could never see any disadvantages of the programme and I honestly don't know how some women could have coped without it. These days they are trying to cut Sure Start programmes all over country but if you take away these lifelines in vulnerable areas then things are going to be a lot worse.

In 2001 my friend Kim had decided to be a midwife for the RAF and was trying to convince me to do the same. Having completed her training she encouraged me to come to her graduation and passing out ceremony, which was to take place at RAF Cranwell.

I'd gone feeling optimistic and excited about the prospect of following in her footsteps. But when I got to the ceremony I found it all a bit strange.

You couldn't walk into certain areas unless you were an officer and people kept referring to me as a 'civilian'. It was all a bit jolly hockey sticks and I was disappointed.

I stayed overnight and, somewhat deflated, I headed home the following day. That night my friend Lesley suggested a night out in Newcastle.

'Nah, I'm staying in,' I told her. 'I can't face the quayside. I'm sick of it!'

'Oh come on! Let's go out,' she insisted.

So we went to a pub and then on to a club called Sea.

'See, you're having a good time, aren't you?' Lesley said as we hit the dancefloor.

'Yes!' I agreed, grinning. At that moment I saw a tall, slim guy with brown hair stood near the dancefloor. He caught my eye and smiled and then he came over to speak to me.

'Hi, I'm Michael,' he said.

He had a very soft Scottish accent and immediately I thought there was something about him that I liked. He had these big brown eyes that twinkled and I could see he had a good sense of humour.

'What ya doing in here?' I asked.

Michael explained he was from Lairg, an hour north of Inverness, and was with a group of lads who'd been watching Scotland in Belgium. They'd hired a camper van and driven to Belgium via Calais.

But on their way home to Scotland on the A1 they'd had a problem. The wheel of their van was damaged and they had to stop off to get it fixed. There had been some discussion about whether to carry on to Edinburgh or not. But eventually they'd settled on stopping in Newcastle and had headed out for the night. They'd originally queued for a different nightclub over the road but some of the lads didn't have the right footwear so they had come over the road to Sea.

The story made me laugh and he was witty and friendly. He had an answer for everything I said.

We spoke for a while, had a dance and then I went back to my friends to chat. As the night finished we chatted outside, had a quick kiss on the cheek and he asked me for my number.

'Sooo?' my friend Lesley teased the next day.

'He lives in Scotland!' I protested. 'I'm not ringing him!'

Then when I didn't hear from him by mid-week I assumed that would be it.

Meanwhile, shocking events were unfolding.

I was in my flat watching TV when a news report flashed up that a plane had flown into one of the Twin Towers in New York. Shortly after, the same thing happened to the other tower.

I couldn't move from my chair. It was unbelievable.

I rang Mam to see if she was watching the news and then headed round to hers. That Sunday I was booked to fly to Cyprus to see Kim, who was posted over there with the RAF.

'You're not going to go, are you?' Mam asked.

'Of course I am,' I said.

On the Sunday I was just finishing off my packing when the phone rang.

'Hi, Maria?' a Scottish accent asked. 'It's Michael.'

'Oh,' I said. 'Thanks for ringing but I'm really sorry but I can't speak for long at the moment – I am leaving now to go to Cyprus! Can I call you when I get back?'

He later told me that he'd had a huge dilemma as to whether to ring me or not, but his brother told him, 'What have you got to lose?'

So after wading through all the high security at Newcastle airport I boarded the plane, arriving in Cyprus five hours later for what would be a very entertaining week hanging out with Kim. The base was on 'red security', which is a very high state of alert, but we still got to have lots of fun.

The RAF base had fantastic beaches and one day as Kim was walking across the beach I saw her stop and salute her commander who was also there.

'Did you just salute him in your bikini?' I teased.

'Yes! I have to!' she said.

'What? Even on the beach?'

'Er . . . yes,' she said, sounding less convinced by the moment.

Well, back at the mess later all her friends fell about laughing.

'Oh well, he won't forget that,' one said as Kim blushed.

We all nodded in agreement; Kim was very pretty!

Back in Newcastle I called Michael and we talked on the phone for ages.

After that we spoke for weeks on the phone and then the natural progression seemed to be that I should invite him down to Newcastle. It was quite a big step having him to stay but I had a good feeling about him and generally I'm quite a good judge of character.

Mam was very excited.

'I'll have to meet him!' she said.

'No, you'll not!'

When I relayed this back to my friend Lesley she laughed.

'So Sheila is not going to meet him? Yeah, tell me that again at the end of the weekend.'

So first thing on the Saturday Michael drove down.

I spotted him pulling up and dashed into the back yard in a fit of panic. 'What am I doing?' I wondered. 'I can't be dealing with this!'

But the nerves in my tummy soon diminished when I went back inside and saw that he was still trying to park his car. I couldn't believe how long it took him in a nearly empty street!

He eventually made it down the path and I made him a cup of tea when he came in. As before, we just hit it off straight away.

My dad had kindly given us his tickets to Saturday's Newcastle match but I'd forgotten to pick them up, so the following morning I drove round on my own to collect them.

'How's it going?' Mam asked, the minute I got through the door.

'Fine,' I replied.

'Am I going to meet him?'

'No.'

She thought for a moment. 'I need to go into Newcastle today,' she said. 'Can you give me a lift?'

I raised my eyebrows.

'I'll not say anything!' she insisted.

'OK,' I sighed. 'You can sit in the front but don't ask him any questions!'

So, heading back to mine, we picked Michael up and I introduced them. Immediately, Mam was turning around in her seat, chatting away.

'So, where do you live, Michael?' she asked. 'Tell me about your family . . .'

'Mam!' I said. 'Are you going to put your seatbelt on or are you not bothered?'

Just at that moment, as we were coming on to the sliproad, another car pulled up alongside us. It was Lesley. She looked in our window and, seeing Mam, she nearly crashed her car laughing.

'I told you so!' she mouthed, shaking her head.

As soon as I got into town I pulled the car up, bringing Mam's interrogation to an end.

'What, here?' she said, looking despondent.

'Yes, get out!' I demanded.

'Lovely to meet you, Michael,' she chirped as I practically pushed her out the door.

Poor Michael: as if meeting my mam wasn't enough of a baptism of fire, he then had to sit next to my brother Peter at the match as well.

As I looked over at the two of them chatting away and getting on famously I suddenly felt a bit freaked out. It was all going so well!

After that weekend I just knew. But I was also very hesitant. '*I* feel like this but does he?' I wondered.

Well, I must have done something right as after that he invited me up to Inverness.

'How long will it take to drive?' I asked.

'Six hours,' he said.

'What? Can't I fly?'

So I went to the travel agent and booked a flight to Aberdeen for the Friday night. When he picked me up at the airport I jumped in the passenger seat, all excited.

'Are we going out tonight?' I asked. 'How long will it take to get back?'

'Oh, about two and a half hours,' he said.

'Oh my goodness!' I said, clasping my hand over my mouth.

'It's fine!' he laughed.

I soon learnt that living up there he thought nothing of driving for two and a half hours.

That New Year, Michael came to Newcastle and spent it with all the family. There was Mam, Dad, my brother Michael and his girlfriend Julie, Peter and his wife Alison, Christopher, me and Michael. It was great that he got on so well with my family. 'This is too good to be true,' I thought.

I noticed Dad watching us.

'You cannot fit a Rizla paper between you two!' he remarked.

I didn't want to let on too much but I was feeling really happy.

A few weeks later I was in the car with my younger brother, Michael.

'How's the romance?' he asked.

'Great,' I confirmed.

'And?'

'Oh well, I'm going to marry him!' I blurted out.

Michael nearly crashed the car. In fact he pulled over.

'Hang on!' he remarked. 'You've only known him five minutes!'

'I just know,' I said.

His girlfriend Julie was in the back just howling with laughter.

Meanwhile there were other developments in the family. In February 2002 my brother Peter and his wife Alison were expecting their first baby. Peter and Alison lived in a cottage around the corner with their dog Patch so I'd pop round when I could and listen to the baby's heart rate to reassure her.

One Saturday they called.

'Fancy a coffee in about five minutes?' Peter suggested.

'Why, what's happening?' I asked.

'Alison is having a few pains.'

'OK, I'm leaving now.'

When I walked into the cottage Peter was in the kitchen. I found Alison in the bedroom, very established in labour. It was clear her contractions were coming one after the other.

'They're getting a bit strong now,' she admitted, before wandering into the other room.

'What's the plan, Peter?' I asked.

'Stay here for a little longer?' he shrugged.

'Can I change your plan a bit?' I said. 'Go downstairs, ring the hospital and tell them you are bringing Alison in now. I'll get her ready. She is well in her labour.'

I hurried them outside. Thankfully the hospital was only five minutes away. We got her in the car and Peter raced off to the maternity unit.

A while later I'd heard nothing so I rang up.

'My sister-in-law is in,' I said. 'I'm just wondering is she all right.'

'She's fine. She is fully dilated and ready to have her baby,' they said.

For the next few hours I paced the flat, frantically washing my floor. I couldn't believe how nervous I felt.

Then the phone rang.

'SHE'S HAD A BABY!' Peter announced comically. 'A girl! She's gorgeous!'

I nipped in for a few minutes later to meet baby Nicole. I'd never seen Peter look so elated.

With things going well, I continued to go to Scotland whenever I could and Michael came down to see me when possible.

I was very busy at work as usual and also giving some lectures at the University of Northumbria on midwifery courses. I got involved with teaching on degree courses to student midwives and also teaching experienced midwives as part of their continuing professional development. In addition, I was still running breast-feeding workshops with Lynne.

But after a year and a half the long distance was taking its toll. Something had to change.

Then a staff midwife job came up at the local hospital, Raigmore, in Inverness. It felt like a sign. I managed to get an interview for a Friday and immediately started swotting up on Scottish health care.

The interview went well and was quite informal. They were more interested in what I had done and checking that I was confident as a midwife.

'Do you have any questions?' Sister Rowntree asked.

So I asked loads of questions about Highlands policy.

'I think you know more than we do!' she laughed.

With the interview over they explained that I'd be likely to hear on the Monday.

Feeling that I'd done the best I could, I walked across the hospital to my car. Just as I was searching for my car keys in my bag, my phone went. It was Sister Rowntree.

'We've made a decision,' she said. 'We'd like to offer you the job.'

Oh my God, I was moving up to Inverness!

Back at Michael's I kept up my poker face.

'How did it go?' he asked.

'Yes, it went very well actually,' I said, then paused, '. . . In fact, they offered me the job!'

'You're joking!' he said, his face morphing into a big grin. We were both very happy but aware of the big step we were taking.

I immediately went home and put my flat on the market. It was sold within a week. Then I began to sort through all my belongings ready for my big move.

It was a nightmare as I am such a bad hoarder but reluctantly I got rid of my furniture, filled up a van and drove up to Inverness.

Poor Michael: his house was immaculate and perfect and then I just filled it with all my stuff. It drove him mad and I felt like I'd completely invaded his space. A month in and it was all getting very tense. Then I found a funny book called *Living Together*, which listed the rules of first moving in together. There were his and her sections on every subject. We had a lot of fun pointing out the pages that struck a chord to each other.

I really wanted us to sell and buy somewhere together so when I saw an advert in the paper for new-build houses for sale in Inverness I persuaded Michael to go along for a look.

You had to say then and there if you wanted it. Luckily we both said yes, as we both loved the look of the house and it was in a perfect location for us. We went back and put Michael's house on the market and waited until we were ready to move.

Meanwhile, I needed to settle into my new role at Raigmore. My job in Inverness was a step down but after all the responsibility I'd had in Newcastle over the last few years I was quite relieved to have a breather.

Everyone was very friendly and women who had their babies were lovely. It was a much calmer place to work and the women seemed a lot more laid back.

It was very different from London and Newcastle. A few days

in I had just delivered a lady's baby and had popped outside to clean up my top and make her tea and toast when the midwife in charge came over.

'How are you getting on?'

'Yeah, fine,' I said. 'She had a very straightforward delivery. I'm just sorting her out with something to eat and drink.'

'Has she delivered the baby?' she said, looking surprised.

'Yes, about five minutes ago.'

'But you didn't call anybody?' she confirmed. 'You do know we always have a second midwife at every delivery?'

I shook my head, amazed that they had the staff to do it.

'Just before the birth you tell the person in charge and another midwife comes in with you to help,' she reiterated. 'We always have an extra person.'

What a privilege for the women! There didn't seem to be as many complications either and ninety-nine per cent of women got one-on-one care from a midwife all through their labour.

No wonder that I've since heard stories about people who get a temporary address in the Highlands just so they can come up and have their baby there.

However, working up in the highlands of Scotland brought its own difficulties. In my first week a lady came in with twinges.

'You're not really in labour,' I explained. 'I'd suggest you go home for a couple of hours.'

She looked at me like I was insane.

'But I live in Skye,' she said.

'How far away is it?' I asked.

'Over three hours!' she exclaimed.

I just didn't appreciate the geography at all and had to look Skye up on the map.

A bit later in the week one of the community midwives from another remote spot called in. A howling wind battered down the receiver as she struggled to get her words out.

'Please can you give me the bleep number for the doctor on call?' she shouted.

I started reading out the number when suddenly I heard a cry of 'Agghh!' and the phone went dead.

A minute later the phone rang once more.

'It's me again,' she said. 'Sorry, I fell off my bike.'

I felt like I'd been propelled back to the 1950s.

'Are community midwives always on bikes here?' I asked one of my colleagues, trying to sound casual.

'Oh, Maria,' my colleague Karen sighed. 'No, they're not normally on bikes!'

My next task was to call a woman who hadn't come in to be induced.

'I can't,' she said grouchily in a thick Scottish accent.

'Why?'

'I'm feeding my animals,' she snapped. 'I'll come in later.' Then she hung up.

'Well, I've heard it all now!' I thought.

Seeing as all the other staff were local they had an absolute field day laughing at my pathetic attempts to pronounce the names of Highlands places.

One day I was in a meeting when I announced that my patient was going home to Kinmylies, or 'King-a-mer-lies' as I pronounced it.

Everyone in the meeting was hysterical.

'What?' I asked.

It was only at the end that someone came up and told me it's actually pronounced 'King-my-lee'.

I thought that was the end of it until one of the other midwives wandered over to me later.

'Do you fancy going for a coffee?' she said.

'Where?' I said.

'Well, you've just started so I thought it would be nice to take you somewhere you've never been. I hear there's a nice coffee shop in King-a-mer-lies.'

Ha-bloody-ha! I must admit, though, it totally broke the ice with me starting there.

Generally the maternity unit had a really nice atmosphere and I started to learn the geography of the area I was living in. I was gradually starting to feel at home in Scotland. I spent my days off sorting out the flat and trying to rummage through my belongings to see if I could declutter them. I did meet a couple of midwives out of work but really I just kept my head down until I got the house sorted out.

There were some real characters at Raigmore, especially the older midwives coming up for retirement.

One, a lady called Effie, was hilarious. She was about sixty and was a very smart woman. She'd constantly laugh at my accent.

'I need to try to teach you Gaelic, Maria,' she'd say, before springing these tongue twisters on me. As I pronounced them badly she'd laugh hysterically as apparently often what I was saying had a very different meaning.

I'd always enjoy chatting to her as I came in for the morning shift and she was finishing on nights.

'Good morning, girls,' she'd say, addressing us all. 'I've told the women they're going to get a nice bunch of fresh faces so you better shake yourselves up.'

She also had a big thing about babies' names.

'You'll never guess what we had a baby called overnight,' she'd whisper incredulously. 'Kylie! I mean, Kylie – in the Highlands?! I told them, "What ever on earth are you calling your baby Kylie for in the Highlands? Get yourself to Australia! That is where they call babies Kylie."' She had us all in stitches.

In October 2003 we moved into our new home, which was incredibly exciting.

Michael wisely gave me full rein to decorate so Mam arranged to come up and help.

During the course of the day I was dismayed to feel a nasty headache coming on. I never suffered from them normally. By midnight I was sitting in bed with the pain getting worse and worse.

Then, without warning, my vision went. It was a sudden onset and very painful. Now all I could see were shadows and nothing else.

Michael phoned NHS Direct who said I should go to hospital in an ambulance. But I was embarrassed as I'd only just moved there, so I made Michael drive me.

When we got to the hospital I promptly fell out the car onto the pavement. I still couldn't see anything. Scooping me up, Michael guided me inside.

The staff immediately found me a bed in a mixed ward. I lay there feeling completely bewildered. From a bed nearby, I could hear someone coughing. It didn't sound like a woman and I felt so vulnerable. I had a heightened awareness of what was going on around me. It is amazing how other senses come into play.

When the doctor came over I could hear them discussing lumber puncture but nobody directly told me what was happening. I was too ill to make a fuss.

The next few days passed in a blur of tests as I slipped in and out of sleep. I was given intravenous antibiotics and then after twenty-four hours my sight came back, which was an enormous relief. But I still felt really unwell.

After four days I was told I'd be allowed to go home but I needed to come back and get my bloods tested again. I got the sense I wasn't being told the full story.

I pleaded with the nurse to tell me what was going on.

'All I know is your white cells came up as less than one,' she said. My heart was immediately in my mouth. I knew that white blood cells were needed to fight infection. When they diminished this rapidly it can be associated with disorders of the blood. 'Oh God, I could have leukemia or something,' I thought.

The doctor was implying they'd have to do further investigations and my life just flashed in front of my eyes.

When Michael came to collect me I insisted he take me into town.

'I need to buy a new pair of shoes,' I said.

He thought I was mad, especially when I bought the first pair I saw, but I needed to do something normal.

The next week was the longest week ever. We carried on getting things done at our new house, getting blinds fitted, furniture organised and so on. Every salesman who arrived at the house to show us something must have thought I was the most laid-back person in the world. I would take the first thing they offered, as I just wanted them to go away.

Meanwhile I had to go back to hospital every day to get my bloods checked. The apprehension was awful.

Every day we would get the results back and eventually my white cell count had gone up one. It was a huge relief, as step by step it headed in the right direction. It took a full six months to go back to normal.

When I went back to the consultant he told me he believed I'd had a viral infection that had affected my blood results, but he thought I'd be fine from now on.

'You just need to take it easy,' he said. 'Make sure you get lots of sleep to allow your body to recover.'

It was such a scary time and it really made me evaluate my life. Even now, whenever I hear people are waiting to get results I feel a bit ill for them, as I know it is the worst feeling. However, I just had to pick myself up and get on with it.

It was really difficult when I went back to work. I felt so worn out – not that I let on. I was still quite new in my job and I felt embarrassed that I'd already had some time off.

I was quite grateful when Christmas arrived. I spent it back home at Mam's for her yearly festive party with all the family.

When the girls at work asked what I had planned for the New Year I revealed it would probably be a quiet one but that Michael had said we were going away for a few days in January.

'Ooh, bet he's going to do something!' they speculated.

'Oh, I don't know,' I said, a little embarrassed.

It was all very mysterious. We were going away on 6 January.

'I'm not telling you where but you need to pack some warm clothes and some really nice ones,' he said.

So there I was, pulling everything out the wardrobe.

'Yes, maybe that but a bit more dressy,' he'd say. In the end I packed loads.

We set off driving at 6 a.m. It was only when we started

turning off towards the airport that I realised we could be going abroad.

'Don't tell me we're getting on a plane?' I said. Grabbing my handbag, I started throwing stuff out: tweezers, nail scissors . . . My bag was not packed to go through security!

After we arrived at the airport, Michael marched me to a gate marked 'London'. 'Aw, lovely,' I thought.

But when we got off at Gatwick airport we didn't go and collect our bags.

'No, we're going a bit further,' he smiled.

The next departure gate said Venice. I didn't want to assume anything but this was proving to be some trip!

At Marco Polo airport, Michael ushered me onto a little luxury speedboat, which whizzed us through gorgeous canalside scenery. It was freezing cold but the skies were blue and bright. Quaint buildings in all different pastel colours passed by on either side of us. Venice really was something else.

Our destination was a secluded island, San Clemente, and my first glimpse of our hotel was breathtaking. It used to be a monastery and was grand and huge. When we parked up and I got to go ashore all I wanted was to run around in circles of excitement. It was just so beautiful.

Inside, the hotel was just as gorgeous, with a dramatic, old-world Venetian style. It was pure luxury. As we were shown up to our room I was just spellbound by all the decor. I'd never seen anything like it.

The first day Michael took me sightseeing. We visited all the hotspots and then sat in St Mark's Square, watching the world go by and enjoying a good bottle of wine.

That night, back at the hotel, Michael told me to get really dressed up so I put on a long blue dress and spent ages doing my make-up.

As we waited to be 'escorted down to dinner', as was the tradition, we sipped on wine.

'Will you get my phone out of the safe?' Michael asked.

As I leant in to grab it I saw a ring on top of a ring box. My stomach flipped.

'Oh my God!' I thought.

Grabbing his phone I passed it to him.

'Um, I wasn't really wanting my phone!' he said, reaching in himself to grab the ring. Then he got down on his knee.

'Will you marry me, Maria?' he asked.

I was speechless and ecstatic and of course immediately said yes! He revealed that he'd already got my dad's permission.

A few minutes later our escort, Luciano, knocked on the door to take us down to dinner. For some reason we were being led through the kitchen where all the chefs were running around cooking up a storm. Well, this is novel, I thought.

Suddenly the maître d' came running over. Apparently Luciano was new and had taken us the wrong way. Poor Luciano! Mind you, as far as I was concerned, nothing could go wrong that night. It was just perfect.

Back at work on the ward a few days later, I was immediately pounced on with screams of delight as my colleagues spied my sparkler.

'How did you not know?' they teased as I relayed my surprise.

'I didn't want to build it up in my head and then be disappointed,' I admitted.

'Well, he's a Scottish man, he's from good stock,' they said. 'We knew he wouldn't let you down!'

Michael and I wanted to get married that October, in just nine months time, so it was a case of hitting the floor running.

Immediately we managed to get a free date at St Paul's in Jarrow, one of the oldest churches in the country. It is a really famous church and people come from all over the world to see it.

Of course, Mam was falling over herself to help.

'We'll not run away with it,' she reassured me on the phone. 'We'll just be sensible.'

'OK,' I agreed.

'Well,' she added, 'so I know a girl about the flowers, there's Joanne for the cake and you'll have to get down here pretty quickly for the dress. Will you get a dress in that space of time? Have you thought about the bridesmaids yet?'

Her voice was getting higher and faster by the second.

'You'll have to have the nieces as flower girls,' she continued. 'Katie Watson got married the other week and she had six bridesmaids! We'll put together a folder. Anyway I'm not getting too involved – you'll make all the decisions . . .'

'Yes, Mam!'

To be fair, having seen Peter marry Alison and Michael marry Julie two summers earlier, I think Mam just could not contain her excitement at finally being the mother of the bride.

A few weeks later we invited Mam and Dad up to Scotland to meet Michael's parents. It was a certainly a culture shock compared to what they'd been used to in Newcastle.

Michael had first taken me to meet his parents, who lived an hour from Lairg, in early 2002. Like Mam and Dad, I'd been quite surprised by just how rural it was. Michael's dad had a farm that had been converted into a croft and it was in a very rural area where they farmed sheep and other animals. But Sandy and Stella made me feel very welcome from our first introduction, which was a relief.

That weekend, Michael had told me we were going to a party in the village hall so I'd got dressed up in a cocktail dress.

When I came downstairs his dad's jaw nearly hit the floor.

'Where you going now?' he asked.

'We're going down to the party in the village,' I said.

'Aye, well, they'll not be missing you,' he said.

Michael appeared in the doorway.

'Is it too much?' I questioned.

'No, you keep it on, it's lovely,' he said.

Of course I'd then arrived at the party and been the most over-dressed by a mile. Everyone else was in jeans.

'I need a drink now!' I said to Michael.

'Don't worry about that. It'll give them something to talk about!' he'd laughed.

Now, with Mam and Dad in the car, we pulled up at the farmhouse.

'I haven't seen any cars or people for miles,' she said. 'Is there even a corner shop? All I can see are sheep!'

'Sssh,' I chastised. 'We're not in Timbuktu!'

We'd been inside the farmhouse for five minutes when one of the lights started flickering.

Before anyone could protest, Dad grabbed a wooden chair. 'I'll fix it!' he announced. I think he was nervous and wanted something to do.

But as he stood on the chair, the whole thing literally shattered! He'd grabbed a broken chair that no one sat on. What a great first impression!

Eventually we sat down to eat and I noticed Mam was twitching a little bit.

'You OK, Mam?' I asked.

'Yeah,' she said unconvincingly.

'Is everything OK with the lamb?' Sandy, Michael's dad, asked.

'Is this fresh lamb?' Mam asked, to my utter dismay. 'All I can hear is the sheep in the fields.'

'No, no, no, it's not one of our sheep,' Sandy laughed. 'We got it from the butchers.'

'Oh God, my dad's broken the chair and now Mam is talking about eating the sheep!' I thought.

But Michael's mum and dad just fell about laughing. They all got on fine.

Later Mam asked if I was planning to buy a place around there.

'No!' I said.

'That's all right then,' she replied. I think she just felt uncomfortable as there was no street lighting and it was so pitch black. I reassured her that Inverness was small enough for me, let alone a village somewhere.

In any case, I was making progress at work in Inverness. When I'd come back to work after Michael's proposal I'd been interested to hear that a job had come up to work on the labour ward. This was an acting charge midwife post. Figuring that while I hadn't worked there very long I should at least try, I applied.

I was still on such a high from getting engaged that nothing was going to knock me down so I went into the interview feeling really positive. Afterwards I reflected that it seemed to have gone well. A week later I was offered the job!

'I'll give you a piece of advice: keep your head down and lie low,' Sister Rowntree told me.

'I've never done that in my life – but I'll try,' I said.

I knew that the other midwives really wanted to promote normal birth, something I too felt passionate about, so I suggested we could start a practice development group. I got the go-ahead from the management. My colleagues all seemed interested and lots of people came to the meetings with great ideas. Together with three other midwives, Fiona, Trish and Alison, we set up the group.

By now I was really beginning to appreciate the rural aspect of the hospital and the different situations that arose because of the geography of the area. The Highlands is the largest area in Scotland and is the least densely populated. It wasn't unusual for women to be airlifted in or to get a phone call about a woman having a home birth over 100 miles away from the hospital.

It was also not uncommon to deliver a baby in a car and recently we'd had that happen just outside the maternity unit.

I'd been alerted by the buzzer from the side entrance.

'Help! Help!' a man shouted. So I legged it downstairs, grabbing a pair of gloves on the way and shouting to the auxiliary nurse to get towels and get help.

The difficulty when you are delivering in a car is it is very hard to get in and to see what you are doing. If the woman is in the front you have to get the car seat back. You develop new skills and thankfully I was able to help the woman's baby to be born safely.

'It's the likes of women such as yourself coming from places like Lairg,' I told Michael's mum. 'People are delivering before they get to hospital!'

'Well, Michael was born in an ambulance!' she replied.

'Was I?' Michael piped up.

'I was having contractions and the midwife came out but they thought I had a while to go as it was my first baby,' she said. 'But when we got to Viewpoint we had to stop. I told them the head was coming out and they didn't believe me so I said, "What's that, then?" You were born a few minutes later!'

Michael and I looked at each other, completely gobsmacked. The Viewpoint layby was a big tourist spot because of the unbelievable view across the Highlands. We'd stopped there so many times to look out across the beautiful mountain scenery.

Travelling down to Newcastle in March I spent an exhausting day trawling various shops with Mam, looking for my wedding dress. It was nearing closing time when finally I stumbled upon the perfect one.

It was not at all what I expected – it was strapless with little pale blue gems on the bodice – but when I tried it on I knew instantly.

'This is it!' I said. Mam just nodded her head in agreement.

When I ordered it at the counter they said it was going to take six months so I picked it just in the nick of time.

'And I'm buying the dress!' Mam said proudly.

I wasn't expecting that at all.

'I've only got one daughter,' she said. 'Please let me buy your dress.'

We even picked out a tiara and I came out of that shop delighted.

'That's a good job done, pet,' Mam smiled.

Determined to tone up for my dress, I immediately started seeing a personal trainer. Very soon, I realised he was killing me. Every time I complained, he'd taunt me.

'You've got to get into your dress, Maria,' he'd say. 'You can do better than that! Dry your eyes!'

The thing I liked the most was the kickboxing. I'd do it before my early shift and really enjoyed letting off steam.

One day I was really giving it some welly when my personal trainer asked, 'Do you know her? There's someone looking through the window.'

I stopped in time to see one of my student midwives peering at me. She gave me a little nervous wave.

'She'll do as she's told now!' I laughed.

With my wedding dress in hand, my sister-in-law Julie started on my case about the hen do. She took on the full organisation with Lynne.

I didn't want a conventional hen do so I decided that a few of my friends and all the women in the family would go to Rome.

Sadly, my sister-in-law Alison couldn't come as her baby was due a week later.

'It's OK,' she said. 'Just make sure you have a drink for me!'

I continued to juggle the wedding preparations with a demanding role at work.

While it was tempting to put my career on the backburner until the wedding was out the way, I didn't have to think twice about applying for a permanent position as a senior charge midwife – which I got! This meant I would be responsible for the coordination of the labour ward and the out-of-hours maternity unit while on shift.

As the practice development group continued, the general consensus was that we should be promoting normal childbirth in the unit. The major hurdle was that we had no money to do this, so we applied for some funding for research through the hospital research department. We were successful and embarked on a clinical research project, which we presented as a poster at the International Confederation for Midwives in Glasgow in 2008.

We were clearly on to something, as not long after the Scottish government decided that they would provide funding to promote normal birth across Scotland. Their initiative 'Keeping Childbirth Natural and Dynamic' promoted everything we were already striving for with our ongoing changes to the unit.

Eventually, September arrived with myself and ten family and friends jetting off to Rome. Meanwhile Michael went to Barcelona with my brothers and his friends.

Arriving at our hotel everyone got ready to go out and as we congregated in the reception I noticed Julie had a twinkle in her eye.

'Julie, you're not going to do anything, are you?' I warned.

'You'll just have to wait and see,' she grinned.

She told me to get in a taxi and we headed off to a restaurant her brother had recommended that overlooked the whole of Rome. When we got there I was mortified when Julie doled out tiaras to everyone – even my Aunty Jean, an older aunt and a real lady, wore one!

As we sat in the restaurant, Mam got an excited phone call from Peter. Alison had given birth to a baby boy called Daniel! It was brilliant news and immediately put us all in great spirits.

Meanwhile, Julie produced a book she'd put together with lots of pictures of me over the years. In addition, all the women gave me something that reminded them of me.

Lesley got me a watch 'because you're never on time!' she said.

'That's a real cheek! I am always on time!' I laughed.

Then there were dancing shoes from Lynne, a doll of a midwife, earrings, lipstick, shoes and lots more.

The next day we visited the Colosseum and had our pictures taken with the gladiators, even Aunty Jean. It was hilarious. After that we just ambled about Rome, laughing and enjoying the atmosphere. It was such a good laugh and when we got home I actually felt a bit sad that it was over.

However, unbeknownst to me, the Inverness lot also had a hen do organised. Michael made himself scarce for the weekend, and my friends Lynne, Mandy and Lesley came up from Newcastle to stay. I thought I'd be fine in Inverness but suddenly I was being given all these things to put on. Looking at a veil, I turned my nose up. 'I'm not wearing that!'

In town we went for a nice meal, about twenty of us, and it was all very calm – until unexpectedly the lights dimmed.

Suddenly, four of the girls dressed as nuns were in front of me singing, 'How Do You Solve a Problem Like Maria?' with their own customised words. It was hilarious.

A week later it was time to travel down to Newcastle.

When I arrived, Mam addressed me with a serious face.

'We're not going to get stressed. We're all going to be calm,' she said.

I nodded.

'But we've got a problem on our hands,' she said in the next breath. 'We need to sort the favours out and I'm worried about the flowers . . .'

'Mam!' I could barely get a word in edgeways.

The most nerve-racking moment was going to pick up the dress. Luckily all the personal training had paid off: to my huge relief it actually fitted.

Before my big day, I had a third and final hen do, this time organised by my Gateshead and Newcastle friends. We went for a meal where they presented me with lots of gifts. Then, much to my amusement, it became apparent that my Gateshead friends had written their own version of 'How Do You Solve a Problem Like Maria?' as well!

'So no one wanted to sing me "Maria" from *West Side Story* then?' I mocked. 'Just the one from *The Sound of Music* about me being a problem. Are you trying to tell me something?'

Then it was back to reality with Michael and I being separated for the wedding. The night before we all congregated at the hotel where a lot of the guests and Michael were staying. I made sure that I left at 11 p.m., ready for my big day.

Chapter Twelve

Opening the curtain I looked out to see thick fog obscuring pretty much everything in my parents' garden.

I almost burst out laughing. With my wedding being in October I hadn't expected a bright beautiful day – but fog! It was just typical.

'Oh that's lovely, it's really foggy,' I announced.

'That's not fog,' said Mam, rushing over and trying to shut the curtains protectively. 'That's God's cloak!'

'What?!' Julie and I couldn't stop laughing.

The church service began at 12 p.m. but I was feeling very relaxed. That morning, in a touching gesture, Michael had sent me a big bunch of red roses and they kept catching my eye as we opened the champagne and chatted while everyone got ready. Soon, Claire, my hair and make-up girl, arrived, so I sent the bridesmaids down first. Then I sat sipping champagne as she did my make-up beautifully, complete with my trademark red lipstick.

Of course, Mam had a bee in her bonnet that a bride shouldn't wear red lippy but I wasn't going to be persuaded on the subject.

'That's me!' I said determinedly.

In fact I was so worried about being able to apply it all day that I'd given one lipstick to each of my bridesmaids to look after.

When I eventually stepped out wearing my wedding dress, Lynne looked me up and down. 'Not bad Joyce-y, not bad,' she announced.

Finally I was ready to set off. But unbeknownst to me, Mam had allowed quite a few of the neighbours to congregate at the bottom of the garden and was handing out a tray of champagne. I thought we'd never get away.

By then 'God's cloak' had dispersed and it had turned into a beautiful bright October day. Mam and the bridesmaids piled into the first car to head to the church.

'Who's got my lipstick?' I asked.

'WE'VE ALL GOT YOUR LIPSTICK!' they chorused in unison.

Suddenly it was just Dad and me left and I felt really nervous. He helped me into the car, an old Rolls-Royce.

'You look beautiful, bonny lass,' he said, smiling proudly. 'Enjoy your day.'

Unfortunately, when I got to the church, I had nobody to help me get out the car as the bridesmaids were inside at the back of the church. So it was down to the priest and my dad to pull me out and sort out my train. All the while stragglers were running past, panting, 'Sorry, sorry, I'm late!'

'In your own time, Maria,' the priest told me with a big smile. 'When you're ready we'll go.'

So the music started and off we went.

It was just magical. All the way down the church I was spotting people I hadn't seen for ages and I couldn't stop smiling.

Then I saw Michael's best man, his brother Alan, looking at me and saying something to Michael. Michael turned and gave me an approving smile.

As we said our vows, I looked into Michael's brown eyes. I felt very choked but managed not to cry. Then suddenly the priest was pronouncing us man and wife! After signing the register we headed back down the aisle to claps and cheers.

'Where's my lipstick?' I asked Lynne as soon as we were out the church.

Climbing into the Rolls-Royce we set off to our reception at Linden Hall, a thirty-five minute drive away.

En route (as I reapplied my lippy) we travelled through the Tyne Tunnel. It was Friday and busy and we were getting toots of congratulations. I felt very nostalgic as the journey took us past the Stannington psychiatric hospital where I'd done my student nurse placement and the spot where I'd broken down.

'This is a much better journey,' I thought.

Arriving at Lyndon Hall everyone was given champagne before sitting down for the reception.

My poor dad was getting greyer by the minute. I felt so nervous for him but his speech was lovely. As was Michael's who – despite forgetting his cue cards – pulled off a blinder.

Following Michael I stood up.

'You didn't expect me to keep quiet on a day like today, did you?' I said.

Later we had a disco. We'd chosen 'Who Do You Love?' by Ted Hawkins for our first dance but despite rehearsing it Michael was frozen to the spot. The video was hilarious. It's basically me dancing around him.

The last song of the evening was 'I've Had the Time of My Life' from *Dirty Dancing* – so of course I had to do 'the lift'! Unfortunately, Michael must be the only person in the world who hasn't seen the film.

As I ran at him and straddled him, the look on his face was pure confusion. Thankfully he caught me. Phew.

It was the most brilliant day. I loved every minute.

The next day we flew to St Lucia for two weeks, to stay at the Sandals resort. We spent our days exploring the island and sunbathing on the beach. It was just lovely.

Aware that I was now thirty-seven and we didn't have much time to hang about, we decided that we'd like to try for a baby – not that we admitted it to anyone despite the fact that, boy, would they not stop asking!

I just wanted to take the pressure off myself. If I was going to give it a go I wasn't going to advertise the fact. 'If it happens, it happens,' I thought. In my head I had decided that if it didn't come naturally then we'd call it a day.

I'd never forgotten a woman I'd met who'd had fifteen attempts at IVF. When I called her in for her booking appointment she came in and immediately burst into tears. It took ten minutes to console her.

'I can't believe I'm sitting here,' she said. In all the years of trying she'd never been pregnant before. Thankfully she had her baby and it was really good to see her dreams finally coming true. But I wasn't sure I could put myself through that level of heartache.

Fortunately I was lucky enough to become pregnant in August 2005.

At the time I had completely buried myself in work and spent a lot of time working with student midwives as a regular practice educator in both a clinical and a university setting. I loved it. I really enjoyed the teaching aspect.

When I was late with my period I absolutely knew. I was lying in bed one day when I suddenly felt very queasy and had to rush to the bathroom to be sick.

'What was that?' Michael asked.

'I don't know!' I lied. 'I feel fine now!'

Luckily I was off that day so I immediately went and bought two twin packs of pregnancy kits from Tesco.

'I think I'm going to do a test,' I told Michael.

'What test?' he asked.

I raised my eyebrows.

So the two of us piled into the bathroom. As we waited for the results I knew as soon as I looked at it. The test stick had already changed colour and it was getting stronger by the second. After a minute I showed it to Michael.

'What do you think?' he asked.

'Michael, it's positive,' I said. He looked unconvinced.

'OK, we'll do another just to be sure.'

In the end we did all four.

For the next fifteen weeks I had horrendous morning sickness. I had decided I wouldn't tell anyone, but it was really difficult as I was just so ill. Sometimes the day room was so hot and it made me feel nauseous. In fact, many things seemed to set me off. The aroma on the labour ward or the smell of the placenta. It all tipped me over the edge.

One morning at half past eight, or 'puke o'clock' as it was now affectionately known in my world, one of the student midwives asked me if I could guide her through the suturing (stitching) after you have a baby.

Just the thought of it made me feel like I could be sick so I wracked my brain for an excuse.

'I'm just doing the handover with the doctors,' I said, knowing that would stall me for ten minutes. Then I went into the kitchen to have a ginger biscuit to see if that would help. I knew everything was mind over matter. I was drinking hot water with lemon by the bucketload under the pretence that I was on a detox.

In addition to the morning sickness, as I was coming up to twelve weeks I was finding the work on the labour ward very physical. In the end I had to tell a couple of people.

When I went for the scan it was all very cloak and dagger. I didn't want people knowing as I didn't want to tempt fate. Michael came with me and as we received the news that all was well we were just delighted.

Heading down to Newcastle I broke the news to Mam and Dad by printing off a piece of paper that said 'Congratulations, you're going to be a granny/granddad again!' and placing it inside their Sunday papers. It worked a treat, with them both opening the pages almost simultaneously.

Mam looked at Dad, Dad looked at Mam, then both looked at me.

'Congratulations!' Dad said.

'Thank God for that!' Mam exclaimed.

'Why?' I said.

'Well, I was just really worried,' she said.

I wanted to tell everybody at that point and as we journeyed on to London I told Michael and Julie who were equally excited.

But on the way back I started to have some bleeding. I was fourteen or fifteen weeks pregnant and really worried.

I had to tell Michael and from then on I lay in the front seat of the car trying to be as still as I could. When we stopped at the services the blood was still coming. So in the end we stopped off in Nottingham where we booked into a hotel and I went into the hospital to be scanned.

The waiting was horrendous. I couldn't bear the thought of losing the baby and I was in floods of tears.

Eventually the obstetrician came to see me.

'Your placenta is a little low but everything else appears to be fine,' he said. 'You just need to take it easy.'

So we did the journey back in stages.

Back at the Raigmore I booked to see the consultant and then I had a big scan at twenty weeks. To our utter relief everything was fine. Now I felt I could finally break the news.

'Have you got something to tell us, Maria?' one of the girls asked.

'I have actually,' I said. 'I'm having a baby.'

'I'm so glad you've told us now,' she said. 'We all said you've either put on a lot of weight or you are pregnant.'

Even though I'd made the announcement I didn't necessarily go round telling everyone and some colleagues took a while to cotton on. I was about twenty-six weeks when one of the doctors said, 'Hi, Maria, how are you doing?' Then he did a double take.

'Can I ask you something?' he whispered. 'Are you pregnant?'

'Whatever gives you that impression?' I said, looking down at my big bump. We wore pink scrubs and I was wearing the largest size available.

It's really saying something when a consultant can't work it out! We had a good laugh at that but secretly I was a bit worried that everyone thought I was just fat.

As the pregnancy continued, I wanted to attend parentcraft classes, as it was an opportunity to meet other women who were pregnant in my area and for Michael to learn about the birth.

'I'm not going to tell anyone I'm a midwife, though,' I warned

Michael, explaining that I'd had a word with the midwife running the class.

I really wanted to be anonymous, as I knew that the moment I revealed my job I would be treated differently and would probably be asked a million questions. I kept up the pretence and managed to avoid discussions about what I did for a living but then the class was taken on a tour of the labour ward.

Of course the minute we walked in, the sister on the ward spotted me and grinned. I shot her a look and she flashed me a knowing smile.

It was weird being being shown around the labour ward and seeing it from a patient's perspective. On the way out I deliberately placed myself in the middle of the crowd but then a female doctor shouted, 'Maria, what are you doing?'

'Hi!' I replied, quickly following the group out the ward doors.

'You!' I said the next day when I saw her. 'I'm anonymous in that group.'

'You came for a tour of where you work?' she confirmed. 'Interesting!'

I actually did come clean during one of our final sessions and told my fellow mums-to-be that I worked on the labour ward.

'We can't believe you didn't tell us!' they all exclaimed.

Then within about five seconds they launched into asking me loads of questions. I had to laugh.

As my bump continued to expand, the fussing was relentless at work.

'Have you had a break?' they'd say. 'Go and have a cup of tea.'

The women on the ward were noticing as well. One day I was looking after a woman who was delivering twins. She'd just had the first and I was standing next to her, encouraging her and telling her what would happen.

'Ooh, when are you due?' she said.

'Oh, I've got a while yet!' I said. 'Ten weeks.'

'Have you?' she said.

The conversation carried on, with her asking lots of questions.

'Um, can I stop you right there?' I interrupted, laughing. 'We've got another baby to deliver yet!'

But as time went on it was getting harder and harder at work, and I felt like the bump was slowing me down. You don't realise how small the corridors are until you start walking around pregnant. It was a mammoth effort just going from one room to another on the labour ward and it was frustrating as I just couldn't get to places as fast as I wanted to.

Trying to get across the car park was also a nightmare. The big problem was wing mirrors. When you slip past with a bump you can't breathe in so I used to pull in wing mirrors all along the car park to get through or I'd have to go the long way round. It was so embarrassing.

When you are pregnant you can't bend in half as nothing squashes, and I felt very conscious in our tiny staff changing room. It was just such a mission trying to get my scrubs on and putting ankle socks on with my shoes. I just felt like a weeble wobbling about. I started to get in earlier so nobody would see me.

I was just too big so in the end I decided I was going to go on maternity leave from thirty-two weeks. The physical side was getting too much.

Over the years I'd given the women all the chat: 'This is your first pregnancy so really take advantage of your maternity leave. Look after yourself.'

Instinctively I knew I really needed to rest and I wanted to enjoy the rest of the pregnancy. I was looking forward to going round coffee shops, finding out more about Inverness and being more social.

I was also becoming more emotional, which was not good for women when they needed someone who could help them and remain stoical.

The final straw was when one night shift we had a baby that died just after it was born. I was resuscitating the baby and I knew it just wasn't going to survive. Emotionally it was just too much to take on while I was so heavily pregnant myself. I couldn't deny that my pregnancy hormones were making me more sensitive.

Afterwards everyone was saying to me, 'Are you OK?'

'Yeah, I'm fine,' I said, even though I really wasn't.

Then the phone rang. It was Michael.

'Why are you calling me?' I asked.

'Are you OK?' he said. 'I just woke up and I needed to ring you and check you're all right.'

'I'm fine,' I said. 'It's just been a bit of a difficult night.' It was really spooky.

I actually had to be interviewed by the police about that baby because it had happened unexpectedly.

The following week I was very grateful to go on maternity leave.

When I was thirty-six weeks I found out that not only was my baby huge but it was also breech. I'd suspected as much. I recalled how nine weeks earlier I'd been lying on the couch when I'd experienced this uncomfortable feeling, like a dragging sensation on my insides. At the time I'd watched my belly move and had wondered if the baby was now legs-first.

With the breech confirmed I immediately tried a range of exercises that I'd previously given women to do. I remembered the way I instructed them, making it all sound so easy:

'What you do is go onto your knees, bring yourself forward and roll yourself back,' I'd chirped. 'It will rotate the baby.'

Well, when I tried it myself, with Michael holding me, what an effort it was. I managed about two before I had to lie on the settee. I was completely out of breath!

'Oh my God, how was I telling women to do this?' I wondered.

At thirty-seven weeks I went for another scan where it was revealed that the baby had turned and was now facing the correct way for birth. Bizarrely this time I hadn't felt a thing.

As the final weeks of my pregnancy approached I was incredibly uncomfortable. The baby's head was quite high and hadn't engaged with the pelvis at all.

I was psychologically preparing myself to have the baby naturally but inside there was a little nagging doubt. Why was the head not going into my pelvis?

I carried on doing all I could. I got my TENS machine out and I did lots of walking around and tried to enjoy the time I had off.

At forty weeks Mam and Dad came up to see me.

'Oh my goodness, are you sure you can get through that?' Dad asked, catching sight of me. 'Your mam had four and she wasn't that big!'

'Thanks, Dad, that's very reassuring,' I said. 'I see you've got your midwifery skills on high alert.'

A couple of days later I started to get contractions. All of a sudden I felt these twinges and when I timed them they were five minutes apart. Mam and Dad immediately started flapping.

'I can't believe this!' Dad said. 'You're never going into labour!'

'Are you sure you shouldn't go to hospital?' Mam fussed.

Then Michael's mum arrived.

'Can you all just leave?' I said. 'Please just go out, go to Boots and get me some stuff.'

The contractions went on all day but then they died down. I could feel my baby's head knocking against my pelvis but it wasn't going in. It was very painful.

I called Helen, my midwife friend, at the hospital and asked her to come round. She took one look at me and her forehead wrinkled in concern.

'Are you OK?' she asked.

'Can you check the baby's head has gone into the pelvis?' I said.

'Sorry, Maria, it's nowhere near,' she said, after giving my abdomen a good feel.

'Do you think this is a big baby?' I asked.

She looked at me and I could tell she didn't want to frighten me. 'Well, it's definitely not a small one,' she confirmed. 'We'll just have to see what happens.'

At yet another appointment with the consultant I asked if the baby's head was not going into pelvis because the placenta was low. She explained that I was starting to get fluid around the baby which can happen in late pregnancy. I then underwent two 'sweeps', where she tried to stimulate contractions by stripping membranes from around the cervix.

Afterwards I saw Mam and Dad off at the train station, getting onto the train myself to give Mam a last hug. Then I waved them off and walked back down the platform.

'Well,' said the guard, looking me up and down. 'I cannae tell you how relieved I am you got off the train.'

'I'm due now!' I said.

'Never!' he said.

I needed to try and get myself into labour so after that I was on a mission!

I went to the bookshop every day for a coffee and climbed up and down the stairs trying to get the baby's head down.

I was starting to get really worried as I was now two weeks over my due date. Eventually, after a visit to the consultant, it was decided the safest decision was to have a Caesarean section.

On the afternoon when I got back from this appointment, another consultant phoned me at home.

'I think this has gone on long enough,' he said. 'I'm going to deliver your baby. Come in this afternoon and we'll get you delivered first thing tomorrow morning.

When I arrived on the ward all the midwives were saying how relieved they were to see me.

'That baby is huge and the head is nowhere near the pelvis!' they said. Even so I was kind of beating myself up. I'd really wanted a natural birth.

The following morning Michael arrived in a bright blue shirt.

'What on earth are you wearing?' I asked. 'That's the first thing the baby will see!'

Half an hour later Kath arrived.

'We'll take you down now, Maria,' she said.

In the theatre I was greeted by the anaesthetist.

'Can I ask you something?' he said, looking at me quizzically.

'Yes,' I said.

'Have you got lipstick on?'

'Oh sorry,' I replied. 'I just put it on without thinking.'

It was really weird being awake during the Caesarean. I couldn't feel anything but as soon as the baby was lifted out it instantly felt like my back had been lifted to a normal level.

'Wow, look at the size of this baby!' I heard the anaesthetist say. The baby didn't give an immediate scream but then it let out a cry, much to my relief.

'What is it?' I asked, focusing my eyes on Michael. He was so overwhelmed that he could not get the words out.

'It's a girl!' he finally stammered, his eyes watering with emotion.

'What a size!' the anaesthetist interrupted. 'You'll never believe the weight! We've had her on the scales three times! She's ten pounds eleven!'

Then they passed her over. It was such an amazing moment. My first impression was that she had really dark hair and that she was very long.

Taking in her tiny features I was just spellbound.

'Hello, Rosie,' I said, calling her the name Michael and I had already settled on if we had a girl.

'She's got my nose, Michael! Thank God she hasn't got yours.'

'What do you mean by that!' he laughed, hardly able to tear his eyes away from our new baby daughter.

The consultant came over and gave me a kiss on the cheek.

'Congratulations,' he said. 'It was the right decision, Maria. She would never have come out naturally.'

After being wheeled back to the ward I had my first go at breastfeeding. I really felt the pressure to succeed after all the advice I'd doled out over the years. It was difficult at the beginning as Rosie was so big and hungry but eventually I started to get the hang of it.

The next day Mam and Dad drove up. The funny thing was

I could see them trying to park up from my bed in the hospital. Dad was whizzing around the car park trying to get a space but Mam clearly couldn't contain herself. Suddenly she'd abandoned the car and was striding purposefully towards the hospital.

I heard her voice and her footsteps before I saw her. Then she raced round the corner, dropped her bag and came flying over.

'Oh my goodness!' she cooed. 'She's just gorgeous!'

The next minute she was pulling out all the presents. 'That's from such and such . . .'

'Er, where's Dad?' I asked.

'Oh, he'll be along in a minute,' she said with a dismissive wave of her hand.

I spent five days in hospital, which I actually didn't mind. It was good to be on the other side with no pressure.

We took Rosie home just in time for the Easter weekend and did that thing that every new parent does. We plonked the car seat in the middle of the room and just looked at her.

'I can't believe it!' I said. 'Can you believe it?'

Well, little Rosie certainly made her mark – she didn't sleep at all!

For the next few weeks we lived on a home-cooked food supply from the freezer as we tried to get Rosie into some kind of routine. I could not believe how much the breastfeeding was taking it out of me. I was drinking pint after pint of water and my blood sugar kept dropping, making me ravenous.

One night Michael made spaghetti bolognaise and brought a dish into the front room for me.

'Oh, you're feeding,' he said and to my dismay took it out again.

He then did the same thing again ten minutes later.

'Michael!' I hissed. 'I'm starving! Please give it to me!'

So with Rosie still feeding I ploughed into my plate like I was ravenous.

When I eventually stopped to glance up, Michael was looking at me like I was out of my mind.

Eight months passed and Rosie was still not settled. All new mums want to be perfect and you really feel a pressure when your baby is not sleeping. I tried every trick in the book but she would sleep for ten or fifteen minutes maximum then wake up. It was just the worst form of torture.

There I'd be at 2 a.m. nearly crying from sleep deprivation, flicking through my *Baby Whisperer* book and repeating, 'Ssh, ssh, ssh' over and over.

Thankfully when I met up with the women in my baby group, a few confessed that they were in exactly the same boat. There just seemed no rhyme or reason to it.

But as weeks turned into months I was getting desperate. When I heard the baby monitor I was having palpitations.

So one night Michael took control and let her cry. It went on for an hour and a half while I sobbed with my head under the pillow. It was tough love but after that she did get better.

Then when Rosie was ten months old we took her to Norway to see my brother Christopher. She was actually quite settled and I managed to discreetly breastfeed on the plane. Maybe I'm finally getting this motherhood thing under control, I thought.

After that I hung out with some of the mothers and babies from my parentcraft group and enjoyed the time getting to know my baby. Then, all too soon, my maternity leave was up and I was back at work, having decided to do three night shifts a week.

Leaving Rosie for the first time I was tearful but concentrated on the job at hand, leaving Michael with lots of instructions and as much expressed milk as I could produce.

Back on the ward I was immediately thrust into the thick of it and the first night I delivered a baby in a car at the front of the maternity unit. The woman was in the passenger seat with her head lying back on the driver's seat.

After hurriedly introducing myself, I quickly checked her over and saw that the baby's head was out.

'Hello!' she said, catching sight of my face. 'You delivered my first one!'

'We'll talk about that later, shall we?' I replied, smiling.

'It's really nice to see you again!' she panted. Then with one last push the baby was out and screaming.

'Your baby is fine!' I confirmed. Then we got her out the car to deliver the afterbirth and cut the cord.

Later, with my shift done, I dashed home at 7.45 a.m. to find Michael and Rosie propped up on the settee. They both looked as white as a sheet.

'How did you get on?' I asked.

Michael just looked at me. 'It was terrible,' he said. 'She didn't sleep at all and she wouldn't take anything to drink.'

'I can't believe I'm going to say this,' I said, sighing. 'But you need to go to bed.'

'What about you?' he said.

'You need to get some sleep so you can look after her when I go to bed later,' I said. 'You sleep until twelve then you can take over.'

Plonking her in the pram, I then took Rosie out in a bid to keep me awake and to send her to sleep, all the while singing nursery rhymes until she was zonked.

Then when midday finally arrived I woke up Michael.

'That's you!' I told him, handing over the baby. Within five minutes I was out for the count.

It did get better and in time Rosie was more settled. And although juggling work and motherhood was hard, I really relished doing both. It was nice to have a challenge. Like a lot of new mums I felt like I'd lost a bit of my identity, so back at work it was nice to have conversations that weren't just about babies. I loved being back in the thick of my colleagues' banter. But some days I did feel torn. I knew Rosie was fine at home but if I had to text Michael to say I was working late I felt very guilty. To be honest no matter what I did I felt bad. When you working and you've got children you have this constant guilt.

One of the worst moments for me came at the start of 2007. I was due to work on New Year's Day but then Rosie, then nearly ten months old, suddenly got really sick. She had contracted the norovirus and had constant diarrhea and vomiting.

I felt really guilty about letting my team down and calling someone else in to cover but I just couldn't leave her. My unwell child was my priority.

Thankfully she started to get better and she was discharged on 2 January.

I went back into work sheepishly and thankfully most people were nice about it.

By now I was thirty-nine and again aware of my biological clock Michael and I decided that we'd like another child.

We didn't want Rosie to be an only child and our lives had already been turned upside down so it couldn't get any worse, right? We might as well add to the juggling act.

Despite my concerns about my age I got pregnant really quickly and discovered I was expecting again in April 2007, not long after Rosie's first birthday.

I woke up once more feeling really sick. And if I thought it was tough before, having morning sickness AND a baby AND a job was something else! There was no chance to rest and I had to just get on with it.

Then when I was twelve weeks pregnant Michael sprang a surprise on me. He wanted to do something really special for my fortieth birthday so he arranged a holiday to St Tropez in the South of France.

We were going to get the train and then the Eurostar followed by the TGV from Paris to Nice. But then five hours into the train journey to London, Rosie, by now fourteen months old, developed a rash. She had a high temperature and, very worried about her, we took her to Guy's Hospital in London.

Tests there revealed she was anaemic and had high blood pressure so they kept her in until 2 a.m. The consultant said it would still be OK for us to travel on to France but that she should be checked out once we got back.

All I wanted was to take her back to Inverness but it was such a long way that Michael went and got the tickets put off for a day and we arranged to stay with Michael and Julie while we reviewed the situation. With Rosie seeming better after a second night's sleep, we finally set off for France.

Bless Michael, we were in First Class. Immediately I saw all the businessmen shooting Rosie a look but she didn't make a peep. Then getting off it was all, 'Isn't she lovely,' of course.

St Tropez was just perfect, although we stayed in a caravan park that did look better in the brochure! But I was lifting buggies up and down when I knew I shouldn't.

A few days after we returned to the UK, I was struck down by horrendous pains in my abdomen. It had started off as a dull toothache-type pain then it had just got sharper and sharper until it was unbearable. Was I going to lose my baby?

When I phoned up my doctor, I couldn't even speak. All I could do was cry into the receiver.

'Go to the hospital straight away,' he told me.

'You are not going to lose this baby,' the consultant told me, when I got to Ward 10. 'It's not miscarriage pain. I think it is either appendicitis or renal colic.'

When I had a scan they diagnosed the latter – kidney stones as they are more commonly known. Thankfully the pain faded with time.

Knowing that the baby was fine, I finally announced to my colleagues that I was expecting again. They all seemed very pleased but I'm sure I tested everyone's patience as I suffered repeatedly from that pain throughout my pregnancy and was admitted into hospital several times because of it.

'Any preference for a room?' one of the midwives, Marjorie, joked, as I rocked up to the antenatal ward for the sixth time. 'Which one haven't you been in yet?

'I feel really guilty,' I said sheepishly.

'Let's get over that, shall we?' she said. 'You're here!'

I really found it hard to consent to having the painkilling injections. A lot of women stall like that. When you're pregnant the protection of the baby comes first but when you're experiencing pain of that magnitude you have to let common sense prevail.

Then on Christmas Eve, when I still had around five weeks to go, I was in church with Rosie watching the nativity play when all of a sudden I started to get horrendous pains.

The pain was searing over my abdomen near the scar from my first C-section. It was almost like contractions and was similar to the pain I'd had when Rosie's head was bashing on my pelvis.

I wanted to shout, 'I'll play Mary!'

Grabbing Rosie, I got to the back of the church and headed home, where Michael was sat in the sitting room.

I crawled to the sink.

'What *are* you doing?' he asked.

Of course, despite my reluctance I ended up in hospital again.

'There is no way I'm being in hospital on Christmas Day,' I told the staff and eventually they let me go. I could have kissed them!

But for three weeks the same thing continued, on and off, on and off.

There was more unsettling news to come. In my thirty-six-week scan they said my second baby would be even bigger than Rosie had been and the recommendation was again made that I should have a C-section.

Once more I had a huge guilt about it. As a midwife I had spearheaded a campaign to encourage women not to have elective C-sections and here I was gearing up for my second one!

Finally I went into theatre when I was coming up to thirty-eight weeks.

This time I was convinced I was having a boy. But then out came this perfect little girl. She was completely different to Rosie, much smaller, weighing eight pounds two ounces and with very defined features. We named her Molly Kate.

I was actually very happy to have another girl. I'd grown up with three brothers. 'This is fantastic,' I thought. 'We can all do girly stuff together.'

'You wouldn't have been able to have had her naturally,' the consultant told me afterwards. 'Your womb was paper-thin and completely see-through from the scar tissue. It could have ruptured if you'd had a normal delivery.'

It really sent shivers down my spine. I felt very, very lucky that I'd had Molly when I did!

I was desperate for Rosie to see her and I'll never forget her expression when she saw Molly. Her face just lit up. Then she threw her toy in the air and it nearly landed on Molly's head. Oh Lord, I thought.

I'd been mentally preparing myself for more sleepless nights but as it happened Molly was completely different to Rosie. She just slept and slept. You could Hoover around her! She soon grew into a happy, chilled baby and it was a real relief to have less hard work the second time around.

But if I'd thought my two girls were a handful I had to laugh when my brother Michael and his wife Julie revealed they were expecting triplets. The whole family were ecstatic for them although I felt a little worried as a midwife, knowing the complications that can occur. But everything went just fine and their three beautiful girls, Lily, Clara and Elise, were born on 8 January 2009.

While I was on maternity leave, Michael decided to become a driving instructor.

I wanted to support him but to be honest it was probably the worst time he could have done it. He was already so busy working with his regular job as a signalling technician on the railways, and now he was doing the driving on top.

All of a sudden it was like every journey was a driving test.

My driving was being analysed, he was asking me questions and then expecting an answer immediately.

'Just stop right there,' I'd say.

It got to the stage where come rain, snow or hail I wore my sunglasses in the car so he couldn't see where my eyes were and whether I was checking my mirror enough.

'Do not say one word,' I'd warn him. 'Stop looking at what gear I am in!'

Yet he'd still pipe up.

In the end I'd pull over in a rage.

'Do *you* want to drive?' I'd ask.

When the time came for him to take his exam he was very anxious. He knew the odds were stacked against him – the test was notoriously hard with only five per cent of entrants passing first time.

I felt so nervous for him when he left the house. Not that I should have worried. He passed with flying colours and was actually the first person in Scotland to pass first time that year!

Meanwhile I had my eye on a new opening at my work. A few months before a new job had come up at the hospital for a consultant midwife.

When the position was advertised I was very excited as it was along the lines of everything I'd been doing. I interviewed for it with an extensive presentation but I didn't get it. Instead it went to one of my colleagues who, to her credit, encouraged me to work alongside her.

I was admittedly disappointed but adapted the attitude I've tried to have all along. I decided that I was still going to develop and learn, and continue with the practice development group. I'd also do my best to promote normal midwifery and keep looking at research and continuing with my teaching. It has been brilliant watching my students increase in confidence. These days I'm a supervisor of midwives and have about seventeen midwives to look after on top of my normal job.

In the last four or five years the birth rate at our hospital has gone up 450 births a year, from 1,750 to 2,200. It's got a lot busier even though we have four staff including me on the labour ward.

Working as a SCM on the labour ward presents new challenges every day. We're at the central point of the whole of the Highlands. Any problems arise on our patch, we have to solve them. The place is busier with more social, drug and child protection problems creeping into Highland living now. With more robust clinical governance and risk management strategies being developed across the area, staff are engaging more with management at varying levels to deliver a safer environment for patients. Local programmes have encouraged each area to work together to provide a safe, efficient service to the public. However, on a day-to-day basis on the frontline, it is sometimes a juggling act to meet everyone's expectations.

Every day you are making life or death decisions. Although we have a special care baby unit we don't take babies less than twenty-eight weeks. So if they are too premature the decision has to be made whether to transfer them out to another hospital such as Aberdeen, Glasgow, Edinburgh or even Newcastle. Then comes the dilemma: do you fly them or send them by ambulance, taking an emergency vehicle out of the area for a few hours? And can you afford to send a midwife to assist?

In the last few years it has been almost like going back to basics. We have had hand hygiene audits to reduce hospital-acquired infections and there has been a huge development in the NHS to go back to matron-style wards in which it is clear who is in charge and who is accountable.

Then there is the constant challenge of the present economic cuts that are constantly stripping the medical profession of its resources and allowing workloads to spiral out of control.

Professor Cathy Warwick CBE, General Secretary of the Royal College of Midwives, has said that midwives need to move forward and redesign our services. We need to fight and justify why we need more midwives on our wards. She's a person I really admire and she is right.

The number of midwives who are being trained is dwindling and midwives are often criticised in the papers for seemingly not being up to scratch. But the truth is all we want is for you to be safe and your baby to be fine too.

And you should have no doubt that the midwives who are out there really are the cream of the crop. In order to keep our jobs we have to maintain our qualification and reregister every three years. Women in the UK actually have incredibly well-qualified individuals looking after them.

We are getting the flack for overcrowded maternity wards and what is viewed a bad quality of care. But 4,700 midwives were cut in England last year (2011). And right now there is a huge worry about where the staff will come from in the future. From 2012 there will be only three centres in Scotland to deliver midwifery training. Aberdeen is the nearest for us – not much use if you live in the Highlands.

It is also a worrying time for recruitment into the profession over the next five to ten years. Management at hospital trusts are not replacing staff and student midwives qualifying after eighteen months training can't get jobs. Previously there was a commitment to take them on but now they are not getting any opportunities at all. In the Highlands we are getting student midwives applying for our jobs from all over the country. Terrified they won't get a job, they are going for every vacancy they find. If these eager, dedicated young students are unsuccessful they'll often go and get another job or go back to nursing. If you don't catch them early they generally don't come back, which is such a shame.

Meanwhile specialist midwives are being cut so don't expect to have a midwife there for you to help you stop smoking or to assist you through a vulnerable situation. Over the next few years we'll see more mortality and problems because of the shortage of midwives.

My peers all over the UK are constantly being put in situations where they are looking after multiple women at once. If something goes wrong then the midwife is accountable. It is a dangerous time we live in. Midwives need to be more politically minded and legally informed.

We're heading for an era where a shortage of midwives has resulted in a workforce of burnt-out midwives off sick, dreading going to work as they can't cope with being constantly on the frontline.

If as a mum-to-be you find yourself in a chaotic maternity unit with the midwives stretched to the limit then you need to lobby your MP and ask him to do something about it.

So why do we do it? Because it's absolutely worth it. Midwifery is not a job; it is a way of life. You have to give a lot of yourself and make it your world. And when you do, you can make a real difference.

I'll never forget one community visit where I sat down with an expectant mother to ask her all about her birth plan.

'Man, you've got a cushy number,' her husband remarked, as he walked in the room to see us chatting away.

'Well,' I replied, staring him straight in the eye, 'if I make my job look easy then I know I'm doing a good job – because the one thing it's not is easy!'

Acknowledgements

I would like to thank the following people for sharing and encouraging me throughout this wonderful opportunity:

Charlotte, my ghostwriter and friend, for helping to capture my 'voice' throughout the book which was so important to me.

To my family for their support throughout my life and in writing this book: Mam, Dad, Michael, Julie, Peter, Alison, Christopher and Katharina. Peter and Jean for everything. Stella and Sandy. Lynne, Fiona, Helen, Kath, Shona, Diane, Lisa, Sarah, Lorraine, Catherine, Irene and Stewart for your friendship.

To the Headline Publishing team: Carly Cook for choosing me to write this book, Sarah Emsley, Richard Roper and Lindsay Davies who have supported me.

To Rowan Lawton, my literary agent for keeping me right throughout this process.

Thanks to Collen Begg (NMC) who read this book as a professional courtesy and the Royal College of Midwives in supporting the writing of this book. To Angela Watt, my midwifery manager, for her support and Susan who gave permission to share her story.